Behind the Badge

History of the Royal Canadian Mounted Police "Depot" Division

By

Dale Sheehan and Redd Oosten

BEHIND THE BADGE –
History of the Royal Canadian Mounted Police "Depot" Division
by Dale Sheehan and Redd Oosten

First Printing – May 2006

Copyright© 2006 by Dale Sheehan and Redd Oosten

Published by Publishing Solutions/Centax Books.

All Rights Reserved. Except for brief passages in a review, no part of this book may be reproduced, by any means, electronic or mechanical, including photocopying and recording, without written permission from the publisher.

Library and Archives Canada Cataloguing in Publication

Sheehan, Dale, 1961-

Behind the badge : history of the Royal Canadian Mounted Police "Depot" Division / Dale Sheehan, Redd Oosten.

Includes bibliographical references.

ISBN 1-897010-25-7

1. Royal Canadian Mounted Police. "Depot" Division – History. 2. Police training – Canada – History. 3. Police training – Saskatchewan – Regina – History. I. Oosten, Redd, 1958-   II. Title.

FC3216.2.S54 2006   363.2'071'071   C2006-900408-0

Project Coordinator – Dan Marce, Publishing Solutions
Editor – Margo Embury, Centax Books
Historical Consultants – Malcolm Wake and William MacKay
Cover design and page design concept by Tom Wieclawski
Cover photo by Chrystal Kruszelnicki
Visual Assets Coordination – Nancy McLaughlan
Book formatting and individual page design by Iona Glabus, Centax Books

Designed, Printed and Published in Canada by:
Centax Books/PrintWest Communications Ltd.
Publishing Director – Margo Embury
1150 Eighth Avenue, Regina, Saskatchewan, Canada S4R 1C9
Telephone (306) 525-2304   Fax: (306) 757-2439
centax@printwest.com   www.centaxbooks.com

TABLE OF CONTENTS

Preface	6
Dedication	8
Foreword by the Commissioner	9
RCMP Academy at "Depot" Division	10

Chapter One – In the Beginning

The Early Years	11
Rules and Regulations 1889	15
Recruiting Notice 1893/1914	16
Recruiting	17
"Depot" Division – Not a Favorite Place	21
Desertion	21
Royalty and Royal Visits	23
Hollywood	30
Postcards	33
Social Activities	34
Game Dinners	38
Christmas at "Depot"	39

Chapter Two – Buildings

"A" Block – A.B. Perry Building	42
Applied Police Sciences (APS)	45
Artisan Shop	46
"B" Block	48
Barber Shop	51
Barrack Life	54
Tent Living	66
Buffalo Detachment/Scenario Houses/Mall	67
"C" Block	69
New "C" Block	71
Centralized Training	73
The Chapel	75
In Memory of Miss Audrey Carden	78
The Chaplaincy at "Depot"	82
Commissioner's Residence	84
Crime Detection Laboratory	86
"D" Block	89
Drill Hall	90
"E" Block	92
"F" Block	93
Firehall	95
Guardroom	97
Prisoners	99
Louis Riel	101
Gym	104
Heating Plant	106
Learning Technology and Creative Services (LTCS)	108
Lecture Hall	109
Medical Treatment Centre (MTC)	111
Messes	114
Division Mess	114
Officers' Mess	118
Sergeants' (Senior NCOs') Mess	123
Corporals' Mess	126
Stand Easy Lounge	127
Canteen	128
Model Detachment	129
RCMP Museum and Heritage Centre	130
The Victoria Cross	135
Officers' and NCOs' Quarters	137
Post Garage	141
Recreation Hall	143
Regina Town Station	144
Resource Centre	145
Riding Schools	147
Stables	151
Swimming Pool	154
Water Tower	157

Chapter Three

Change of Command Ceremony 158
Commissioners/Commanding Officers 160
Reflections of "Depot"
    Commanding Officers 171
        Assistant Commissioner R.J. Mills 171
        Chief Superintendent H. Boucher 171
        Chief Superintendent L. Twardosky 172
        Chief Superintendent C. Tugnum 173
        Chief Superintendent P. Ménard .. 174
Sergeants Major 177
Sergeant Major's Parade 180
Church Parade 182
Sunset Ceremonies................. 183
RCMP Memorial Service Parade..... 187
Musical Ride 190
Musical Ride Horses 194

Chapter Four

Carden Estates Campground 195
Cemetery 196
Unmarked Graves................. 201
Cenotaph 202
Entrances to "Depot" 205
Footbridge....................... 207
St Roch Memorial................. 208
Sleigh Square 209
Street Names of "Depot" 211
Gardening....................... 217
Weather at "Depot" 219

Chapter Five

Curriculum...................... 221
Cadet Training Program........... 224
Actors 227
Canadian Law Enforcement
    Training (CLET) 229
Dress/Deportment................ 230
Drill and Tactical Unit 233
Duties 237
Facilitators/Instructors.......... 240
Female Recruits 242

Firearms 249
    Connaught Cup 254
Forming Up...................... 255
G8............................. 257
Graduation Ceremonies 259
    Oath of Allegiance 269
    Regimental Numbers 272
    50,000th Member.............. 272
Memories of "Depot" 273
    Commissioner M.J. Nadon....... 273
    A/Commissioner R.J. Mills...... 273
    Constable R. Cyr 274
    3/Constable C.N. MacKinnon..... 275
    Inspector J. Dowling........... 277
    Sergeant R. Gill 278
    Constable M. Coulibaly 280
RCMP Families................... 282
    The MacRae Family 282
    The Hadley Clan............... 286
    The Clare Brothers............ 286
    The Gibson Family............. 287
    The LaFosse Family 288
Life at "Depot" 289
How to get in trouble 289
Leave Pass...................... 291
Marriage 293
To the Wives.................... 294
Native Special Constable Training 295
Pay/Salary...................... 297
Pay Parades..................... 298
Physical Training 299
Quick Change Artists 302
Let's make a Deal 303
Police Defensive Tactics (PDT) 305
Police Driving Unit (PDU) 307
Recruit Training 310
    Recruit Training 1932 310
    Recruit Training Syllabus 1960 ... 311
    Recruit Training 1962 312
    Training and Discipline 1969..... 312
    Regular Basic Recruit
        Training 1977 and 1988 313
Reserves 315
Reveille 316
Rites of Passage 317

Saturday Inspection 319
Sports 320
Swimming..................... 326
Training....................... 328
Training Journal of
    Superintendent Religa 334
Training day 1977 334
Training day 1987................ 335
Training day 2005................ 335

Chapter Six

RCMP Regimental Badge 336
Force's Name Change 338
Guidon 339
How the Divisions Came to Have
    Their Letters 342
Regions and Divisions............. 342
Insignias 343
RCMP Corps Ensign 344
Mounties "Always Get Their Man" ... 344

Chapter Seven

Horses........................ 345
Fun at "Depot" Division........... 349
Horse Troughing 351
Horse Auction................... 352
Cars.......................... 353
Sergeant G.W. Brinkworth 354
Constable A.A. Lunkie 357
RCMP Bands................... 359
The Nine-Pounder Field Guns 363
The Seven-Pound Bronze Mark II 364

Chapter Eight

Evolution of the Uniform 365
List of 1901 Kit.................. 367
RCMP Tartan 367
Uniform Modifications 368
The Stetson..................... 369
The Buffalo Coat................. 370
Kit – Stores 371
Cost of Placing a Member in
    Red Serge.................... 375
Tailor and Leather Craft Shop 377

Chapter Nine

Historical Calendar................ 379
Through the Decades 391
Historical Centre of "Depot" 396
"Depot" – an Overview 398
Honour Roll 400

Footnotes 402

Bibliography 410

Acknowledgements 414

Preface

It was seven years prior to the first puck being dropped in the inaugural Stanley Cup Championship game and 24 years before Toronto won the first-ever Grey Cup. It was in 1885, nine years before the province of Saskatchewan was created. In terms of Canadian institutions, there are few that have played such a significant and constant role in shaping, not only a Canadian icon, but also Western Canada and the Province of Saskatchewan. The institution is "Depot" Division, home of the Royal Canadian Mounted Police.

In 2006, "Depot" Division, the Royal Canadian Mounted Police Training Academy, celebrates its 121st Anniversary. In the middle of the Canadian Prairies, before Western Canada became part of confederation, the North-West Mounted Police were formed. In 1904 they received the "Royal" prefix to become the Royal Northwest Mounted Police and in 1920 they became the Royal Canadian Mounted Police. "Depot" currently showcases one of the world's best-known and best-regarded police training academies.

There have been hundreds, perhaps thousands, of books dedicated to Canada's national police force. None, to our knowledge, have been solely and specifically dedicated to "Depot" Division. As an Honourary Aide-de-Camp to Her Honour, Dr. Lynda Haverstock, Lieutenant Governor of Saskatchewan, Dale Sheehan visited many places throughout the province and had the opportunity to observe the respect that Saskatchewan citizens had for the RCMP. One night, while flying back to Regina, he mentioned to Her Honour that "Depot" Division deserved a history book of its own. Her Honour, a self-professed Canadian history enthusiast, simply replied, "I agree. And I think you should start writing it." The result of that conversation is this book – *Behind the Badge : History of the Royal Canadian Mounted Police "Depot" Division*.

The history between the stories of the original three hundred members who rode west in 1874 and the thousands of members who have since served the Force is truly a national and historic account that essentially needed to be recorded. Aside from the thousands and thousands of members who have passed through the gates of "Depot" and left proudly wearing the world-famous Red Serge, "Depot" is a place that every Canadian should want to know more about, given its direct impact on Canadian history. In 2003, a badge inscribed with Regimental Number 50,000 was issued to Constable Jason Pole. That number alone accounts for the great impact "Depot" has had on Canada and on policing around the world.

There are three groups of people that would see "Depot" from different perspectives. The first being the recruits or cadets, who have spent six months in barracks, separating themselves from their family and loved ones to pursue their dream of becoming a member of the Royal Canadian Mounted Police. The second would be the tourists, taking in the Sergeant Major's Noon Parade, a Sunset Ceremony, or a tour of the facilities and Centennial Museum. The third group would be the employees of "Depot," both Public Service employees and members of the Force who returned to "Depot" as instructors and facilitators. These are the people who truly experience the "behind the badge" history, stories and anecdotes. There have been few incidents that have occurred over the past 121 years at "Depot" that were not known by the employees while they occurred, after they occurred and, in some cases, before they occurred. These rumours, myths, stories, almost-forgotten historical details and facts have been passed on from generation to generation.

There is not one recruit or cadet that does not remember his or her instructors and facilitators, especially their drill instructor. Whenever members meet, one of the first questions is "What troop were you in?" or "What is your Regimental Number?" Often, these members end up working together in the field again at some time in their careers, with the common denominator being "Depot."

Pouring through thousands of photographs and researching every RCMP Quarterly, Annual Report, Pony Express, and speaking with employees who have spent decades working at "Depot," every effort has been made to confirm, deny and obtain as many facts about the history of "Depot" as possible. Countless publications and stories proved to be very difficult to reconcile when separating fact from myth, and the authors accept responsibility for any errors or omissions.

Writing a book about "Depot" was not a simple task. Over 50,000 members of the Royal Canadian Mounted Police have marched across the infamous Sleigh Square, which has been in place since 1885. Each one of those members has seen it with his or her own eyes and thus has formed their own perspectives about "Depot," from the training, to the barrack life, to the food, to the separation from their loved ones. Resurrecting and assimilating these individual memories can be a daunting task, as we know. It is simply impossible not to overlook some detail that someone will remember and wonder why it was omitted.

Reliving the sense of dedication and loyalty to the Force shown by tens of thousands of former and present RCMP members has been an inspiration to us. As you turn the pages on the history of "Depot," put yourself in the place and time of each photograph. Examine the living conditions and experiences of the recruits and cadets. For those of you that have lived it, enjoy reliving it. For those of you that have not, this is your chance.

Dale L. Sheehan

Redd Oosten

Dale Sheehan was born in Montreal, Quebec, and joined the Royal Canadian Mounted Police in 1986. After graduating from "Depot," he was posted to Prince Edward Island. He has since served in Nova Scotia, Saskatchewan, "Depot" and Ottawa Headquarters. Dale also completed a tour of duty in the former Yugoslavia in 1993, representing the RCMP with the United Nations Civilian Police Force. He is currently serving in Ottawa as Superintendent. Dale is a freelance writer and has co-authored a RCMP 125th Anniversary Yearbook about "Depot." He has been published in several national magazines and newspapers.

Redd Oosten was born in Vancouver, British Columbia. Prior to joining the force as a regular member, she was a telecom operator at the Burnaby detachment. She is a Sergeant with the Royal Canadian Mounted Police. Sworn into the Force in 1985 in Burnaby, British Columbia, Redd has served in Manitoba, "Depot" and Ottawa Headquarters.

DEDICATION

Dedicated to all of the men and women of the
North-West Mounted Police,
Royal Northwest Mounted Police and
Royal Canadian Mounted Police
who sacrificed their lives in the line of duty.

Foreword by the Commissioner

Commissioner G. Zaccardelli

There are some places that are more than the sum of their geography, structure and purpose. The Royal Canadian Mounted Police Training Academy at "Depot" in Regina is one of these.

For me, "Depot" represents the very heart of the Force. The one place where virtually everyone who ever wears the red serge will pass through. A shared experience, a historical symbol, a cutting-edge training academy, a home for chapel, cemetery and cenotaph, a constant presence in a changing world – "Depot" is all of these and more.

I have now served with the Royal Canadian Mounted Police for more than 35 years and "Depot" has been a part of my experience throughout that time. I'll never forget how nervous, how excited and how proud I felt when I arrived for basic training in 1970. I'll always remember the stimulation of later training programs that I went through during my career – advancing my skills, deepening my knowledge, continuing in my quest to be worthy of being part of the best police force in the world. I will never forget the pride of being part of many parades at "Depot," or later, the honour of inspecting row upon row of proud members. And I will never forget the hurt and difficulty of those terrible times when we have paused to remember our fallen comrades whose names are etched on our memorial cenotaph.

As Commissioner I have the great privilege – and, on some days, the challenging responsibility – to oversee this great Force. To steer the "good ship RCMP" on sometimes stormy seas, making sure all is in order, protecting the well-being of tens of thousands of members as they in turn live out a commitment to serve and protect Canada and her people. And through it all "Depot" is like an always burning lighthouse – providing guidance, lighting our way forward, illuminating our past.

For those who pass through "Depot," whether in training, in service, to remember a colleague or loved one, or maybe even only as a visitor, I know you will find something for yourself in this place.

To me, always, "Depot" represents the best of what the Royal Canadian Mounted Police has been, is today and will be in the future: the embodiment of duty and service, the determination of thousands of men and women to make a difference, the covenant made with Canadians to work with them and for them, the ethos of a great country.

I have said on occasion that as goes the RCMP, so goes Canada. I'll add to that as goes "Depot" so goes the Royal Canadian Mounted Police. May we always live up to the values and history of this place, take from it what we need and give back as we can.

RCMP Academy at "Depot" Division

"Depot" is the oldest Division in the RCMP. It is the only Division to have had a Commissioner as its Commanding Officer. It has seen all three changes in the name of the Force and it has been a training facility for 120 years.

"Depot" Division is the heart and soul of the RCMP, where most young men and women attracted by the dream of wearing the "Red Serge," take their first steps toward achieving that goal. It is synonymous with the thorough training required to prepare every member of the Mounted Police for their role in policing the communities in which they serve.

"Depot" is also where the history, traditions and the esprit de corps of the Force are first instilled in every new trainee. "Depot" is almost as old as the Force itself and has witnessed the departure of ten of thousands of newly trained members.

Oldest aerial of "Depot" – 1919

"Depot" Division was established on the recommendation of Commissioner A.G. Irvine. Based on a model of the training facilities of the Royal Irish Constabulary at Phoenix Park, Dublin, "Depot" was created on November 1, 1885 as a training centre for the North-West Mounted Police. There is no doubt that "Depot" has a certain mystique about it, enhanced for many years by the fact that RCMP Headquarters, including the Commissioner's office, was located in Regina until 1920.

The nature of policing and the training methods have changed dramatically since the 1880s. "Depot" Division has changed as well to reflect the modernization of the Force in every respect. The RCMP, however, is keenly aware of its history and traditions and "Depot" Division is that valuable and all-important link between the present, modern-day police force and the frontier force that brought law and authority to the prairies and the north.

– Depot 1998 – 125th Anniversary of the RCMP, compiled by Bill Chisholm, Garth Cunningham and Dale Sheehan

Aerial of "Depot" – 1998

CHAPTER 1

IN THE BEGINNING

The Early Years

It seems to me that the best Force would be, Mounted Riflemen, trained to act as cavalry, but also instructed in the Rifle exercise. They should also be instructed, as certain of the Line are, in the use of artillery. This body should not be expressly Military but should be styled Police, and have the military bearing of the Irish Constabulary.

Sir John A. Macdonald, December 1869

On May 23, 1873, the Dominion Parliament passed an Act to provide for the establishment of a "Mounted Police Force for the Northwest Territories" which included the precise provisions regarding responsibilities of the Force. This included, "to gain the respect and confidence of the natives, preservation of the peace, prevent crime and apprehend criminals, stop liquor trafficking in the North West." The North-West Mounted Police (NWMP) as it was soon called, actually came into existence on August 30, 1873 when the provisions of the Act were brought into force by Order-in-Council and recruiting began.

By 1882 the need for relocating the headquarters of the Force from Fort Walsh to a point on the newly constructed Canadian Pacific Railway called "Pile of Bones," was determined by Edgar Dewdney, Lieutenant Governor of the North-West Territories. It was not a popular choice amongst the Officers given that it was a wide open, wind-swept, barren, flat stretch of prairie. The new barracks was to be built immediately west of

Photo credit from Sam Steele – Lion of the Frontier

Inspector Samuel Benfield Steele

Chapter 1 – In the Beginning   11

Saskatchewan Legislature under construction – circa 1909

Lieutenant Governor Dewdney and Mrs. Dewdney

"Depot" Division Regina – 1885

the Wascana Creek, two and a half miles from Regina's core. Inspector S.B. Steele recommended a different site, which is now occupied by the Legislative Building for the Province of Saskatchewan.

Frederick White, Comptroller for the Force had little say in the final decision as the Lieutenant Governor was adamant that the new headquarters site be located at the Moffat homestead, where it remains to this day.

Forty prefabricated buildings, manufactured in Ottawa and Sherbrooke, Quebec began to arrive via the Canadian Pacific Railway at the end of October 1882. The basic structure of the base, centred around the barrack or parade square, was laid out by Inspector Sam Steele. The sectional buildings which were used for barracks consisted of two sizes, 48 feet by 16 feet and 24 feet by 16 feet – both with 11-foot walls. The kitchens were 18 feet by 10 feet and by 12 feet. The stables were 50 feet by 30 feet. The accommodation was for 100 men and 60 horses. When the NWMP Barracks at Regina was completed, there were over 30 separate buildings, none of which were considered to be permanent. All of the buildings have been replaced, but the modern infrastructure is still centred around the Parade Square, which is in its original location. (1)

Until the establishment of "Depot" in 1885, training was the responsibility of each division. Recruits were simply engaged at headquarters and then transferred to the field without any training, sometimes without uniforms. At some divisions they might receive some training immediately, or they might not, depending on how busy the senior non-commissioned officers (NCOs) were with police duties, and whether or not the division was short of staff. It was not unusual for recruits to find

"Depot" – circa 1885 – #1 Orderly room, #2 Guardroom, #3 Recreation Hall, #4 Sergeants' Mess

North-West Mounted Police Barracks – "A" Block under construction on the left – 1887

themselves on detachment with no training at all. Training in most divisions was left to the winter months when many detachments and outposts were closed and the men were brought into headquarters.

In 1880, Commissioner A.G. Irvine visited Ireland to study the organization of the Royal Irish Constabulary. He was impressed with its permanent training centre, "The 'Depot' of Instruction" in Phoenix Park, Dublin. All recruits were posted there for a regular period of training, and advanced courses were provided for senior ranks.

Upon his return to Canada, Commissioner Irvine strongly recommended the establishment of a "Depot of Instruction." All recruits being engaged into the NWMP would be sent for training under experienced instructors before being sent into the field. His request fell on deaf

Commissioner A.G. Irvine, popularly known as "Old Sorrel Top"

CHAPTER 1 – IN THE BEGINNING

ears. The fact was that the government of the day gave a low priority to affairs in the North-West Territories, and the NWMP was still believed to be a temporary force that would be disbanded once the railway was completed and settlement had begun.

In 1884, Irvine complained that the exigencies of police work made it impossible to employ NCOs as instructors, and that all the recruits for that year had been posted to divisions as soon as they were engaged as members.

Within a year the situation had changed dramatically. The rebellion in 1885 finally convinced the federal government that affairs on the prairies had been neglected for too long. One of the corrective measures was the reconstruction of the NWMP, increasing the strength of the Force from 500 to 1,000 men.

On November 1, 1885, "Depot" Division was established. It was located in the territorial capital of Regina, on the site which had been the headquarters of the Force since 1882. The Mounted Police established a permanent training facility with full-time staff whose role would be to instruct recruits.

At its establishment on November 1, 1885, Commissioner Irvine placed himself in that position. Commissioner Herchmer continued to hold the command when he replaced Irvine on April 1, 1886. However, it seems that in May of that year he had second thoughts about his ability to run the Force and a division, and the command was handed over to Supt. E.W. Jarvis. From that point until 1920 when headquarters was transferred to Ottawa, the headquarter's staff, the commissioner, adjutant, supply officer, quarter master, senior surgeon and the like, were simply "attached" to "Depot" Division for administrative purposes. In the meantime, the commanding officer at "Depot" was in the unenviable position of knowing that the Commissioner could see everything that happened on the parade square from his living room window.

The creation of "Depot" enabled the Commissioner to revive the position of senior NCO of the Force. By a General Order of April 1886 the Sergeant Major of "Depot" Division became ex officio regimental sergeant major (R.S.M.). The first to hold the position was R.S.M. Robert "Bobbie" Belcher, who served in the 9th Lancers prior to coming to Canada and joined the Force as an "original" in 1873. The R.S.M. was to be a key figure in the maintenance of discipline and the smooth running of the training program.

The original instructors, Staff Sergeant George Kempster, the senior riding instructor, had served in the 11th Hussars and the 2nd Life Guards. The Riding Master, Inspector W.G. Mathews, had held a similar position in the 3rd Hussars, serving in India and West Africa. It was Kempster and Mathews who were the principals in producing the Force's first Musical Ride in 1887.

The senior drill instructor must surely be the only one the Force has ever had who had a Master of Arts degree, and was a classicist to boot. Staff Sergeant Charlie Connon, onetime head boy at Upper Canada College, had graduated from the University of Toronto with an M.A. in Latin and Greek. He was assisted by a Scotsman, Sergeant Joe White, who was a pensioner of the 12th Lancers. He had emigrated to Montreal, and when the Northwest Rebellion broke out, had gone west with a militia regiment. The Commissioner happened to see him drilling militiamen in Regina, and was so impressed he persuaded White to join the Force.

In addition to men, the government doubled the annual expenditure on the Force to over one million dollars. Most of this was spent on new buildings and other physical facilities. The days of portable huts and log detachments put up by the men themselves were coming to an end. In 1885, the responsibility for the erection and repair of Force buildings was transferred to the Department of Public Works. "Depot" was one of the main beneficiaries of the post rebellion construction program. – S.W. Horrall – RCMP historian (2)

Rules and Regulations 1889

Under the direction of Commissioner L.W. Herchmer, the first "Regulations and Orders," for the North-West Mounted Police was established in 1889. Section XXVI details the basic guidelines outlining the mandates for the rank and file who were posted to "Depot" Division during the later years of the 19th century.

1) The "Depot" Division is formed for the instruction of officers and men of the Force generally.

2) All non-commissioned officers and men of the Force will, from time to time, be ordered by the Commissioner to headquarters and attached to the "Depot" Division.

3) The course of instruction in "Depot" Division will include mounted and dismounted drill, as adapted to the Mounted Infantry Regulations: manual and firing exercise for the Winchester carbine, the Enfield revolver, musketry instruction and the duties of a Constable as laid out in the Constable's manual.

4) Every officer, on appointment, will report to the Commissioner at headquarters and will be attached to the "Depot" Division for instruction.

5) Newly appointed officers will not be passed as fit for duty until they have qualified themselves, not only in drill, riding, etc., but in the regulations and orders of the Force.

6) No officer or other member of the Force ordered or applying to be sent to the Headquarters for drill or instruction is to take any command there, but is to obey, under the superintendence of the adjutant or the officers commanding the "Depot" Division, such orders as the Commissioners may deem necessary to the object in view.

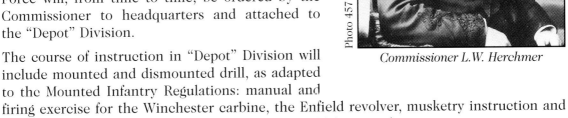

Commissioner L.W. Herchmer

"Depot" – circa 1890 – #1 Riding School, #2 Stables, #3 Recreation Hall, #4 "A" Block, #5 Guardroom, #6 Water Tower under construction, #7 "B" Block, #8 Sergeants' Mess, #9 Officers' Residences, #10 Commissioner's Residence

CHAPTER 1 – IN THE BEGINNING

Recruiting Notice

Recruits Wanted poster – July 1893

The recruiting standards have always stressed physical fitness and good character. In addition, recruits have always been required to be British subjects (Canadian citizens or British subjects residing in Canada), but prior to World War I, men of many nationalities, particularly American, were recruited. (3)

The recruits numbering 163 that have joined during the last year are generally very fine men and well adapted for our service, few of them being over 25 years of age; when enlisted beyond that age, unless already good horsemen, they seldom become so, and after that age are slow to pick up the ways of the country. – NWMP Annual Report 1890

Medical Examination form – circa 1900 – completed and approved prior to engagement

Recruiting

Recruits Wanted poster – August 1914

You are Invited to Join the RCMP – Recruiting poster – 1953

When the North-West Mounted Police was established on May 23, 1873, expectations were clearly outlined. The duties were to preserve the peace, prevent crime and apprehend criminals. Members were to act as court orderlies, jailers, customs officers, and escort prisoners and lunatics.

With the duties came the requirements for recruiting. The RCMP, to this date, attracts thousands of applicants a year. In 1873, no person was to be appointed to the Force unless "of sound constitution, able to ride, active and able bodied, of good character, and between the ages eighteen and forty. Furthermore, the men were required to be able to read and write either the English or French language." (4)

From the *North-West Mounted Police Annual Report 1887*, Superintendent R.B. Deane reports:

I received 183 applications for engagement exclusive of about 25 of which I kept no records, such as drunken men, tramps, etc. I, in all, engaged and sent to Headquarters, 63 intelligent and able bodied men, who produced recommendations or testimonials, which I believe to be authentic.

I am deluged with applications from all parts, even the old country and the United States, for admission to our ranks. A very large proportion are farmer's sons and I still prefer this class to all others.

I gave every man fully to understand the conditions of service in the Mounted Police, set forth its disadvantages and well as its advantages, pointed out that discharge by purchase being rarely permitted, unless a man had made up his mind to serve for the five years of his engagement, he had better not sign the papers.

Sixty-two applicants were rejected by the examining surgeons, varicoceles and varicose veins being prominent disqualifications. Of the remaining 58 some were rejected as being under height or age. Two could not read or write. Some were sent to the doctor for examination and did not go to him, others who underwent examination ascertained that they were sound and well and went their way. – NWMP Annual Report 1887, Superintendent R.B. Deane

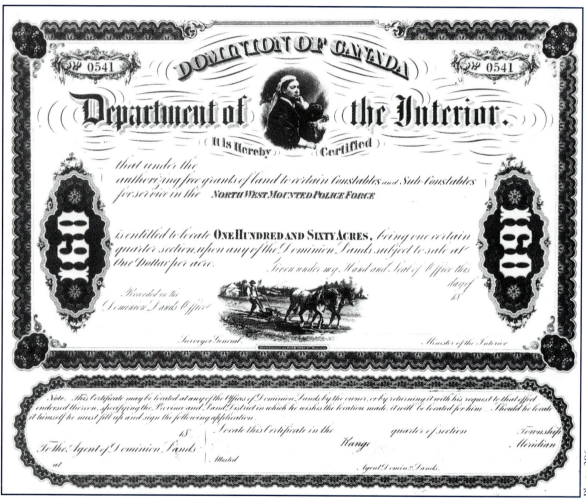

Free land grant of 160 acres in the North-West Territories was provided to members upon expiration of their three-year commitment to the Force

Engagement was for a period of three years and, as an incentive, upon expiration of their service, men would receive a free land grant of 160 acres in the North-West Territories. The salary scale ranged from $2,000-$2,600 for the Commissioner to $1 per day for constables and seventy-five cents for sub constables. New members could not be married and could only marry after 5 years service with approval from senior officers.

In the late 1880s and early '90s, the Force's attrition rate averaged 15-20 percent. With an establishment of 1,000 it needed to recruit 150-200 men every year. The typical recruit of the time was a native Canadian from the farms of Ontario, Quebec and the Maritimes. He had some public school education (a few were illiterate) was between 18-25 years of age and was 5'9". He may have had some experience in a trade or semi-skilled work. With his rural background he was used to hard manual labour and long hours of work; he could handle an axe, knew how to fish and hunt and understood the care of domestic animals. This was exactly what the commissioner was looking for. Herchmer regarded "townies" as soft, easily discontented and not likely to be satisfied with the pay of 50 cents per day. Recruiting officers were warned, before leaving for the east to recruit men, to look closely at the hands of the applicants. – S.W. Horrall – RCMP historian (5)

Qualifications to be considered for the Force in 1933 included:

- not less than 21 and not more than 30 years unless he has had previous naval, military or police experience, at the discretion of the Commissioner, age limit may be increased to 40
- minimum chest measurement of 35 inches
- minimum height of 5'8"
- minimum weight of 185 lbs. (6)

In the RCMP Annual Report of 1937, Superintendent T.H. Irvine noted:

These men were recruited from the provinces of Alberta, Saskatchewan and Manitoba, and were as fine a type of manhood as I have ever seen. They were keen to the n'th degree, each individual, without exception, putting his whole energy into the work with a view of gaining a permanent position in the Force, and it was with great difficulty and only with the greatest of care that the selection was made to fill our quota.

Over the years, basic qualifications for applicants have changed little. Age (18-30 years) and height restrictions (5'8"-6'5"), as well as unmarried applicants only, have all been removed from the process. An applicant today must possess a valid Canadian driver's license and high school education as minimum standards.

Current minimum qualifications include:

- be a Canadian citizen
- be of good character
- be proficient in either of Canada's official languages
- have a Canadian secondary school diploma or equivalent
- possess a valid unrestricted Canadian driver's licence
- be at least 19 years of age at the time of engagement
- be able to meet the physical/medical requirement
- be willing to relocate anywhere in Canada (7)

Today's cadets are a diverse and multicultural population representing Canada's demographics.

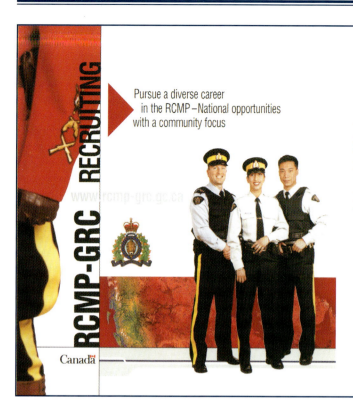

THE ROYAL CANADIAN MOUNTED POLICE, is in terms of the Canadian police community, a large, multifaceted organization which is charged with a broad mandate encompassing federal, provincial, and municipal policing responsibilities. Organizationally, the RCMP is divided into four Regions which, in turn, are split into fourteen Divisions for operational purposes with Divisional boundaries being established primarily on the basis of provincial/territorial boundaries. Divisions are further divided into districts, which are specific geographic boundaries and these are, in turn, divided into detachment areas. The Commanding Officers of Divisions are directly responsible to the Commissioner of the RCMP, and receive functional direction from Directorate Heads and Branch Officers in Ottawa, Ontario.

BASIC REQUIREMENTS
- Canadian citizen
- Proficient in either of Canada's official languages (English and/or French)
- 19 years of age or older at the time of enrollment
- Min. Grade 12 or equivalent (GED) from a Canadian educational institution
- Possess a valid Class 5 Canadian Driver's license
- Meet the physical and medical requirements
- Be of good character

RCMP RECRUITMENT— OUR COMMITMENT TO CULTURAL DIVERSITY

In terms of recruitment, the RCMP encourages the participation of women, visible minorities and aboriginal peoples. The RCMP is seeking to employ more persons with disabilities in non-peace officer roles. The RCMP is committed to a membership which is representative of our diverse Canadian society and to promoting and supporting equity within its employment practices. The RCMP is committed to policies and practices which reflect all laws, regulations and government commitments confirming and dealing with cultural diversity, including all laws prohibiting discrimination on any ground not related to effective performance on the job.

Current RCMP Recruiting Campaign Information

"Depot" Division – Not a Favourite Place

"Depot" Division was not a favourite location for most recruits. Their stay was something to endure and get over with as soon as possible. Commissioner Herchmer was determined that it would be a showplace for the many distinguished visitors who came to see the famous North-West Mounted Police. There was a constant grind of parades, escorts and fatigues, and every change in the day's routine was signaled by a bugle call, from reveille at 5:30 a.m. (6:30 a.m. in winter) to "lights out." Discipline was stricter there than anywhere else in the Force. A recruit could find himself in the guardroom, minus a few dollars pay, for having a button undone.
– S.W. Horrall – RCMP historian (8)

Looking south on Sleigh Square. The Chapel is prominent in the background – circa 1935

Desertion

Once signed on to join the North-West Mounted Police, there was no turning back. Charges of desertion were laid to those that decided to leave Regina without authorization. In one famous case, a recruit named Joe Clark started training at "Depot" in 1892. Having come from Ontario, he did not enjoy the regimental training or barracks life. He deserted from "Depot" and was pursued to Ontario, where he was brought to justice. A normal desertion charge was usually six months in jail, but because the magistrate was his uncle, he was handed a $100 fine. Joe Clark completed law school and went on to a controversial life in politics in Edmonton. – *Edmonton Journal*, Sunday October 3, 2004, by Christopher Spencer (9)

Conduct and Discipline

The conduct of the division has been good, very few breaches of discipline of a serious nature being recorded, and of those the majority were due to negligence. A good many minor offences were committed, and this is only natural amongst a number of recruits unused to discipline and barrack routine. In the case of new men I make it a rule to try admonition and advice before giving them entries in the defaulters book, and also try if possible to make a man take a pride in keeping his sheet clean.

I regret to report eleven desertions during the year, as compared with six last year. Two of these were captured. The cause of these desertions I attribute to new men fearing the responsibilities that are likely to be placed upon them, and to the fact that recruits joining have a particularly hard time at the outset of their career. – RNWMP Annual Report 1907, Superintendent G.E. Sanders

RCMP Rules and Regulations 1935

165. Should a Non-commissioned Officer or Constable be absent without leave, for seven full days, he will be classed as a deserter.

166. Where there is good ground for supposing an absentee to have deserted, a report is to be forwarded to the Commissioner within twenty-four hours after his absence has been discovered, and a description of the man circulated with a view to effecting his arrest.

168. In the case of deserters, the word "discharged," where it appears immediately after the statement of service on (Form 54) viz: "and is now discharged" is to be struck out and the words "struck off" substituted, so that the sentence will read, "and who is now struck off in consequence of having deserted and is transferred to the deserters' roll at Headquarters."

RCMP Rules and Regulations 1936

59. Every Constable on engagement will be posted to the "Depot" Division (except as otherwise thought advisable by the Commissioner) for instruction and training in his duties and is not, except when authorized by the Commissioner, to be employed on any Police Work until he has qualified.

Royalty and Royal Visits

Royal Visits have played a prominent role in the history of "Depot" Division. Kings, Queens, Heads of States and Canadian Prime Ministers have regularly visited "Depot" Division to tour the site, make official presentations, partake or observe parades and ceremonies, and inspect the troops.

Superintendent R.S. Knight, Commanding Officer "Depot," and His Royal Highness, The Duke of Connaught inspected the division in 1925. A squadron of three troops under Knight took responsibility for the tour. Afterwards, the entourage pitched camp in the cricket field.

It was reported that His Royal Highness expressed himself as highly pleased with the smartness of the troops and the fine appearance of the horses.

Preparing for the 1911 Coronation of His Majesty King George V in front of the Officers' residences at "Depot." On May 20, 1911, a detachment of 82 men and 80 horses left Regina to participate in the coronation in London, England

HRH the Prince of Wales in 1919 in front of "B" Block

CHAPTER 1 – IN THE BEGINNING

Left to right – Cst. R. Portelance, Sgt. W.H. Williams, Queen Elizabeth, A/Commr. LaNauze, King George VI, Cst. J.C Coughlin, Cst. S. Langois in front of the Chapel

May 25, 1939 Regina – Their Majesties were greeted by Commissioner S.T. Wood and Assistant Commissioner C.H. King after descending from their automobile and about to enter the Officers' Mess – Regina Leader-Post

On May 25, 1939, Their Majesties King George VI and Queen Elizabeth, accompanied by Prime Minister W.L. MacKenzie King, as part of a tour of the City of Regina, also honoured the Force by visiting the barracks. Their Majesties partook in a tea at the Officers' Mess while the RCMP band played musical selections. Their Majesties spent an hour resting, and conducted an informal tour of inspection.

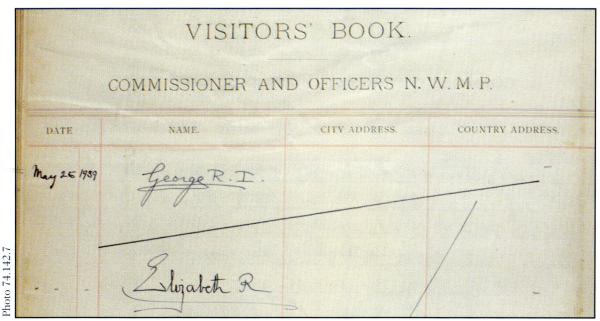

Signatures of Their Majesties in the visitors' book at the Officers' Mess

Today, the chairs which seated Their Majesties are on display in the Officers' Mess. They each have a plaque inscribed with the names and the date of the Royal Visit. Their Majesties signed the Guest Book in the Officers' Mess and reportedly thoroughly enjoyed their visit to "Depot" Division.

Prime Minister W.L. MacKenzie King returned to "Depot" in 1940 for an informal visit and tour of the base. He was shown the cenotaph, the scientific laboratory, the swimming pool and the museum. The Prime Minister concluded his visit by declaring that the history and traditions of the Royal Canadian Mounted Police were among Canada's proudest heritages.

On April 23, 1941, The Governor General, the Earl of Athlone and Princess Alice toured the base.

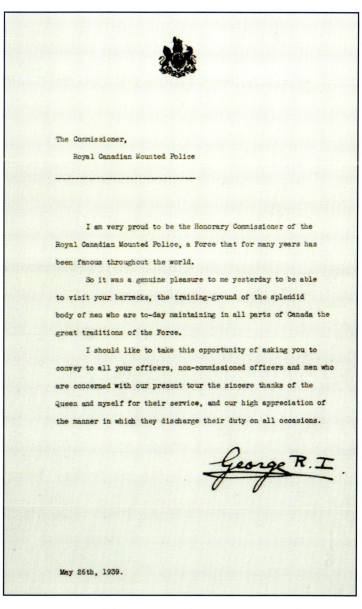

Letter of appreciation from King George VI, complimenting members of the Force for their service to Canada

CHAPTER 1 – IN THE BEGINNING

Queen Elizabeth II and Prince Philip visit "Depot" in 1959

Her Majesty Queen Elizabeth II is the Honourary Commissioner of the Royal Canadian Mounted Police. Queen Elizabeth has visited "Depot" Division on several occasions, each time marking significant and often personal events in the Force's history.

On one occasion, a member of the RCMP was requested to attend the Royal Suite at the Hotel Saskatchewan during the Queen's visit to Regina. Inspector Herbert Robertson received a call at the barracks in 1959. Inspector Robertson, who was born and raised on the Royal Estate at Balmoral, had been connected with the Royal Family since Queen Victoria's reign. Inspector Robertson reported that the "seven or eight minute conversation with the Queen was like talking to my wife or sister," and that the visit was more or less a discussion of his family connections.

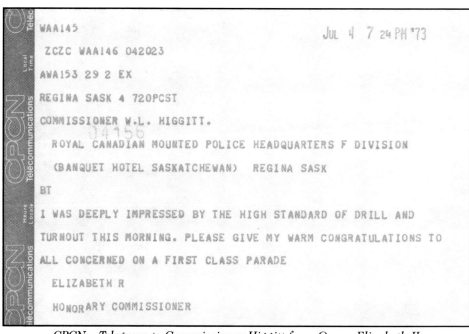

CPCN – Telegram to Commissioner Higgitt from Queen Elizabeth II

Her Majesty's Visit to "Depot" – 1973

Queen Elizabeth II escorted by Supt. W.F. MacRae at "Depot" in 1973.

S/Sgt. Harry Armstrong presenting "Centenial" to Her Majesty with Commissioner W.L. Higgitt looking on

On the occasion of the 100th Anniversary of the Force in 1973, Her Majesty presided over the official opening of the RCMP Centennial Museum, the presentation of the RCMP Guidon to Commissioner Higgitt and the troops on parade.

Her Majesty Queen Elizabeth II – presenting the Guidon to Commissioner W.L. Higgitt – 1973

Prince Edward inspects troops in August of 1994 escorted by Supt. L. Chipperfield and C/Supt. J.R.A. Gauthier

Her Majesty Queen Elizabeth II, Honourary Commissioner of the RCMP, and Commissioner G. Zaccardelli – 2005

In 2005, during a Royal visit to Saskatchewan and Alberta to celebrate the 100th anniversary of the two provinces, Queen Elizabeth requested a private audience in the RCMP Chapel with the families of four members of the Force who were slain on March 3, 2005 in Mayerthorpe, Alberta.

The RCMP has had a long and proud association with the Honourary Commissioner of the Royal Canadian Mounted Police, Her Majesty, Queen Elizabeth II.

Her Majesty Queen Elizabeth II inspects RCMP veterans during her visit to "Depot" on May 19, 2005

Commanding Officer of "Depot" C/Supt. Pierre Ménard with Her Majesty Queen Elizabeth II and Saskatchewan children – 2005

Her Majesty Queen Elizabeth II and C/Supt. Pierre Ménard inspecting "Depot" Facilitators – 2005

Her Majesty Queen Elizabeth II and Prince Philip laying a wreath in honour of the four RCMP members slain at Mayerthorpe, Alberta – 2005

Chapter 1 – In the Beginning   29

Hollywood

Since the Force's inception, Hollywood and the motion picture industry have been fascinated with portraying the legacy of the Canadian Mountie. Motion pictures were filmed about the Scarlet-Clad Mounties and often the barracks at "Depot" were utilized in the films. England also expressed interest in Mountie training and filmed a motion picture titled *The 49th Parallel*.

"Sneak" previews, such as the Metro-Goldwyn-Mayer film *Maintain the Right* which dealt with training activities in Regina highlighting the progress of recruits, were held for Officers of "Depot" Division. Members were detailed to attend Hollywood to supervise barrack and drill scenes.

Cst. Foley-Bennet and Cst. Ball training for Hollywood – July 1927

Film being shot in barracks – circa 1930

North West Mounted Police

When the world premiere of North West Mounted Police, *starring Gary Cooper and Madeline Carroll, was held in Regina in 1940, the* Leader-Post *published a special pictorial addition detailing the growth and development of the Force. These were major events for the Force, the city and even Canada as the publicity generated was world wide. The city of Regina was decorated with flags and bunting, store fronts mirrored log settings and people travelled from far away to participate in the show. The* Leader-Post *special edition was sent to over 400 detachments country wide, as well as to the detachment fighting in Britain's battle overseas.*

Some of the movies stars, Madeline Carroll, Preston Foster, Lynne Overman and Robert Preston attended the Regina premiere and were greeted by the A/Commissioner LaNauze and C.O. T.H. Irvine of the day, who entertained them at a luncheon at the Officers' Mess and a tour of the barracks. Miss Carroll also opened the RCAF flying field extension while in Saskatchewan. A grand street parade was held, led by a Mounted Police officer flying the Union Jack. All other units of the Army and Air Force training in Regina at the time (over 1,000) participated in the parade as well. (10)

Scene from North West Mounted Police *– Hollywood, California 1940, where Canadian history is rewritten as Gary Cooper, the Texas Ranger, arrives in time to win the girl, Madeleine Carroll, and the Riel Rebellion*

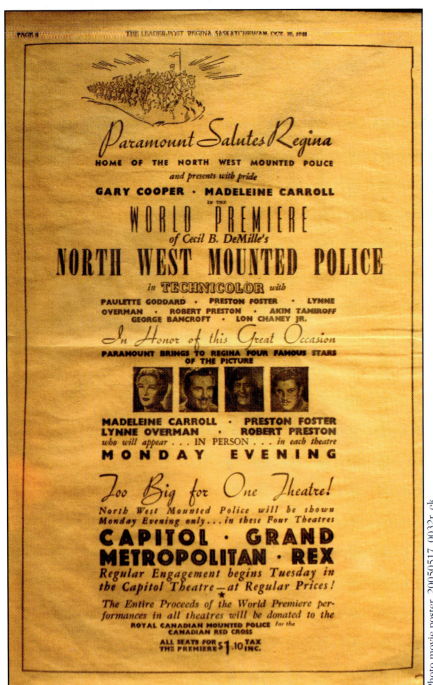

The Leader-Post *ad promoting the movie North West Mounted Police – on premiere night in October 1940, Cecil B. DeMille's North West Mounted Police was shown at four Regina theaters, the Capitol, Rex, Metropolitan and Grand. It was followed by a Premiere Ball at the Armouries*

Frequent visits were made by producers for other films including Universal Studio's Canada Carries On series. The Force has proudly been the subject of, and participated in hundreds of motion picture and television shows during its history.

Films on the Force generally followed two themes, "Love versus duty" and "The Mountie always gets his man," leading many to believe, to the annoyance of members, that the latter was their motto. The romanticized Rose Marie, set in the northwest, stared Eddy Nelson as a singing sergeant in the RCMP and Jeannette McDonald as a French Canadian opera star looking for her brother who had escaped from jail. Rose Marie gave the RCMP more publicity than any other film, resulting in the Force's members detesting the term the, "Rose Marie police force."

To combat misrepresentations, the RCMP has often provided production crews with technical advisors. These advisors were hired to ensure that a film's costumes, characters and storyline were accurate representations of the Canadian Mountie. (11)

Postcards

The Royal Canadian Mounted Police are world-famous and are often utilized on postcards as part of Canada's portrayal of its national police force and tourism. Many of the historical postcards provide a pictorial record of "Depot" Division, including parades, residences, training, buildings, horses, uniforms and life at the early police academy.

R. N. W. M. POLICE ON PARADE.   REGINA, SASK.

R. N. W. M. POLICE – ADMINISTRATION BUILDING.   REGINA, SASK.

Chapter 1 – In the Beginning   33

Social Activities

Invitation to a Dance At "Depot" – 1935

In the late eighteen nineties, the halcyon days of the Force, Regina Barracks was the centre of society and hospitality for a large region. Monthly balls were held during the winter and attracted the youth and beauty, not only of Regina, but of the whole surrounding countryside. The ballroom on these occasions would be decorated with flags and trophies; and floors were waxed until they were as slippery as ice. The red tunics of the men and the brilliant mess jackets of the Officers, the pretty frocks of the ladies and the black coats of the civilian guests, all combined to add a touch of colour and gaiety to a shifting swirling scene. But the main feature of these balls was the NWMP band which kept such excellent time that the dancers just couldn't keep their feet still. Sergeant Walker was always in the limelight out in front conducting, he face beaming with pleasure and good humour. (12)

With the construction of the new elaborate gym in 1937/38, it proved to be an ideal place for the festivities and, provided with good music by Russ Isadore and his orchestra, everyone spent a very enjoyable evening. This was not only the first "Depot" Division dance for 1938, but also the first even to be held in the new building. In the basement is the rifle range which proved to be a most suitable place for the buffet lunch which was served at midnight. (13)

Members of Troop #26, New Year's Eve Ball – 1955/56

34 BEHIND THE BADGE

Some downtown Regina establishments became well ingrained in RCMP history as "Mountie bars" where recruits, free on a leave pass, looked for entertainment.

For the most part, social activities on the base usually revolved around sporting events. Inter-troop rivalry and competition most often ended up with an evening of dance and entertainment in the Drill Hall. Monthly dances were held and one comment in an annual report indicated that "monthly dances have been interesting as usual this winter, telephone calls being fast and furious about the first Friday in the month." (14) "Dances, sponsored by the Officers, NCOs and Constables attracted in excess of 600 people on a Friday night." (15) Recruits had to be issued passes so they could enjoy a full evening and later see their guests safely home.

Prior to females being permitted to join the Force, arrangements were made to ensure that there would be female attendance at the dances for the all-male cadre of recruits. "The dance area was colourfully complemented by an encouraging representation of attractive student nurses from local hospitals. (16)

As with any institution that houses hundreds of young people at a time, "Depot" Division, over the years, has promoted social activities that encourage esprit de corps and allow for some rest and relaxation time. Given that the cadets are mostly isolated with their troops during the day, social events provide the opportunity for cadets to get to know each other.

New Year's Eve Ball in Post Gymnasium at "Depot" – 1956

Recruits "volunteered" for busboy duties – circa 1960

A formal Officers' Mess place setting

CHAPTER 1 – IN THE BEGINNING

Packed dance floor at the Drill Hall – circa 1960

In the new millennium, social activities still exist at "Depot." Events such as "Who Wants to Be a Mountie," based on a popular television show, pit troop against troop as contestants answer questions about RCMP history, academic subjects and other training issues.

The Annual New Year's Eve ball at the Drill Hall continues to be one of the main events for the city. Tickets are sold out well in advance to this popular event. "The bright scarlet uniforms of the officers and men of the force, interspersed with the dress uniform of the other Services, the black evening gowns of the feminine guests, formed a colourful combination with which to give the New Year a most happy welcome at the annual New Year's Eve Ball. (17)

The RCMP also supports many charities which hold events at "Depot."

Charity Ball "Depot" – 1962

Saskatchewan Hard of Hearing Charity Ball – 2003 – Grand March (left to right) Mrs. Moulton, C.O. "F" Division A/Comm. Moulton, C/Supt. Tugnum, Mrs. Tugnum, Commissioner G. Zaccardelli, Their Honours Lieutenant Governor Lynda Haverstock and Mr. Harley Olsen

Saskatchewan Hard of Hearing Charity Ball – 2003 – one of the many charities supported by the RCMP

Game Dinners

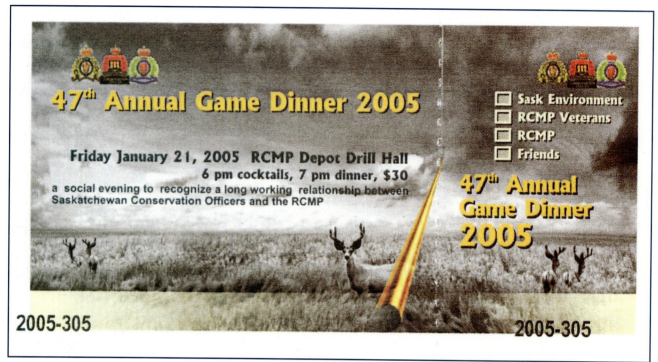

Ticket to the 2005 Annual Game Dinner

One of the traditions that has continued at "Depot" Division for 48 consecutive years is the Annual Game Dinner. The event, which is held in the Drill Hall, was conceptualized by Ernest L. Paynter, then the Director of the Wildlife Branch of Saskatchewan, and Staff Sergeant Major James Robinson of the Forensic Laboratory in Regina in 1958. The objective of the dinner was the recognition of the outstanding service and cooperation between the two agencies. The initial agreement was that the Game Branch provide the various species of game (including elk, moose, caribou, mule deer, white-tailed deer, buffalo, black bear, fish and pheasant) and the Senior NCO Mess would provide the venue, their cook and program for the dinner. The annual dinner, as it still stands today, is a tribute to its founders, S/S/M Jimmy Robinson and Mr. Ernie Paynter.

Until his death in 2002, Staff Sergeant. C.J.W. (Jack) Chester (rtd.), Reg. #12524, was the only person who had attended every dinner.

Christmas at "Depot"

NWMP Christmas menu at "Depot" – 1888

Christmas greetings from "Depot" – 1894

Preparing for Christmas festivities in Division Mess – circa 1940

CHAPTER 1 – IN THE BEGINNING

"A Merry Christmas" card – circa 1895

Christmas greetings from "Depot" – 2005

Since 1882, Christmas has always played a large and important role at "Depot." Because the recruits and cadets, as well as the majority of facilitators, were separated from their families, extra effort was made to ensure everyone had an opportunity to celebrate Christmas.

Christmas scenes of the base at the festive season were often used as cards to send to family and friends. Christmas feasts were prepared, followed by entertainment in the Messes. It is believed that during this time the tradition originated of the senior officer serving dinner to the junior constables, fostering esprit de corps and camaraderie.

"Christmas was also a time for the Mounties to celebrate with the residents of Saskatchewan. Festive galas were held, levees and, of course, the children were not forgotten. In 1933, the 'Mounties' held their annual Christmas party, and Santa hosted ninety-six children, all under the age of twelve." (18) "500 members and friends were entertained by the RCMP Regina Band in a 1950 Christmas concert held in the gymnasium." (19) The RCMP remains an active participant within the community.

Christmas Dinner in the old Mess, Members of Troop #26 1955/56, December 1955

Christmas Dinner – Special Constable Troop – circa 1980

To this day, Sleigh Square and the base are still elaborately decorated with bright Christmas lights and ornaments. Christmas carols can be heard playing from the public address system and walks in the winter wonderland looking at the bright Christmas decorations en route to the Chapel for a Christmas Eve mass can not help but put everyone on the base in a festive spirit.

A.B. Perry Building at Christmas

Chapter 1 – In the Beginning

Chapter 2

BUILDINGS

"A" Block
– Building No. 14

The biggest additions of 1887, were the construction of the two, two-storey barracks buildings, on the west side of the square, known as "A" and "B" Blocks. These buildings were built with basements and were the first buildings in Regina to have central heating – coal-fired furnaces. (1) "A" and "B" Blocks replaced the portable huts that had been erected in 1882. (2) One of the huts became the Herchmer District Public School, employing Miss O'Flynn as the teacher. She taught the rudiments of education to a handful of "Depot's" children. (3)

"On the night of March 21, l912, a most disastrous fire burnt down the "A" barrack block; this building being of old well-dried wood, was soon a mass of flames and nothing was saved from it, everything being consumed; some of the men had difficulty in getting clear, one having to jump from the second-story window. This building is being replaced by a modern structure, which has been commenced, but owing to the strike of bricklayers and carpenters, work has been at a standstill for the last few days, and a temporary covering put over to protect the work already completed from the winter storms. It is to be hoped that this building will be completed as early as possible next summer. The contract was awarded to Messrs. Smith Bros. & Wilson, of Regina. – RNWMP Annual Report 1913, Inspector R.S. Knight – "Depot"

The original two-storey "A" Block on the left, "B" Block on the right, both constructed in 1887

"A" Block and the second Riding School – circa 1900

The structure originally housed the artisan's shops, with stores in the basement and offices on the upper floors. The armorer shop was also housed in "A" Block and many of the Ross & Lee Metfold carbines were also lost in the fire. The north portion of the building was occupied by the Sergeants' Mess with bedrooms and a billiard room. The basement housed supply stores, quartermasters' store and tailor shop while the remainder of the building was Divisional and Headquarters' offices.

"A" Block, the most architecturally significant building, is designed in a derivative Tudor Gothic style. Its stone decorated red brick exterior, gable roof form and distinctive stone-capped end gables were also emulated in most of the major "Depot" buildings constructed between 1929 and 1943. (4)

Since its construction in 1912, the grandest building at "Depot" has been "A" Block, the new administrative building constructed in the Tudor Gothic style. This building which was once the Headquarters of the Force was designed with a projecting central entryway, steeped parapets

"A" Block designed by Regina architect Neil R. Darrach and built in 1912-13 by the construction firm of the Smith Brothers and Wilson at a cost of $77,800. "A" Block became the showcase of Commissioner Perry's rebuilding plans for the Academy as the most stylistically elaborate of all "Depot" buildings

CHAPTER 2 – BUILDINGS

The A.B. Perry Building – 2005

and corner towers or buttresses. It has, at various times, included the offices of the Commissioner, both the Commanding Officers of "Depot" and "F" Divisions, the Post Adjutant, a telephone switchboard, Quartermaster's Stores, support offices, the mail room, the Senior NCOs' Mess and living accommodations. A two-storey brick addition, to house extra officers was added at the rear of the building in 1937-38. This annex was erected on the foundation of the original sub-grade boiler room, accessible from the central cross corridors of the main building.

In 1998, as part of the RCMP's 125th anniversary celebrations, the building was renamed in honour of former Commissioner Major-General Aylesworth Bowen Perry. Major-General Perry holds the distinction of having been the only Commissioner of the Force under the three different names by which it has been known: The North-West Mounted Police, the Royal Northwest Mounted Police and the Royal Canadian Mounted Police. He was Commissioner from 1900 to 1923, the longest-serving Commissioner of the Force. The administration building at the RCMP Training Academy Regina is dedicated to his memory. The office now occupied by the Commanding Officer of "Depot" Division was once the Commissioner's office, prior to the Force relocating its Headquarters to Ottawa in 1920.

Commissioner A.B. Perry

Applied Police Sciences (APS)
– Building #96

Main entrance to the Applied Police Sciences Building – 2000

As the focus on training changed, so to did the need for expanded and modern facilities for the day-to-day academic instruction of the recruits. In 1972, Commissioner W. L. Higgitt officially opened the new academic building at a cost of $796,803.00. The two-storey structure contained 16 classrooms, four syndicate rooms, an auditorium and facilitator offices.

This was the first time in the Force's history that a building was specifically constructed for academic use and, given its modern intercom system, air conditioning and carpeting, it marked a significant change in direction for the RCMP. At the time, approximately 60 per cent of a recruit's studies was spent in the classroom.

In May of 2000, in order to accommodate a large increase in the number of cadet troops in a fiscal year, an addition was built onto the north end of the academic building, containing additional facilitator office space and four classrooms.

The present day has seen a shift in traditional classroom teaching to a program that requires several of the classrooms and Hall #1 dedicated to the use of computers and the internet.

Hall #1 – 2005

CHAPTER 2 – BUILDINGS 45

Artisan Shop
– Building 24 – the original "D" Block

"The artisan's workshop was designed by Reilly, Warburton and Reilly and built in 1935-36 to accommodate the urgent need for the consolidation of support artisan services and an overflow dormitory for twenty men in its dormered upper level." (5) "Old 'D' Block now houses the painters, carpenters, electricians, saddlers and tailor shops." (6) Storage was also the main requirement for this building in 1976.

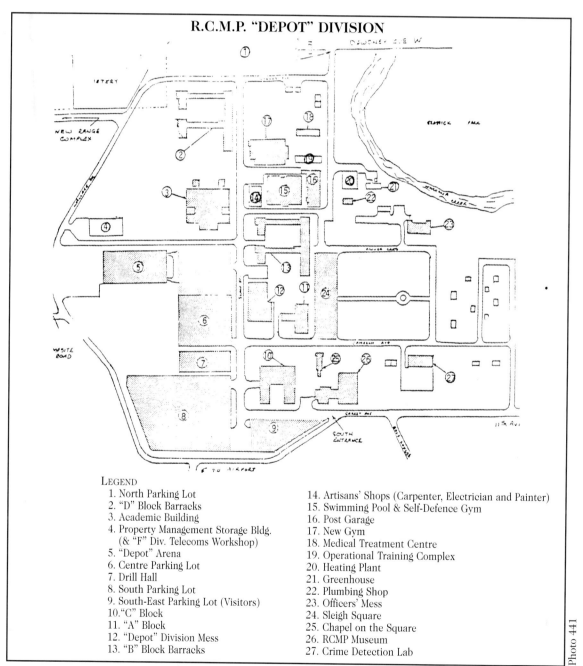

LEGEND
1. North Parking Lot
2. "D" Block Barracks
3. Academic Building
4. Property Management Storage Bldg. (& "F" Div. Telecoms Workshop)
5. "Depot" Arena
6. Centre Parking Lot
7. Drill Hall
8. South Parking Lot
9. South-East Parking Lot (Visitors)
10. "C" Block
11. "A" Block
12. "Depot" Division Mess
13. "B" Block Barracks
14. Artisans' Shops (Carpenter, Electrician and Painter)
15. Swimming Pool & Self-Defence Gym
16. Post Garage
17. New Gym
18. Medical Treatment Centre
19. Operational Training Complex
20. Heating Plant
21. Greenhouse
22. Plumbing Shop
23. Officers' Mess
24. Sleigh Square
25. Chapel on the Square
26. RCMP Museum
27. Crime Detection Lab

Map of "Depot" 1988, showing Artisan's Shop as #14

BEHIND THE BADGE

By the 1980s the upper floor of the building was converted to storage space, removing the dormitory space that had originally occupied the floor.

The building was used continuously for artisan purposes until 1995, when a large artisan shop and maintenance yard were constructed off of Barker Avenue, allowing for the renovation of the current resource centre which was once housed on the lower floor of the APS building.

"D" Block Barracks, which subsequently became the Tailor Shop – 1940

Artisan Shop – currently the "Depot" Resource Centre – 2000

The current Artisan Building – 2005

CHAPTER 2 – BUILDINGS 47

"B" Block
– Building #72

"The biggest additions to 'Depot' in 1887 were the construction of 'A' and 'B' Blocks on the west side of the parade square, replacing the portable huts that had been erected in 1882." (7) "B" Block was erected at a cost of $26,010.00 and for the first twenty-five years of its life the building remained a frame structure, at the mercy of cold winter winds, the trademarks of prairie winters.

"B" Block was originally built in 1887 on the west side of the Parade Square – a third floor and dormers were added in 1934, allowing additional capacity

Both "A" and "B" Blocks were built at a time when there was no plumbing or sewage system. A buffalo coat was necessary to face a very cold walk on a winter's night to the unheated latrines beyond the square. "Electric lights were installed throughout 'Depot' in 1896 but it was not until 1907 that flush toilets were placed in 'A' and 'B' Blocks." (8) "They were connected into a septic tank which drained into the Wascana Creek." (9) Hardwood floors were

Night shot of "B" Block – 1936

The appearance of Sleigh Square was vastly altered when the last original barrack, "B" Block, was demolished in 1956 – circa 1930

New "B" Block – under construction and as completed in 1956. The Division Mess is located in the centre of both photos

added to all barracks rooms and stairways were fitted with oak steps. In 1913, the structure was "bricked over," to fully secure "B" Block and fireproof it. In 1934, a third story was added to the building allowing the top two floors to accommodate 100 men. The lower floor housed an additional thirty-five men, with the remaining space occupied by an orderly room, pay office, interior economy staff, canteen, restrooms, typing and lecture rooms.

"B" Block was demolished and replaced in 1956 with a horseshoe-shaped building which is currently in use. It contains eleven 32-man dormitories, nine single-man rooms, laundry and polishing facilities and the Post Barber Shop.

Cst. J.R.R. Bourget, Reg. #35591, Troop 6, 1979/80, in "B" Block

CHAPTER 2 – BUILDINGS

"B" Block under construction – looking south – Division Mess, once connected to the former "B" Block, is in the centre of the photo – 1956

"B" Block third floor, prior to the placement of furniture – February 1958

Interior of "B" Block – 2004

Barber Shop

Short haircuts are part and parcel of life at "Depot" Division. A barber shop is located in the basement of "B" Block to provide members with hair cutting facilities. Recruits are scheduled as a troop and the troops will be advised well in advance of their appointments, by the head barber, through mail service. Hairdressing facilities for females are not available, however females may obtain minor trimming if they arrange this ahead of time with the barbers. (10)

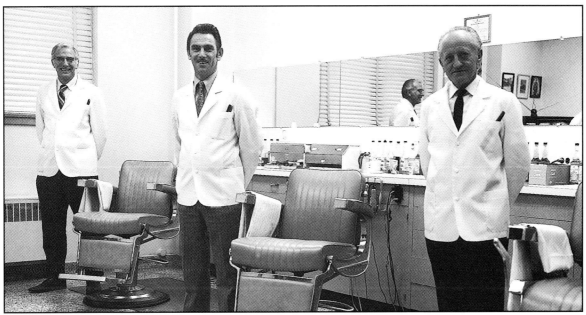

Barber Service – in the basement of "B" Block – circa 1970

One of the first, and sometimes most traumatic, stops a new recruit makes upon arrival at "Depot" is at the Division Barber Shop. Dress, deportment, and grooming play a fundamental role in the development of future RCMP officers. The Force followed military traditions for short hair as long hair had been found to be a health hazard in cramped, hot barrack rooms. This also applied to beards, which to this day are not permitted in the RCMP.

The highest standards are enforced by the Drill, Deportment and Tactical Training staff, as well as the rest of the facilitators at "Depot." It was not uncommon for a recruit, upon being inspected in troop formation, to be ordered to trim, or shave off, his moustache and report to the Drill Hall at 6:30 a.m. for re-inspection as a result of having a moustache longer "than regulation." Regulations in the Administration Manual 2005 dictate "keep your face clean shaven," however:

"I. 2. b. If a mustache is grown, keep it:
1. neatly trimmed with ends not extending more than .625 cm below your mouth or 1.25 cm beyond the corners of your mouth; and
2. conservative and not excessive or unsightly."

Trainees were expected to exhibit the ability to present themselves in a professional manner while undergoing basic training, and it was ingrained through discipline and rigid standards.

Regulations on hair include, 'keep your hair short and ensure that it does not cover any part of your ears.'

1. Keep your sideburns above the bottom edge of the opening of the ear within 2.5 cm width and .625 cm thickness."

Haircuts were scheduled into the syllabus on a weekly basis, whether the recruits needed them or not. The cost of a haircut was minimal for many years; today, although not scheduled, a haircut costs $8.00. Although tipping was not mandatory, a recruit would be remembered the next time he sat in the chair.

One's first acquaintance upon reaching 'Depot' was the regimental barber. This writer's last civilian act before departing for Regina was to get a haircut, but upon arrival was soon ordered to get a haircut – regimental style. The cost was a modest 25 cents out of that day's pay of $1.50 plus 50 cents bonus per diem. Regardless, no hair beneath the hat. If the horses' manes were clipped, why not the men and they both looked neat. – ex-Cst. G.V. Wellman, Reg. #9948 – 1923 (11)

A strict military haircut was the rule, "short up the sides and back," and this meant short! Ideally no hair should be visible when wearing headgear. – ex-Cst. T. Jamieson Quirk, Reg. #11951 – 1932 (12)

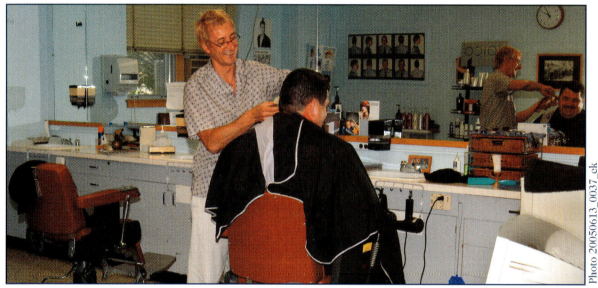

Damien Mauro in the current Barber Shop – The Barber Shop was previously located in both "A" and "C" Blocks and is currently in the basement of "B" Block – 2005

In June 1953 Mike Carroll was working for the Force at "Depot." Mike managed the Post Hospital and was the unofficial "barber." It was Mike who gave new recruits what was often their first "close" haircut. Many a tear was shed as the locks fell onto the floor. Frequently, during the haircut, Mr. Carroll would dip the blade of the clippers into a jar of oil. This was meant solely to keep the clippers running smoothly, not to put a shine on the recruit's hair. Mr. Carroll's main responsibility was as the I/C (In Charge) of the Post Hospital. At morning Sick Parade, he would screen the recruits (a triage of sorts) and decide who the doctor would see and who would receive some over-the-counter remedy from his nearby medicine cabinet. – Supt. John Religa (rtd.), Reg. #0.947, "H" Troop, 1953/54

Familiarization Booklet for Recruits – "Depot" Division 1969

Grooming – Section 3, Page 3

The Commissioner's Standing Orders state that:
A male member shall always appear clean and correctly dressed with boots, badges, buttons and accoutrements polished. He shall be properly shaved and the hair of the head kept "short."

A full-time regimental barber is employed at this Post. Hair cuts are by appointment only. You will require a hair cut at least once a week. Because of the vigorous physical activity required of members in training, it is necessary to keep the hair on the top of the head short, no longer than two inches. Side burns are not acceptable and every member should start to shave approximately 1/8 inch below the point where the ear joins the head. Care should be taken to hold the razor level when shaving the sideburns.

Shaving is a man's job. You must shave daily, even though you have a very light beard. The proper time to shave is before breakfast. This is a habit that must be firmly implanted during training.

A haircut in the Force means just that. At "Depot" Division the Hospital Orderly is authorized to cut hair at times not conflicting with his duties. Your hair is to be kept neatly cut at all times. At "Depot" Division a fee of 25 cents is charged. Prelude to Duty 1947 (13)

Barrack Life

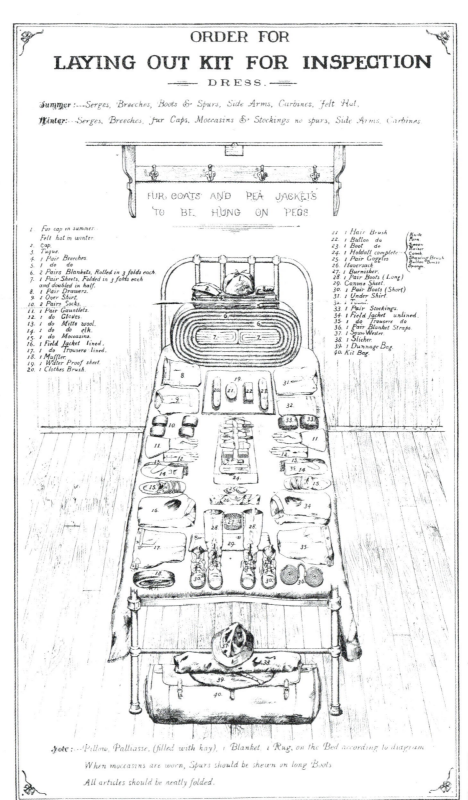

Kit Inspection Layout – 1909

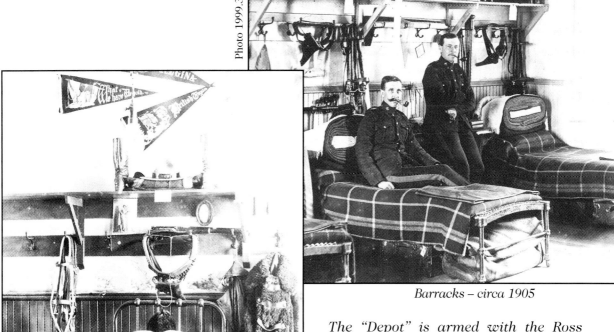

Barracks – circa 1905

Barracks circa 1905

The "Depot" is armed with the Ross rifle, Mark 2 and colt revolver. The Sam Browne equipment is used. All arms and accruement are in good condition. In addition to the inspection at the drills and parades, they are regularly laid out in the barrack rooms for inspection by the orderly officer on Monday morning of each week. I trust that a more suitable method of carrying the rifle will shortly be decided upon.
– RNWMP Annual Report 1911

Kit Inspection Layout – circa 1960

Chapter 2 – Buildings 55

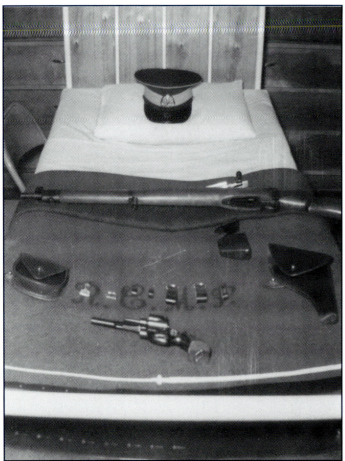

Cst. Alex Herchuk's kit laid out for inspection in "C" Block – circa 1956

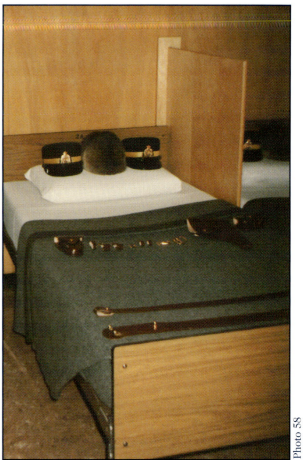

Cst. G. Warkentine's bed, Reg. #40887, Troop #22, "B" Block – 1990

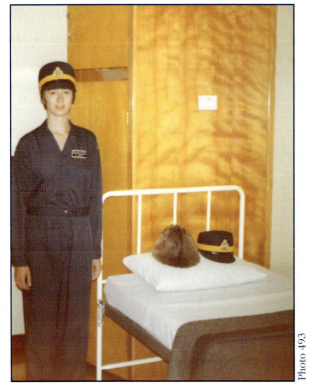

Cst Judy Schaumleffel, Reg. #32727, Troop #8, "C" Block – August 1975

Bed card – mounted above every bed – Cst. J.F.D. Marquis, Reg. #40399, Troop #12, 1988/89. If the bed card was found on one's bed at the end of the day, it meant a visit to the Sgt. Major's office to address a deficiency.

Closet Layout

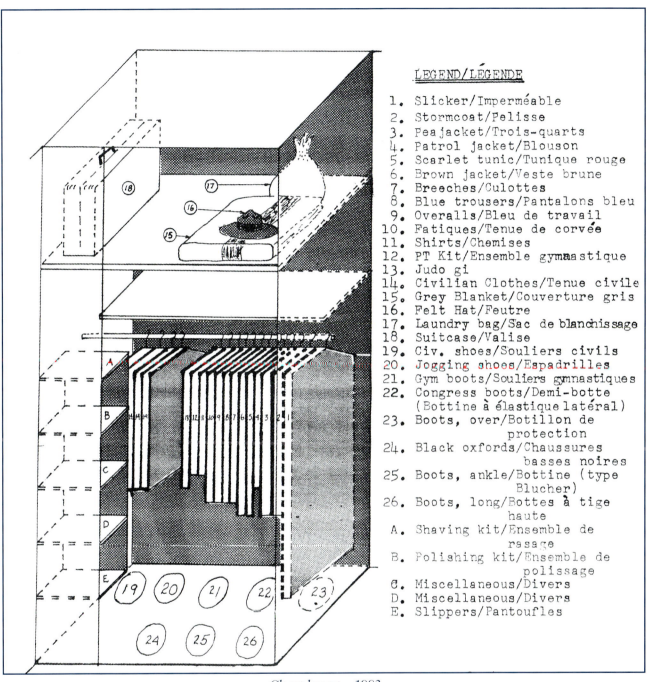

Closet layout – 1983

LEGEND/LÉGENDE

1. Slicker/Imperméable
2. Stormcoat/Pelisse
3. Peajacket/Trois-quarts
4. Patrol jacket/Blouson
5. Scarlet tunic/Tunique rouge
6. Brown jacket/Veste brune
7. Breeches/Culottes
8. Blue trousers/Pantalons bleu
9. Overalls/Bleu de travail
10. Fatiques/Tenue de corvée
11. Shirts/Chemises
12. PT Kit/Ensemble gymnastique
13. Judo gi
14. Civilian Clothes/Tenue civile
15. Grey Blanket/Couverture gris
16. Felt Hat/Feutre
17. Laundry bag/Sac de blanchissage
18. Suitcase/Valise
19. Civ. shoes/Souliers civils
20. Jogging shoes/Espadrilles
21. Gym boots/Souliers gymnastiques
22. Congress boots/Demi-botte (Bottine à élastique latéral)
23. Boots, over/Botillon de protection
24. Black oxfords/Chaussures basses noires
25. Boots, ankle/Bottine (type Blucher)
26. Boots, long/Bottes à tige haute
A. Shaving kit/Ensemble de rasage
B. Polishing kit/Ensemble de polissage
C. Miscellaneous/Divers
D. Miscellaneous/Divers
E. Slippers/Pantoufles

A recruit smelled like a horse, but it was a good clean smell. His uniforms and civilian clothes were jammed together in a tiny locker, his spare blankets and sheet folded in rigid regimental pattern with revolver belt and bridle decorating the front of the locker and the rifle bucket and Lee Enfield at the foot of the cot. Each morning he made his bed to conform precisely with every one of the other 20 or 30 beds, the top sheet folded down to the exact number of inches prescribed. No man left the barracks on a Friday night; he was far too busy cleaning and polishing for the Saturday morning inspection. – ex-Cst. T. Jamieson Quirk, Reg. #11951 – 1932 (14)

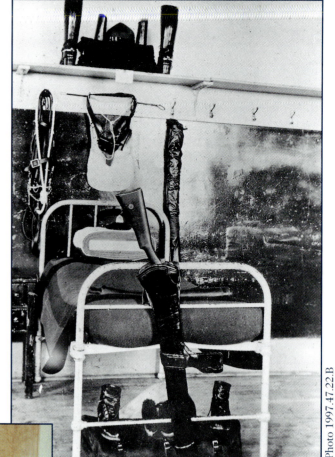

Bed and kit – Lee Enfield in bucket – 1923

"B" Block dorm – circa 1960

Your barracks rooms are inspected daily and your bed must be made up neatly and tidily as instructed. Particular attention will be paid to the cleanliness of your sheets and pillow. Do not allow dust to accumulate in the blankets or on your equipment. – A Guide to Success – 1960 (15)

When a large group of men live together, for the sake of each one and all, cleanliness is one of the first things to be considered. It will be necessary for you to keep your barrack room clean and it will be necessary to keep the buildings clean. If you are detailed to do this type of work, do it cheerfully. Apart from cleanliness, if you make enquiries, there are usually rooms provided where you might store your trunks. You will find showers and baths in every building. Make use of them. Before leaving the barrack room at any time, check to see that everything is in its proper place. After a while this becomes automatic. – Prelude to Duty – 1950 (16)

Since the days of its inception, "Depot" Division has grappled with the issue of suitably accommodating its personnel and the barracks has been always been high on the agenda of "Depot" Division management. The lodging of a large number of people who are often training for more than fifteen hours a day, and returning to their barracks physically and emotionally exhausted is a significant challenge.

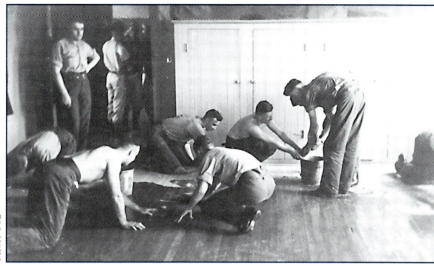
"Depot" Barracks – 1936

"From the very beginning, according to early reports of 1882 and 1884, requests were made for furniture, especially beds." – NWMP Annual Report (17) "There were no beds in the early years of 'Depot.' Each recruit received two wooden trestles and a supply of boards to stretch between them. On these he placed his palliasse, filled with straw from the stables, and made himself as comfortable as possible." (18) The straw palliasses attracted bedbugs, and there were recurring infestations of them in the warm summer months.

I would suggest that more attention be paid to supplying suitable barrack furniture, more particularly iron bedsteads, the same as are in use in the Imperial Service. These, instead of the present makeshift trestle and board style, would materially add to the comfort of the men and greatly improve the appearance and cleanliness of the rooms. – NWMP Annual Report 1886 (19)

As five hundred men descended upon "Depot" in 1885, no provisions were made for extra accommodation, with the exception of one large room which was built for prisoners. Men were lodged in the Quarter Master's Store, or anywhere else where space could be found. – NWMP Annual Report 1885 (20)

The barrack rooms were sometimes so crowded that the men's health was affected and it was necessary to send recruits away to outposts before they were properly trained. – NWMP Annual Report 1885 (21)

In 1887 new barracks were completed, although there remained the difficulty of obtaining heating wood. Commissioner Irvine pleaded in his annual report for the appointment of an architect, as "the ordinary Clerk of the Works did not understand 'Depot's' requirements." – NWMP Annual Report 1887 (22)

"D" Block Barracks – members of Troop #9, 1986/87

Chapter 2 – Buildings

Barrack Life – Troop #13 – 1988/89

The daily task of ironing one's bed – Cst. M.L. Parsons

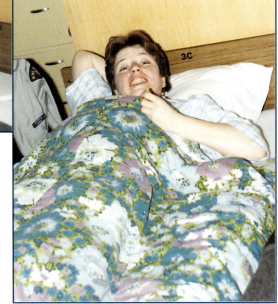
Recruits often slept on top of their beds to save time in the morning by not having to make them. This was deemed to be a shortcut and resulted in disciplinary action by the Drill staff

The aftermath of a dorm inspection

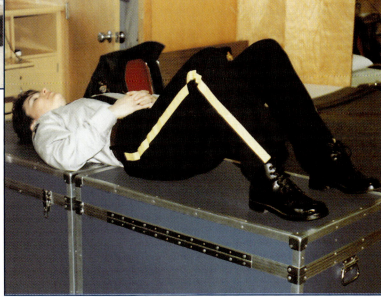
Recruits not wanting to mess their beds could be seen catnapping on their trunks between classes

60   Behind the Badge

With the additions of "B," "C" and, much later, "D" blocks, dormitory-style rooms housed recruits. An entire troop was normally placed in the same dormitory, although the integration of male and female recruits made this difficult. Experiments in the early 1990s with coed troops led to the creation of shared dorms, with a sheet placed as a temporary wall between males and females. It was eventually decided that the sexes would be lodged in separate accommodations, while the troops remained mixed-gender.

Cadets are still housed in communal dormitories in "B" and "C" Blocks; however, several floors in "D" Block have been converted to single rooms, each containing a private bathroom.

The spit-and-polish approach to the training of an RCMP officer also applies to the appearance of their "pit," which includes a recruit's desk and bed space. Proper instruction is passed down from troop to troop on how to properly make and iron the bed, lay out kit, prepare for barrack inspections and assign duties that ensure that the living area is kept at a high standard of cleanliness and hygiene at all times.

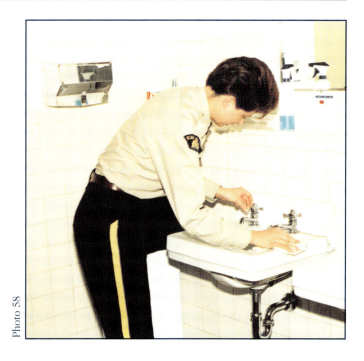

Photo 58

Challenges of maintaining cleanliness – "B" Block 1988/89

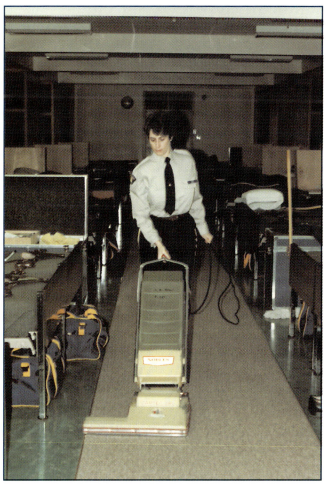

CHAPTER 2 – BUILDINGS   61

Speaking of beds – I remember, as a recruit, being advised to get some baling wire from the stables to repair my bed, a chain link affair, lest I fall through it to the floor. I suspect we had a considerable number of old army surplus beds. I know my mattress had the army ordinance mark on it (an arrow inside the letter C) and it was clearly dated 1915.
– ex-Cst. T. Jamieson Quirk, Reg. #11951 – 1932 (23)

On reaching the barracks, new recruits were issued their first uniform of brown pants and tunic made from heavy cotton, or "duck" as it was called. They soon found out that this uniform was "fatigue dress" to be worn in carrying out the many chores required to keep "Depot" spick and span. They were also assigned to a barrack room and issued with a palliasse and blankets. There were no beds in the early years of "Depot." New arrivals were kept as fatigues until enough of them were assembled to form a squad, then training began. (24)

The Division designated thirty-one other new members and me as "H" Troop. They housed us in a long room in an old one-storey wooden building. Three things caused me to detest my new home. The first was that it was unbearably hot in the room during summer. The second was the hundreds of flies in the room. To take a well-needed nap on a weekend afternoon that I was off, I had to cover myself with newspapers to keep the flies from marching up and down on me. The third was the lack of privacy, living in one room with thirty-one people. – Supt. J. Religa (rtd.), "H" Troop, Reg. #O.947, 1953/54 (25)

Cst. R. Bangs, Reg. #38628, Troop #13, 1985/86 – ensuring ultimate cleanliness

Familiarization Booklet for Recruits – "Depot" Division 1967 – Barrack Rooms

Beds – All beds must be uniform and made up as shown on the diagram posted on notice board.

Bed Cards – Each bed has a bed card bearing the individual's name, regimental number, troop, revolver number. In the event a member is hospitalized, or absent on duty or leave for more than 24 hours the bed card holder must have a suitable white card placed in front of the bed indicating the whereabouts of the individual (e.g. AOD – absent on duty, Post Hospital – etc.) Under no circumstances is the back of the bed card to be used for this purpose.

Bed Making – The foot ends of all beds must be lined up when the room is set up for inspection. When making beds, folds of the sheets and blankets must be measured from the foot of the beds to make a uniform appearance.

Blankets – All blankets must be taken outside early every Friday morning and shaken to assure they are free of dust. It is your responsibility to assure the blankets are kept clean. In the event of accident, and the blankets require drycleaning, permission must be obtained from the troop supervisor to send them out. A note must be left on the bed explaining a lack of uniformity in the make up of your bed – "Bed Rug at Cleaners," etc.

Smoking – Pails of salt are provided throughout the block for the purpose of discarding cigarettes. Every effort must be made to keep these containers free of other refuse to avoid the possibility of fire. There will be no smoking in barracks after "Lights Out" (10:45 p.m. daily). You will not smoke while lying in bed.

Caps – Your cloth caps and fur caps when not being worn must be on your pillow in a clean, tidy condition.

Sam Brownes – No attempt is to be made to shine the leather until the Sam Browne has been fitted. The Sam Browne is to be placed on a hanger in the locker until it has been fitted. After fitting, the leather is to be shone and laid out on the bed as shown on the posted diagram. When the Sam Browne is required for foot drill, it may be laid out on the bed assembled, for the full half day on which it is to be used. Otherwise it is to be disassembled and the components laid out. Special attention must be given to brass on the inside of the Sam Browne (such as the "D"s on the holster).

Floor Savers – Due to the sharp leg ends of the beds, it is compulsory that each bed leg be resting on a floor saver. You are provided with enough for your bed, and it is your responsibility during training to replace any which become missing.

Painting of Beds and Chairs – Every member is responsible for maintaining a neatly painted bed and chair at all times. To minimize the amount of painting required, care should be taken to avoid placing boots, etc., on the beds and chairs. Paint for these articles may be obtained when required from the janitor, 2nd floor of "B" Block. When painting, make every effort to keep paint off the floor and other articles. The brush and painting equipment must be cleaned immediately after use, and returned to the janitor.

Dormitory Doors – Care must be taken and every effort made when entering and leaving the dorm, to prolong and maintain its tidy appearance. Avoid using feet to open doors, or bumping doors with other objects such as garbage pails, in order to offset damage by scratching, denting, etc.

Washroom Care – Each member of the troop, in turn, will assure that sinks, showers, toilets and floors are clean and ready for inspection at any time during working hours, as well as being responsible for reasonable cleanliness after work hours. Cleaning equipment may be obtained from the janitor.

CHAPTER 2 – BUILDINGS

Barrack Room Floors – Must be cleaned and polished for daily inspections from 8:00 a.m. to 5:00 p.m. Efforts should be made to use a minimum of floor wax. Periodically, heavy accumulations of wax in light traffic areas must be removed with Varsol. The floor is to be washed with Ajax and warm water containing disinfectant. It should not be necessary to use solvent on the floors more often than every two or three months. Normal cleaning should consist of sweeping, mopping with clean mop, hot water with a reasonable amount of soap, a small amount of disinfectant. After drying, wax and polish. Prior to each inspection, all radiator vents at floor level must have the grating removed and the area under the drawers cleaned.

Closets – Clothes will be hung as shown in the detail drawing and will be clean. Rags, cleaning equipment may be stored in containers, neatly on shelves. Boots must be laced with the loose ends of the laces placed inside. Shoes must be laid out in pairs, civilian shoes at the rear. At no time will socks be left in the shoes. Spurs may be placed inside the high boots when not in use, but must be clean. A magazine or newspaper may be placed inside, to hold the high boot upright. In view of the short interval when returning from stables in the a.m., you are to ensure that boots are scraped off outside the block on the boot scrapers, to avoid manure being tracked into the building. The boots must then be wiped clean, with particular emphasis given to the instep, then placed on the floor or the closet for inspection. It is realized that the boots will be wet and cannot be shone in such short time. Boots will not be placed at the foot of the beds, in foot lockers or in janitor rooms. Light footwear may be stored on the bottom two shelves only, if desired.

Inspections – The barrack rooms are inspected daily between the hours of 8:00 a.m. and noon, 1:00 p.m. and 5:00 p.m. by either the troop supervisor or the NCO i/c Block, and on some occasions, by both. Each troop has two supervisors, whose names appear on door cards. These instructors are responsible for the troop members and the barrack room. Any questions which might arise should be directed to them. In their absence contact the NCO i/c Block. Troops are allowed approximately one month to familiarize themselves with the procedure. After that period all irregularities are noted on the reverse side of the bed card. When the 3rd irregularity is noted, the member concerned is PARADED to the Sergeant-Major for disciplinary action, and on each successive time. Every effort should be made to keep the reverse side of the bed card free of noted irregularities.

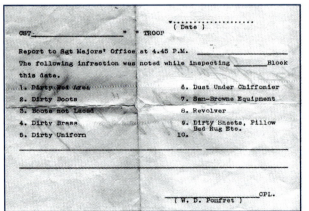

Barrack inspection form used by Cpl. Pomfret in "Depot" 1955/56 and his comments

On allotted Fridays, various troops and their dorms are inspected by the Commanding Officer at 8:30 a.m. Members stand-to at the end of the bed, facing the aisle and the following information should be available upon request by the O.C.:

(1) Your name

I am regimental number _____, Third Class Constable Jones, T.R., Sir

(2) Any complaints?

The senior man of the troop proves (extends right arm, fingers extended), and answers loudly and clearly, either "None Sir" or "Yes Sir, — gives the complaint"

(3) When did you write home last?

(4) Why is this bed empty?

Other requirements

(5) Fingernails neatly trimmed and clean

(6) Feet in proper position of attention

(7) Belt buckles in center

(8) Sideburns cut evenly (not on an angle)

(9) Buttons crown upright

(10) Speak up, answer any comments with "Sir."

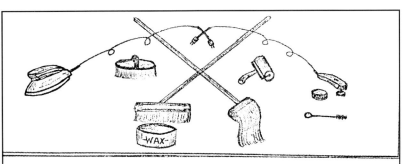

******* C L E A N I N G   T I P S *******

A POLICEMAN IS EXPECTED TO BE NEAT AND TIDY AT ALL TIMES. HE IS CONSTANTLY IN THE EYE OF THE PUBLIC AND BECAUSE OF THIS MUST BE A PUBLIC RELATIONS MAN FOR THE FORCE. THE FOLLOWING ARE SOME HELPFULL HINTS WHICH CAN HELP YOU SAVE MONEY AND LOOK SHARP.

1. Ironing saves money and time(EXTRA). By pressing a crease with a damp cloth first and then afterwords with a piece of brown paper gives rewarding results. By pressing twice a week or whenever needed gives your clothes a fresh look.

2. Spots on ties, serge or pants are easily removed with special spot cleaner or lighter fluid.

3. TIES should be kept clean. The dry cleaners will do ties cheaply. They are not expensive to purchase and a quantity on hand will be useful. The tie should be worn with a full Windsor knot and the knot itself tight.

4. Tattered gloves present an unsightly appearance. Repairs are often necessary to make them presentable. Trimming and sewing up the seams can only last so long. Always keep a new pair of gloves on hand for parades etc.

5. Cracks in leather should be polished by applying polish with the crack instead of against it.

6. It is not necessary to apply a lot of polish to obtain a good shine. Too much polish causes a buildup and darkens the boot. A little polish goes a long way with small amounts of water. ~~Lighter fluid is useful in taking off excess buildup.~~ Another tip on a higher gloss is to use a ladies nylon. Buff lightly.

7. Spurs will leave a black mark on the heel of your high boots. Floor wax will remove this but to avoid it use a little adhesive tape on the inside of the spur. Make sure the tape isn't visable.

8. A toothbrush is ideal for polishing the welts of your boots.

9. Shirts should be pressed sharp in summertime and replaced when fraying occurs.

10. Always keep a close check on your hair and personal cleanliness.

Tent Living

Tent accommodation at "Depot" – 1935

In June of 1935, "Depot" was jam-packed with members from all over western Canada to prepare for the anticipated trouble with the hundreds of "On to Ottawa," unemployed who were arriving in Regina daily via freight trains. To accommodate newly arrived members, 10 bell tents of First World War vintage were set up in a lot between the riding school and the chapel. "After a brief welcome, the members were escorted to the Quarter Masters stores in the basement of 'A' Block to be issued with a paillasse. They then proceeded to No. 4 Stable to fill the paillasse with straw with an odd cricket or grasshopper, continuing on to their new accommodation." (26)

Sleeping in tents was considered fun, however was not as rosey (sic) as we had initially hoped. After a few days, the grass dried up and died inside the tents, leaving nothing but dust and grasshoppers. Regina is also noted for its violent thunderstorms which often arrived in the middle of the night. This meant piling outside to dig a ditch around the tent to prevent a flood inside. It was quite a sight – during flashes of lighting – to see grown men, without pyjamas, scrabbling at the ground trying to make little ditches, sometimes with their bare hands. – S/Sgt. E.C. Parker (rtd.), Reg. #12640, 1935 (27)

Inspection 1935

"On to Ottawa – March of the Unemployed" Identification Parade in front of "B" Block – 1935. The Regina Riot broke out on July 1, 1935

Buffalo Detachment/ Scenario Houses/Mall

– Buildings – Mall #155, Scenario Houses #157 and #158, Buffalo Detachment #103

Buffalo Detachment

In 1994, "Depot" Division officially opened Buffalo Detachment on the base. Founded on the characteristics of an everyday detachment complex in the field, Buffalo Detachment was designed to provide cadets with actual scenario-based training and prepare them for their future duties.

Buffalo Detachment consists of a fleet of 27 police vehicles, four interview rooms, a telecommunications office, classroom, computer area, a police garage, portable radio and camera-storage area, fingerprinting rooms, cell blocks and front counter area.

Front entrance to Buffalo Detachment at 103 Arnold Mews, Buffalo, Saskatchewan

The original Buffalo Detachment was located on the lower floor of the Applied Police Sciences building – circa 1990

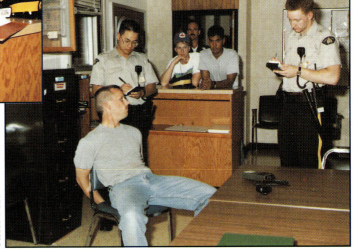

CHAPTER 2 – BUILDINGS   67

Scenario residence – 158 Pedersen Street in fictitious "Buffalo, Saskatchewan"

All rooms are equipped with a camera monitoring system, which permits facilitators to monitor the cadets during training and provide them with additional feedback. The cadets utilize Buffalo Detachment and telecoms during all scenario training and police driving exercises. Cadets are taught basic radio communication and procedures while training.

On any given day, the staff in the telecom unit can receive between 300 to 400 radio calls from cadets. This realistic training complex permits cadets to become familiar with a realistic view of policing in a structured, training environment.

Mall and Scenario Residences

A medley of businesses – a bank, variety store and café form part of the Mall

The Mall, built in 1995, was added to the machine storage building. It once contained the Royal Bank and a travel agency where their representatives offered services to members and recruits. It now houses a bank, variety store and café for scenarios.

The Residences, a bungalow, 157 Barker Avenue, and a two-storey house, 158 Pedersen Street, are completely furnished and were added to the complex in 1995.

The Mall and Residences are used exclusively for scenario training.

A complaint of graffiti followed up by a cadet in training

"C" Block
– Building #16

A view of the principle north facade of "C" Block – circa 1922

Night view of "C" Block on the south side of Sleigh Square – circa 1927

"C" Block was hastily erected in the summer and autumn of 1919 due to the return of several hundred men of the A & B overseas mounted police cavalry squadrons from Europe and Siberia, swelling 'Depot's' numbers to 902 officers and men. This structure designed like the 1907-08 officers' quarters by the Regina architectural firm of Van Egmond and Storey. It was an important factor in the architectural evolution of the depot as its styling deliberately echoed several of the salient Gothic elements of the nearby 1912-13 Administrative Block A. (28)

The original "C" Block, situated to the east of the Chapel, served for many years as barracks. The block also housed a scientific laboratory, post hospital, library, recreation room, canteen, museum and guardroom throughout its lifespan.

"C" Block was well remembered by many members who had experienced the thrill of a speedy ride down the fire-escape chute. The recruits also found that snow would blow in through the cracks and cover their beds. Retired Superintendent Saul recalls having a corner bed on the third floor. He had to remove his high browns off the shelf at the head of his bed as the wind would blow them off. This, with all the windows closed.

By 1966 its use was limited to storage facilities. It was subsequently demolished in 1971 to allow for the construction of the new museum, which was being built on the site as a project for the Centennial of the Force.

"C" Block – showing the fire escape

In early October, it was goodbye horses, and hello books, foot drills, firearms, physical training and swimming. We had started the first of the two parts of the training program. At the same time, we moved into an old brick building located at the south end of the Parade Square.

The building had the colourful name of "C" Block. A billiards room and library were on the first floor and a museum in the basement. My room was on the second floor. To be truthful, it was not just my room. I shared it with fifteen other members of my squad. At least we had gone from thirty-two members in a room to sixteen. The building was so old that snow came into the room through the cracks around the window frames during the winter. The fire escape in the room was unique. To reach it you had to open two small doors in the wall at the end of the room. Inside was a metal tube that went down to the ground. It reminded me of a child's slide at a playground, except it was covered, longer and steeper. Someone had enough foresight to put a pit of sand at the bottom to cushion the landing. I once saw a member in another squad thrown down one of the fire escapes on his way to be horse troughed. – Supt. J. Religa (rtd.), Reg. #O.947, "H" Troop, 1953/54 (29)

It seems this was a common form of "barrack room justice." Stories are told of members being stripped naked before being thrown down and a pail of water being thrown down after them.

New "C" Block
– Building #64

"C" Block in April 1956

The new "C" Block was erected at the cost of $921,743.48 in 1953-54 to the west of the Chapel, providing accommodation for 180 men. The building contained lecture and study rooms, the Museum, recreational facilities and a canteen. The men's quarters ranged in size from single rooms to two- and six-man dorms. Each member had his own private clothes cupboard, chest of drawers, and writing desk. The Corporal's mess was situated in the basement. In 1974 preparation for the arrival of female recruits, included a female lounge and increased washroom facilities.

"C" Block currently houses the guardroom, canteen (store possessing basic necessities), stores, tailor and leather shops, the Chaplain's office, SRR (staff relations representative) office, facilities and dormitories for cadets in training.

"C" Block – August 2005

CHAPTER 2 – BUILDINGS

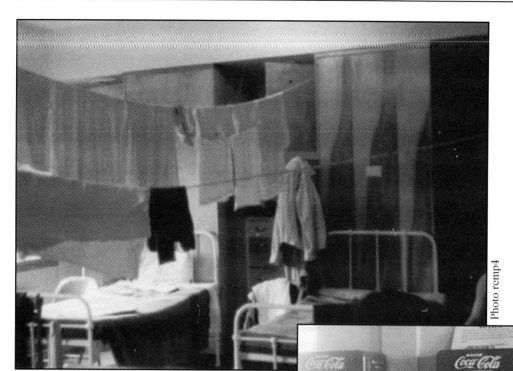

Interior of "C" Block Barrack – 1955

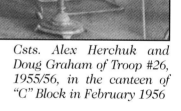

Csts. Alex Herchuk and Doug Graham of Troop #26, 1955/56, in the canteen of "C" Block in February 1956

Csts. Bob Galbraith and Peter Whittemore of Troop #26, 1955/56, playing pool in "C" Block

Centralized Training

Centralized Training – 2002

In 1996, Treasury Board authorized the construction of a Centralized Training Building at "Depot" Division, with a projected cost of $5,960,752. (30)

The mandate of the facility was to provide specialized operational, technical and administrative courses to employees of the Force. The building was designed to accommodate continuous adult and problem-based learning principles in three large classrooms, nine syndicate rooms and ninety hotel-style rooms. Centralized Training was opened September 16, 1998.

The branch was originally located in Ottawa but, following a reorganization of the Training Directorate in 1996, became the responsibility of the Commanding Officer of "Depot" Division. In 2002, the responsibility returned to Learning & Development – Ottawa, under the name of National Learning Services.

In 2006, the single rooms were converted into two-person dorms to accommodate an increased cadet intake at "Depot" to train the greatest number of cadets in one year in the history of the Force.

Centralized Training room – 2006

CHAPTER 2 – BUILDINGS

Construction of Centralized Training Building

"D" Block prior to construction of Centralized Training – March 1997

May 1997

July 1997

September 1997

May 1998

74 BEHIND THE BADGE

The Chapel
– Building #13

The Chapel, originally a mess hall (shown on the left) with the kitchen on the west side, was later a canteen to supply comforts to the men, e.g., tooth powder, boot polish, etc., were set up at certain times of the day on a table. This 1885 photo shows that next to the chapel (left to right) is the Sergeants' Mess with the Sergeant Major's residence attached to the rear, Recreation Hall and the Guardroom

The Chapel, which commands a prominent place on the Sleigh Square, is the oldest, locally best-known and most historically significant building of all the structures at "Depot" Division

CHAPTER 2 – BUILDINGS   75

On either side of the altar are a set of beautiful-stained glass windows. To the right of the altar, the window portrays a trumpeter of the Force sounding Reveille – symbolic of the Resurrection – and underneath is the quotation "For the Trumpet Shall Sound." To the left of the altar the window bears the figure of a Constable of the Force in Review Order. Beneath is the quotation "Blessed are they that Mourn." These windows are a gift of the Maritime Provinces Association of Regina and at the top of each are the Coats of Arms of Nova Scotia, New Brunswick and Prince Edward Island. In June 18, 1944, the windows were dedicated "to the memory of the men of Maritime birth who died while in the service of the Force." The Association initially wished to donate a copper plaque but, due to the war, they were not permitted to use copper.

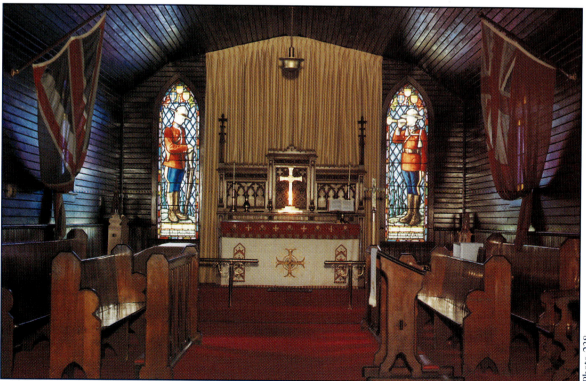

The Chapel is rich in symbolic significance for the RCMP – much enhanced by its rough wooden pews, its dedicated stained-glass windows and the many memorial plaques dotting its walls. The Chapel was designated a municipal heritage structure in 1983

The funeral of Inspector Sampson, Reg. #O.281, May 11, 1933, which was held at "Depot." Reverend E.H. Knowles conducted the service. Inspector Sampson, was in charge of the RCMP troops in Saskatoon during the riot. He had exchanged horses with a constable when the horse reared, throwing Inspector Sampson back. His boot got caught in the stirrup, resulting in his death. Inspector Sampson is buried at the "Depot" Cemetery Block A, row 9, plot 121.

"By 1918, the Chapel was in very poor structural condition, the floors and foundation having rotted away. Commissioner A.B. Perry was recommending its demolition and replacement as part of his program for the rebuilding of 'Depot.' In 1924, the Chapel was extensively rehabilitated by Poole Construction of Regina. The Chapel was moved five feet to the west and twenty-one feet to the south to align it with the other 'Depot' buildings." (31) The chapel was enlarged in 1939 and structurally upgraded in the 1940s.

Looking eastward with the Chapel in the foreground and the old "C" Block in the background – circa 1935

CHAPTER 2 – BUILDINGS

In Memory of Miss Audrey Carden

One of the six stained glass windows created for the Chapel in memory of Miss Audrey Carden

Miss Audrey Carden (spinster) died in London, England in 1936 at the age of 38. Her estate was valued at 70,000 pounds; by the standards of the day she was a very wealthy woman. In her will, she left 15,000 pounds to two close friends and the remainder of her fortune to be divided equally between the Professional Fire Brigades Association of England and the Royal Canadian Mounted Police. Shortly after her death, Sir John Carden indicated he would contest his aunt's will. The family charged that Miss Carden was mentally incapable of making a will. They pointed out the eccentric manner in which she lived and her excessive drinking, reportedly a bottle of champagne a day augmented by brandy and Benedictine. Upon legal advice, the beneficiaries, including the Force, agreed to settle out of court, receiving a sum of $31,000.00. While no precise reason can be given for Miss Carden's gift, she clearly admired and respected the Force. As a result of her very generous gift, six stained-glass windows were created for the chapel bearing the inscription "To the Glory of God and in Memory of Miss Audrey Carden." (32)

The money was initially used to provide comforts for the men and was distributed at Christmas time known as "the moyadee" (sic). However, as the size of the Force increased, and inflation hit the economy, the amount dwindled. It was decided to put the money to better use by purchasing the stained-glass windows and pay for the construction of the campsite which was named in her honour.

The RCMP Chapel, also known as "the spiritual home of the Force" or the "chapel on the square" is the oldest remaining building in Regina. Utilized as a chapel since 1895, this historic building has been the setting for graduations, weddings, funerals and Long Service Medal presentations, the majority being Red Serge events. The sacred walls of the small yet powerful structure are lined with citations of bravery, commendations and plaques dedicated to those who have lost their lives in the line of duty.

The most recognized building at "Depot" Division, and in Regina, is the Force Chapel

CHAPTER 2 – BUILDINGS

"The mess hall was built in the latter part of 1883 as a supplement to the prefabricated post buildings erected during the winter of 1882-83," (33) under the direction of Inspector Sam Steele. "Constructed under a contract awarded to William Langtree and assigned to James A. McCaul of Regina, it consisted of a 26 ft by 60 ft woodframe mess room with an attached kitchen measuring 20 ft by 26 ft." (34) In 1889 the building was converted into a reading room and post canteen, providing beer at five cents and a range of other items at a low cost, with the intention of keeping members close to home and not straying downtown. This move produced an unsuccessful outcry from Regina merchants as the going rate for beer in town was fifteen cents. This was based on an experiment by the U.S. Cavalry to control the drinking habits of their men.

In 1895 the kitchen section of the canteen was destroyed by fire and at that time Mrs Herchmer, the wife of Commissioner L.W. Herchmer, suggested the structure be converted into a Chapel. Arches were added and an addition to the south end of the building was completed.

The Chapel was dedicated on December 12, 1895 and Reverend W.E. Brown, rector of St. Paul's, preached the sermon. It was well attended by townspeople. At a rededication ceremony in 1924, Prime Minister W.L. Mackenzie King was among the dignitaries in attendance.

The Chapel has undergone some minor alterations and repairs over the years and has hosted numerous dignitaries. In 1931 The Right Reverend and Right Honourable A.F. Winnington-Ingram, Lord Bishop of London visited. One of the highlights in the Chapel's history was on May 25, 1939, when His Majesty King George VI and Her Majesty Queen Elizabeth visited. They were very interested in the memorial windows and tablets.

During that same year, the steepled entry tower was designed and constructed by "Depot" staff. On December 10, 1939, it was dedicated to the Glory of God and in loving memory of the officers and men who participated in the "March West of 1874, from the Dufferin Camp in Manitoba to the foot hills of the Rocky Mountains in Alberta."

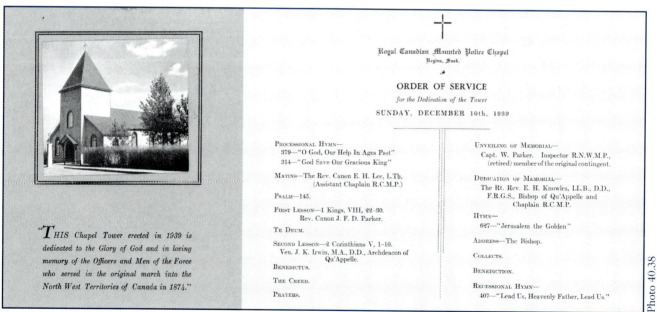

Photo 40.38

On June 18, 1944, a mural tablet and stained glass windows on either side of the altar were installed in honour of "the Sons of the Maritime Provinces whose lives have been given in the course of their duties as members" of the Mounted Police.

On November 4, 1951, two stained glass windows were dedicated: "Nativity" in memory of sons of members and ex-members who gave their lives in the Second World War and "Resurrection" in memory of members and ex-members who gave their lives in the Second World War. During that same year, Her Royal Highness, Princess Elizabeth, and Her Royal Consort, the Duke of Edinburgh, visited the Chapel.

In honour of the Force's Centennial in 1973, Assistant Commissioner D.O. Forrest donated a stained glass window dedicated to the wives of the Force and a second window was donated by recruits in training with the wording, "Donated by Recruits in Training to the Glory of God and in Commemoration of the Centennial of the Force." There are six other stained glass windows in the Nave which are in memory of Miss Audrey Carden, an English woman who bequeathed part of her estate to the Force.

Numerous articles which have been donated to the Chapel over the years are on display. The pulpit was manufactured at the Saskatchewan Penitentiary and the wooden pews were constructed by prisoners. There is also a Display Cabinet for the Honour Roll book which was completed in 1967, containing the names and service dates for those members who have died in the line of duty. The original Guidon, retired in 1973, is proudly displayed in the Chapel.

In 1990, 64 handworked needlepoint kneelers were installed and dedicated in the Chapel for the RCMP veterans' 40th anniversary by members' and veterans' wives.

For over 100 years, recruits on parade have stood and faced this symbol of the Force. One of the final ceremonies for recruits, and now cadets, is a Graduation Church Service held on the Sunday of Graduation week. With families, friends and troop mates present, an official blessing is given to the Red Serge-clad members embarking on a new career. They leave "Depot" with powerful and everlasting memories of the Chapel, filled with reminders of the proud history of the force, its beauty illuminated by the fading sun.

For cadets and members of other faiths, alternate space for worship is made available, reflecting the multinational composition of the Force as part of the Canadian mosaic.

Her Majesty Queen Elizabeth II exiting the Chapel with Commissioner G. Zaccardelli (right) and A/Commr. W. Sweeney (left) – 2005

CHAPTER 2 – BUILDINGS

The Chaplaincy at "Depot"

Force Chaplains, left to right Fred Salerno, Blair Dixon and Allan Higgs – 2003

The history of RCMP chaplaincy officially began at "Depot" in 1882 when Reverend Osborne provided spiritual care to members of the North-West Mounted Police.

The North-West Mounted Police Annual Report, Volume 1, indicates that prior to Reverend Osborne's involvement, spiritual events such as services, funerals and weddings were the responsibility of the ranking officer.

Senior Superintendents and Inspectors presided over the Anglican, Presbyterian and Methodist services in the absence of a clergy member. Other officers in the various North-West Mounted Police forts provided similar services.

In the event a minister or priest was nearby, his services would be requested.

In 1882, when the Force headquarters were located in Regina, the officers were able to delegate the responsibility of spiritual support to the clergy in the community. Reverend Osborne was asked to be the chaplain.

In 1901, the Chaplain's position was given official recognition and was adopted by the Force. Since its inception, the chaplaincy role has grown considerably.

In 2005, Reverend Fred Salerno became the first full-time Chaplain in the Force when he was hired as a public servant Chaplain at "Depot." In 2006, his status changed to that of a civilian member.

Chaplaincy is part of the rich history and tradition of the Force. The Chaplains provide spiritual support at the Veterans' Parade, Change of Command ceremonies, dedication ceremonies, weddings, regimental funerals, baptisms, reunions, dinners, special occasions, parades and the all-important annual Memorial Parade at "Depot." The Chaplains are also available to provide counselling to cadets and staff.

Force Chaplains at the Memorial Parade (left to right) Rev. Bob Harper, Commr. G. Zaccardelli, Solicitor-General of Canada Wayne Easter, C/Supt. Curt Tugnum, Rev. Allan Higgs, D/Commr. Bev Busson – 2003

Prayer for the Force

Almighty God who has called men and women to your service for the protection of your people and the maintenance right, we beseech your blessing upon the Commissioner, Officers and members of the Force. Endue them with loyalty and grant that wherever they may be called to duty or danger they may be under your protection. Amen

CHAPTER 2 – BUILDINGS

Commissioner's Residence
– Building 2

Commissioner's Residence

The Commissioner's Residence, with three storeys and twelve rooms for Commissioner Herchmer's large family, was built in 1887 on the northeast corner of the Parade Square. The house was described as having a dumb waiter and a narrow stairway at the rear, used by maids in reaching the upper floors. The Herchmer's had been very uncomfortable in the small residence used by Commissioner A.G. Irvine, who was a bachelor. Commissioner Irvine's house was significantly renovated, becoming the new home of the Officers' Mess.

Servant Wanted –
Wanted, good general servant, who can do plain cooking, washing and ironing. Apply to Mrs. Herchmer at the barracks.
(Regina newspaper ad)

The Commissioner's Residence was torn down in 1979 due to the significant costs of necessary repairs

Behind the Badge

On the northeast side of the Barrack Square was the residence of the Commissioner. The Officers' Mess, with its prominent peaked roof, can be seen to the left – circa 1914

The Commissioner's Residence became the home of the Commanding Officer of "Depot" Division in 1920 when the Headquarters of the RCMP moved to Ottawa. The current residence of the Commanding Officer has a spectacular view of the surrounding historic buildings and sites. It is situated directly behind Sleigh Square and the flagpole off Stick Sam Way. This residence is usually the home of the Commanding Officer of "Depot"; the house to the south was once the residence of the Commanding Officer of "F" Division.

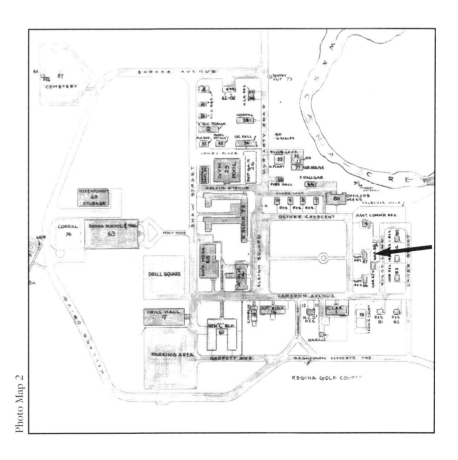

CHAPTER 2 – BUILDINGS

Crime Detection Laboratory
– Building #1

Once the Crime Lab, this building is currently being shared by the Police Driving Unit and the Informatics Section

As criminal science evolved, the Force adapted to providing state-of-the-art facilities for investigational purposes. A Crime Detection Laboratory was conceptualized by Commissioner J.H. McBrien in 1936. The first location of the lab was a small room on the second floor of the Officers' Mess, moving to "C" Block in 1938.

The first crime detection laboratory at "Depot" Division was one of the most advanced of its kind in the world. It was organized and directed by Dr. Maurice Powers, B.A., M.D., C.M. who received his Doctorate of Medical Science in Forensic Medicine from New York University shortly after accepting the post in 1939. This was the first such degree issued in North America.

A wintery night view of the Crime Lab – circa 1955

The lab staff and equipment outgrew its accommodation in "C" Block and building commenced in 1951. By 1953 the new laboratory was occupied on the southeast corner of Sleigh Square. The two-story structure, 51 feet by 105 feet was designed in the same Redcliffe brick that was utilized in other "Depot" buildings. The main entrance contains glass doors edged

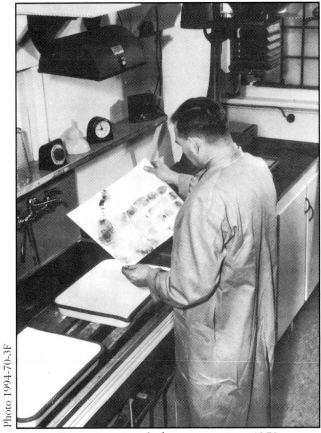
Preparing visuals for court – circa 1950

Photographing a bottle – circa 1950

with an aluminum alloy, set in a arch of limestone. One of the sections of the right-hand column of this arch is a stone laid by Commissioner L.H. Nicholson on July 25, 1951. This stone encloses an airtight container, treated to withstand corrosion, which contains material of interest embodying the functions of the lab.

The building serviced clerical, serology, firearms identification, spectroscope, instrument rooms, exhibit lockers, hair and fibre section, photography section, an autopsy room, a sound-proof firing chamber and a radio room for "F" Division. (35)

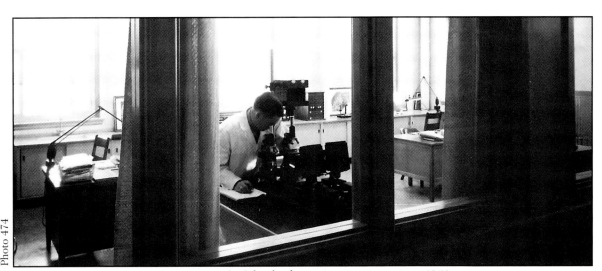
A view into the life of a forensic scientist – circa 1960

CHAPTER 2 – BUILDINGS

The walls with large glass partitions enabled the functions of the lab to be seen without interruption. Originally intended to permit tours of the lab, it was never acted on due to the potential of contamination of evidence – circa 1960

The lab building, as it is still called today, holds the Police Driving Unit on the 3rd floor and the Informatics LANWAN staff, which serves both "Depot" and "F" Divisions, on the second floor. A new state-of-the-art Forensic Laboratory was constructed on Dewdney Avenue west of "F" Division Headquarters in September of 1984.

Surgeon – Dr. Maurice Powers

Dr. Maurice Powers – Father of Forensics

Dr. Powers first assembled equipment in a vacant bedroom off the Officers' Mess while more suitable accommodation was being prepared. He had at his command perhaps the most comprehensive collection of scientific instruments under one roof in Canada – perhaps in North America. Powers quickly found himself swamped with work as the men of the Force availed themselves of his skill and knowledge. In 1939, Mounties from all parts of Canada sent in exhibits from 297 cases. Autopsies were performed, blood samples tested, hair examined under the microscope, markings on bullets and even a crowbar were studied. "With additional staff, Powers soon expanded the lab's facilities, adding sections specializing in instruments, toxicology, spectrograph analysis, firearms and toolmarks. Dr. Powers was killed tragically when the plane in which he was travelling crashed near Battleford, Saskatchewan in 1943." (36) Dr. Powers was attempting to get home for his daughter's birthday party.

88   BEHIND THE BADGE

"D" Block
– Building #124

"The original 'D' Block, currently the Resource Centre, was constructed in 1935-36." (37) It housed on its ground floor the workshops of the post carpenters, painters, saddler, electrician and tailors. One large room on the second floor has been utilized as a barrack and for instructional classes for non-commissioned members.

The new "D" Block was opened on November 29, 1976. Although some driving classroom instruction was done in the basement of the building, it was constructed primarily as dorms for recruits. Renovations in recent years converted several dorms into single rooms. The lower floor of the building currently houses the "Depot" major capital projects, French and English language training/testing and laundry facilities.

"D" Block – circa 1989

Originally built for barrack accommodation, "D" Block now holds 191 single rooms.

CHAPTER 2 – BUILDINGS

Drill Hall
– Building #17

The Riding School was built to replace two previous riding schools which both burnt down, in 1888 and 1920

The current drill hall was originally built as a riding school in 1929 by Van Egmond and Storey of Regina at a cost of $56,968. It was built near the site of an earlier riding school which was destroyed by fire in 1920. With the construction of a new combined stable/riding school in 1953-54 to the north of this site, this building was converted into a drill hall. A wooden floor and acoustic ceiling tile were added. Additions to the drill hall on the north side, which consisted of office space, classroom, washrooms and storage area, were added in 1977-78 by the Saskatoon design firm of Ferguson, Folstat and Friggstad. (38)

The interior of the former Riding School as it appeared when His Excellency the Earl of Bessborough, the Governor General of Canada, presented the Force with the Guidon in 1935

Female recruits of Troop #8 practice drill in the Drill Hall – 1975

Drill Hall with the addition under construction in 1977-1978

Recruits reinforcing a strong sense of esprit de corps through foot drill in the Drill Hall – circa 2004

The Drill Hall is used to this day for graduations, charity balls, citizenship court, award ceremonies and, of course, drill.

The Drill Hall – 2006

CHAPTER 2 – BUILDINGS

"E" Block

"E" Block was one of the wood frame buildings, known as 14X structures, that were obtained from the Department of National Defense at the end of World War II. They were moved to "Depot" in 1946 and 1947 and used for various purposes. "E" Block was demolished circa 1970 to make room for the new Physical Training Building.

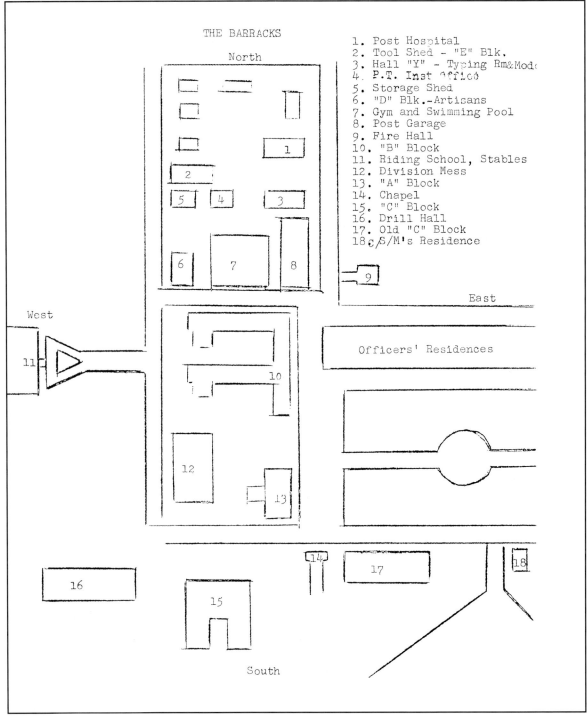

Map of "Depot" – 1967

"F" Block

"F" Block was believed to be constructed of three old army buildings used by RCAF members stationed in Regina. After World War II they were fitted together to form a capital E and placed to the north of the Riding School as accommodation for the squads. These buildings, known as 14X structures, were moved onto "Depot" property in 1946-1947. It was in poor condition in 1957 when retired Superintendent Ralph DeGroot did his basic training.

Denis Ling, a former C.O. of "Depot," recalled that it was a draughty military building, and on one occasion when he was on barrack patrol on a weekend, a tourist touring the facility commented, "You mean to say the horses live in there and you live in here?"

Retired members recall finding snow on the night tables and floors when they awoke in the morning. The building was demolished in either late 1958 or early 1959.

Entrance to "F" Block – circa 1955

Members of Troop #26, 1955/56, awaiting inspection in "F" Block

"F" Block (F-1, F-2, F-3) – December 1955

Pete Whittemore cleaning his new .38 calibre revolver in F-2 Barrack Block at "Depot" Division Regina – November 21, 1955

"G" Troop Special
by Mac and Moose

(TO THE TUNE OF "THE YELLOW ROSE OF TEXAS")

THE BOY'S THAT LIVE IN "F" BLOCK, - ARE PRETTY HARD TO SCARE.
THEY LIVE AND WORK TOGETHER, - AND EVERYTHING THEY SHARE.
THE GIRLS DOWN AT THE TRIONON, - THEY LIKE US ALL, YOU SEE.
THE SHORT HAIRED LADS FROM "G" TROOP, - ARE WITH THE MOUNTED "P".

THE CLASSES ARE TERRIFIC, - THEY WORK US HARD YOU SEE.
THANK GOD WE AIN'T GOT PERRY, - TO LECTURE ON P.T.
WE'RE UP BEFORE THE SUNRISE, - TO SHOVEL ONE MORE LOAD.
WE FINISH GROOMING HORSES, THEN - INDULGE IN CRIMINAL CODE.

WE FALL ASLEEP IN LECTURES, - AND DON'T KNOW HOW TO DRILL.
BUT WHEN WE RODE THE HORSES, - WE GAVE THEM ALL A THRILL.
THE BOY'S ALL GET THE SHOWERS, - AS COLD AS THEY CAN BE.
BUT WE CAN TAKE A LOT OF DIRT, - WE'RE FROM THAT TROOP CALLED "G".

"G" Troop Special

Interior of "F" Block – 1958

Cst. Henry Jensen, Reg. #17842, went through "Depot" training in 1952. As a recruit in "P" Squad, he recalls that "F" Block had no heat. A heating system was installed in December and commenced working in January 1953. Cst. Jensen remembers sleeping in his breeches, underneath his Force-issue Buffalo coat, brown bed rug (blanket) and two Force-issue grey blankets. At that time, "O" and "P" Squads were designated Ride Troops, which spent one half-day on equitation training and one half-day on basic recruit training.

Fire Hall
– Building #62

The Fire Hall – 1974

History records at "Depot" Division regularly document the fear of fire and its effect on the base. Numerous buildings, most noticeably the Riding Schools in 1888 and 1920, were decimated by fire. Causes of fire were attributed to the combination of very dry timber, lanterns and spontaneous combustion.

In 1952, a new Fire Hall, at a cost of $14,375.00, was completed on Moriarty Road. In later years, service was provided by the Regina Fire Department. By the time the "Depot" staff was mustered up, the Regina Fire Department would be on site. Retired Superintendent Dave Pearce recalls the fire engine as "the most polished and least-used vehicle in the world." The building was later converted into a mock courthouse where cadets practice testifying in a courtroom setting.

Fire truck – Sgt. Red Smith, standing, seated in cab, Vern Greenman, mechanic at Post Garage – 1948

Fire helmet used by members at "Depot" in 1940

NWMP Annual Report – 1891

At Regina we have four large tanks and the creek; also an engine, water tower, 70 feet high, is about completed, from which we expect to get sufficient pressure for fire purposes. These, with babcocks, and an efficient distribution of fire pails, represents our artificial water protection. Our chief protection is, however, the watchfulness which the discipline of the Force ensures.

The last occasion that the fire truck was used was when a fire broke out in the under-construction Academic Building in 1972. The bar at the back of the truck that the recruits held on to broke off as the fire truck lunged forward out of the fire hall, throwing them all to the ground. By the time the truck arrived at the fire and hooked up the hose to the fire hydrant, the Regina Fire Department had arrived and strongly suggested to the recruits that their services were no longer required.

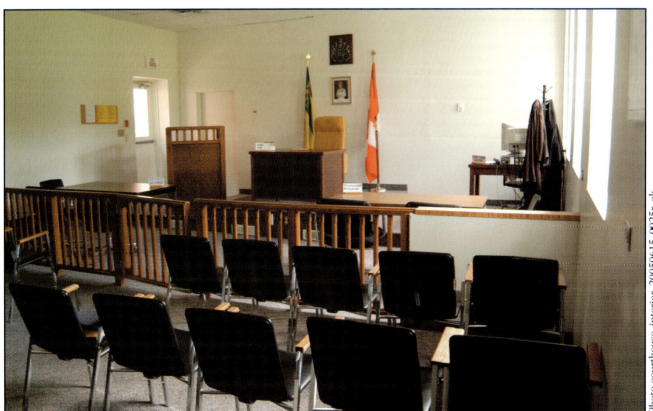

Interior of the Courthouse, formerly the Fire Hall – prior to this the courtroom was located on the lower level of the Applied Police Sciences building – 2005

Guardroom
– Building #3

The Guardroom, a portable wooden structure erected in 1882-1883, contained 10 cells. The walls, ceilings and floors were reinforced with steel to prevent the prisoners from escaping

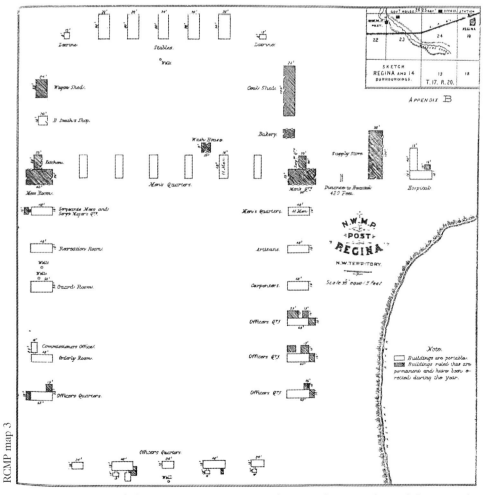

An 1883 site map of the Regina NWMP post – the Guardroom is located between the Commissioner's office and Recreation Room (Annual Report of the NWMP 1883, Appendix B)

Photo of the NWMP Guardroom by G. W. Brinkworth – circa 1905

Our guardrooms at Regina and at Moosomin are common jails and their capacities have been taxed to the utmost. The care of prisoners and the number of men taken away from their legitimate work for this purpose is a serious drain on the force. On the other hand, at Regina, the prison labour is most valuable and during the past year the prisoners have laid about half the water and sewer pipes for the barracks. The new prison uniform supplied is something we have wanted for a long time, and adds to the safety of the prisoners. – RNWMP Annual Report 1908, Superintendent G.E. Sanders (39)

Gathering on the porch of the Guardroom – Recreation Room, Sergeants' Mess follow left to right – circa 1885. The weather-recording equipment is visible to the left of the Guardroom – the NWMP were initially responsible for recording the weather. This duty was later turned over to the Dominion Meteorological staff at the Regina Airport in 1932

Prisoners

Prisoners tending to daily tasks – RNWMP Barracks – circa 1920

*I*n the early years, "Depot" Division in Regina also had the responsibility of providing secure facilities for prisoners serving short sentences and a holding area for subsequent court appearances. In addition, "Depot" lodged prisoners awaiting transportation to institutions in which to serve their sentences.

Both prisoners and members of the Force who were serving sentences for internal breaches were assigned laborious duties, including farming, trade work and anything deemed appropriate to assist in the daily operations of the base. The Chapel, the oldest building in Regina, to this day houses pews that were constructed by the prisoners.

The results of the prisoners' labour was reported on in the annual reports.

Connection with the waterworks system at Regina is nearly completed, and water will be laid on in the Commissioner's house, at the new barracks and stables. A considerable portion of the work has been done by prisoners. – RNWMP Annual Report 1908, Superintendent G.E. Sanders (40)

Prisoners at work – February 1936

CHAPTER 2 – BUILDINGS

Cst. Bradley and Andrews on prisoner escort Regina – February 1936

Work Done by Prisoners:

During the spring and all of the summer, from 14-20 prisoners were taken to barracks every day (except Sundays) for work there. The remainder were kept employed as follows; Last fall some 8 acres of ground were manured and ploughed. During the winter, hauling straw and care of herd horses. In the spring, hot beds and hot house produced vegetable and flower plants, many of the latter being supplied to the barracks for planting there. The 8 acres of garden ground was prepared and planted; noxious weeds and grass kept cut and the weed burned. About twenty-five loads of hay cut, eight or ten being sent to barracks, and balance stored here, of which about eight loads remain. On rifle-range, a mound for temporary use was built at the 800-yard firing point. – RNWMP Annual Report 1914, Inspector R.S. Knight (41)

Prisoner rations were also in effect and in an annual report it was remarked that "the quality has been very good, and few complaints have been made, the chief one being the want of salt, which I believe is barely sufficient, especially in cooking large quantities of oatmeal and meat, particularly the meat is very fat." – RNWMP Annual Report 1914, Inspector R.S. Knight (42)

About 1 o'clock am on the 7th, a sentry apprehended another man who he found lurking in the neighbourhood of his post, and who was unable to give a satisfactory account of himself. This man received three months imprisonment with hard labour, as a vagrant. – NWMP Annual Report 1888, Superintendent R.B. Deane (43)

Louis Riel

The most famous prisoner ever in custody at "Depot" was Louis Riel. Upon being sentenced to death for High Treason, Mr Riel was hung on the grounds outside the Guardroom.

Louis Riel, the Metis leader convicted of treason, was sentenced to death by hanging. The trial garnered national attention. Canadians had many different views regarding Louis Riel's actions, some felt they were treasonous and others that they were heroic.

On May 23, Louis Riel arrived here by special train, in charge of Captain Young, of the Winnipeg field Battery, and was taken into custody by police. He was, from the first, strictly guarded and secluded, although allowed as much latitude as possible, in a way of exercise and other indulgence, which was not incompatible with the object in view. During the time I was in command no person was permitted to hold any communication with him, unless furnished with proper authority. – NWMP Annual Report 1885, Superintendent R.B. Deane (44)

Louis Riel

A platform and fenced-in yard was specially constructed behind the NWMP Guardroom at "Depot." The hangman was Jack Henderson. Strangely, Mr. Henderson had been a prisoner of Riel's at Fort Gary in 1870. After the execution, the body was handed over to Riel's family for burial.

Fully aware of the atmosphere across the country, documentation at the time showed that the Force took every precaution to quash rumours and quell public unrest.

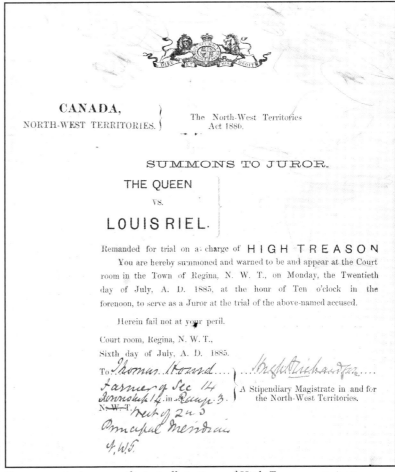

Summons to juror, outlining allegations of High Treason against Louis Riel

CHAPTER 2 – BUILDINGS

Scarth Building, located at the corner of Scarth Street and Victoria Avenue, Regina – The Dominion government rented it as a courthouse for Riel's trial in 1885

This is supported by an entry in Superintendent. A.G. Irvine's Annual Report dated December 31, 1885:

> On the 16th of November last, Louis Riel was executed within the precincts of the gaol here. The body was subsequently handed over to Mr. Bonneau, by order of the sheriff. Unfounded and malicious reports were circulated, after the execution, that the body had been mutilated and to disprove this rumor, the coffin was opened and the body examined in the presence of myself, Mr. Bonneau and other persons, before it was allowed to leave the barracks. (45)

Rear view of the old NWMP Guardroom at "Depot" built in 1882-1883 and demolished in 1919-1920. Louis Riel was hanged in the structure built in the rear on November 16, 1885. He entered the scaffold through the window seen at the rear of the building

November 16, 1885
The Death Warrant
Riel Informed that He Will be Executed To-day
The Prisoner Said to be Perfectly Resigned to his Fate.

(From our Correspondent)

Regina, N.W.T., 15th. "The special messenger bringing the warrant signed by the Governor-General of Canada directing that the execution of Louis Riel should take place, arrived here on special train at 8 o'clock to-night. There is no longer a doubt that Louis Riel will meet his fate at some hour to-morrow. The arrival of the warrant was a surprise to many of the officials, who, owing to the late hour and previous delays, had argued that another respite would follow.

Riel received the formal intelligence at 9 o'clock to-night in his cell in the guard-room of the Mounted Police barracks, three miles west of this city. The intelligence was conveyed to him in person by High Sheriff Capleau. The scene was in many respects remarkable. The famous rebel's cell is immediately adjacent the guard room of the troops doing night patrol duty, fully five of whom occupied the room. Through the iron gate in front of the cell was seen an armed sentinel on duty and outside the building a cordon of armed men were pacing their beat. The iron gate was thrown open on the approach of sheriff Chapleau and Col. Irvine, commandant of the Mounted Police.

Riel, who had been conversing with the surgeon of the post, arose and welcomed the Sheriff in a hearty and thoroughly unconstrained way. His voice was modulate, and he displayed no sign of excitement. His initial greeting was, "Well, and so you have come with the great announcement. I am glad." Sheriff Chapleau replied that the death warrant had come. Riel, continuing in the same cherry way, said: "I am glad that at last I am to be released from my sufferings."

He then broke off into French and thanked the Sheriff for his personal consideration. He proceeded again in English: "I desire that my body shall be given to my friends to be laid in St. Boniface." (This is the French cemetery across the Red River from the City of Winnipeg.) the Sheriff then asked him if he had any wishes to convey as to the disposition of his personal estate or effects.

"Mon cher," replied he. "I have only this," he said touching his breast above the region of the heart, "this I gave to my country fifteen years ago and it is all I have now." He was asked as to his peace of mind, and replied, "I long ago made my peace with my God. I am prepared now as I can be at any time. You will find that I had a mission to perform. I want you to thank my friends in Quebec for all they have done for me."

He continued, in reply to another question, "I am willing to go. I shall be permitted to say something on the scaffold," he said in a tone of inquiry. When told that he would be allowed to do so, he said, smilingly, "You think my speech will be too long, that it will unnerve me. Oh, no! I shall not be weak, I shall feel that when the moment comes I shall have wings which will carry me upwards."

The reverting again to the French tongue and in an inimitably winning way, for which he is famed to all those who have known him closely, he spoke again of the glad remembrance he would retain of those who had espoused his personal cause. He closed by saying to Sheriff Chapleau, a he held out his hand in parting, "adieu mon ami." His eye was clear and unflinching, and his bearing throughout was such as to evoke a sense of admiration by the absence of any tremor of excitement. If he ever showed the white feather under fire, or on any occasion he succeeded in keeping himself admirably under command in the presence of his own approaching fate. Pere Andrew, his spiritual adviser, then arrived, and he was left with him to celebrate mass.

(Source unknown)

Gym
– Building #25

Physical activity has always been prominent in the training at "Depot" Division. A new gymnasium was built in 1937-1938 which was 113 feet by 56 feet in size, joined with an entry service structure 26 feet by 113 feet. (46) The main floor of the gymnasium wing consisted of an open area well adapted to large-scale physical training exercises while the basement contained offices, an indoor rifle and revolver range for shooting from ten to twenty-five yards. The basement also contained a lecture room and emergency accommodation for twenty men. The basement of the entry structure was left unoccupied while its main floor contained an entrance hall, dressing rooms and toilets. The gymnasium wing was erected by Poole Construction at a cost of $54,292.00. (47)

In 1938, to celebrate the opening of the new building, the first dance of the year was held with music provided by Russ Isadore and his orchestra.

In 1940-1941, the swimming pool was added to the east side of the building.

Currently, the PDT Gym is specifically used for police defence tactics classes, and the basement contains three large dressing rooms and custodial services.

Looking north at the original Gym with the Artisan Shop to the left – this Gym is specifically used for Police Defensive Tactics today – 1938

C&D Squads in Gym performing gymnastic display – 1940

The current Gymnasium was completed in 1971 at a cost of $459,228.00. This area can be divided into two separate gymnasiums with an electronically controlled divider. Seating for four hundred spectators, on rollaway, self-stacking bleachers is located on the west wall. In 1988 an annex was added to the original structure housing additional weight equipment and facilities. Many thought that the addition of a sauna was considered a "luxury" and was not meant for recruit training. Documentation stated at the time that it was "not, as might at first be thought, simply another indication of the degenerate depths to which today's recruit is being reduced during the course of modern training methods, but rather a complement to the overall fitness program to which he is exposed during his stay at 'Depot.'" (48)

Police Defensive Tactics Gym – 1986

Weight room added to the Gym in 1988

Interior view of the Gym – 2005

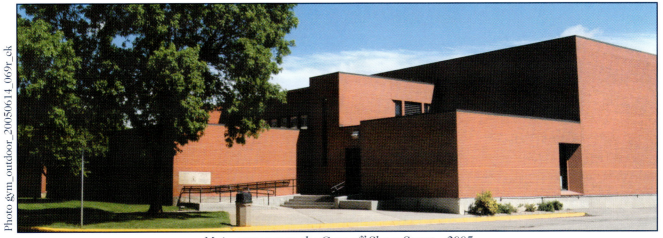

Main entrance to the Gym off Shaw Street – 2005

CHAPTER 2 – BUILDINGS

Heating Plant
– Building #33

Excavating for the heating plant – 1934

The current heating plant

In 1914, much to the pleasure of the staff and recruits at "Depot" Division, a new central heating plant was opened. Comments from the staff reported that it was one of the most significant improvements in the barracks in years. All buildings on the base were heated by the plant.

In 1934-1935, the current heating plant, designed by Reilly, Warburton and Reilly of Regina, with the assistance of John Guildford, a consulting heating engineer, was built. "The new building was erected and heating installed at an estimated cost of $100,000, replacing the old system by providing a separate heating source in each of the "Depot" buildings. A walk-through tunnel system for the heating piping was commenced in 1949." (49)

To this day, the central heating plant is responsible for providing climate control to the entire base.

In the 1950s the Heating Plant smoke stack (seen in the background of this photo) was higher than any other structure at "Depot" and could be seen from well beyond the base

106   BEHIND THE BADGE

Aerial view of the RCMP Academy at "Depot" Division – 1976

CHAPTER 2 – BUILDINGS 107

LTCS and Applied Technology
– Learning Technology and Creative Services

Feed Storage Shed – November 1956

This building was used for machine and feed storage prior to significant renovations in 1994. Currently, Learning Technology and Creative Services includes the "Depot" Division video conference suite and graphic area on the second floor. On the ground floor, LTCS' production and photo studio share space with the workshop of Informatics Applied Technology Section and printshop.

On the north side of the building a facade was built around the ground floor to depict a strip mall containing a variety store, a bank and café. These storefronts are used as scenario locations for cadet training.

Main entrance to Learning Technology and Creative Services – 2005

Lecture Hall
– Building #34

Domestic violence scenario in the practical training complex – circa 1982

"X" and "Y" Lecture Hall – A lecture hall with no basement was built in haste with wood and brick north of the post garage in the winter and early spring of 1934. "The public works design fell under the responsibility of Van Egmond and Storey. The building, erected by Bird Construction of Regina at a total cost of $11,515.73. This building, one of the first to depart from the gothic-style buildings at 'Depot,' was a one-storey brick-veneered wood-frame structure measuring 30 feet by 105 feet. The building consisted of a large single room that was divided into three separate lecture rooms by means of long folding partitions that were suspended from roof trusses. The building has been utilized as a part-time residence, and later converted into a practical training complex which included a living room, store, and office where recruits practiced searches, arrests, and domestic interventions." (50)

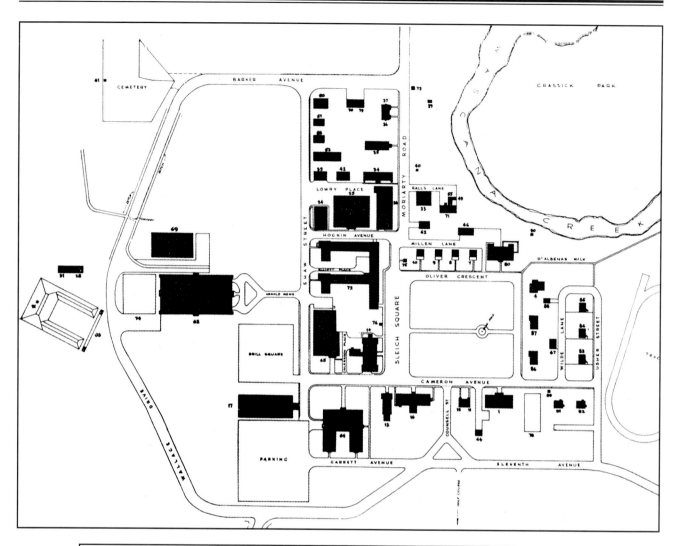

LEGEND—"Depot" Division, Regina, Sask.

#	Name	#	Name	#	Name
1	Crime Detection Lab	40	Scales	69	Feed Storage
4	Asst. Commr. Res.	42	Model Detachment	70	NCO Garage
7	Officer's Residence	44	Garage	71	Greenhouse
8	Officer's Residence	45	"C" Block—New Room 107-65	72	"B" Block
9	Officer's Residence	46	Tool Shed	73	Gatehouse
10	Officer's Residence	49	Storage—Gardener	74	Corral
11	NCO Residence	50	NCO Residence	75	St. Roch Monument
12	NCO Residence	51	NCO Residence	76	Cenotaph
13	Chapel	52	NCO Residence	77	Skating Rink—Demolis
14	"A" Block	53	"E" Block	78	Tennis Courts
16	"G" Block—Old	54	Salt Storage—Demolished	79	2-Stall Garage
17	Drill Hall	55	Tool Shed—Gardener	80	Officers Mess
24	"D" Block	58	Pump House	81	Inspector's Residence
25	Gymnasium & Pool	59	Outhouse	82	Inspector's Residence
26	Post Garage	60	Outhouse	83	Inspector's Residence
28	Storage	61	Tool Shed—Cemetery	84	Inspector's Residence
31	Storage	62	Fire Hall	85	Inspector's Residence
32	Auxiliary Garage	63	Riding School	86	Supt's Residence
33	Heating Plant	64	"C" Block—New	87	Supt's Residence
34	"X" & "Y" Lecture Hall	65	New Mess	88	Garage
35	Hospital	66	5-Stall Garage	89	Tunnel Entrance
36	NCO Residence	67	3-Stall Garage	90	Tunnel Entrance
37	NCO Residence	68	Pistol Range	91	Storage—Pistol Range
30	"A" Magazine				

"Depot" 1960 – the Lecture Hall is #34

Medical Treatment Centre (MTC)
– Building #35

NWMP Annual Report 1887 – Assistant Commissioner Irvine:

Owing to the comparatively large number of epidemics which have broken out there during the past two years, city hospitals have been filled to capacity at Regina, Saskatchewan and, as a result of this, members of the Force at "Depot" Division who became ill had to be cared for at the barracks, where no facilities were available for such an emergency. To overcome this situation, a new Post Hospital has been erected on police property at Regina and will be used for the accommodation of patients who are not seriously ill, but who need isolation and medical attention.

The MTC was situated where the Royal Regina Golf Course parking lot is now located – circa 1935

The Pharmacy at "Depot" in the 1880s – Dr. Dodd, centre left, was the doctor who declared Louis Riel dead

The MTC prior to its addition – 1974

In 1887, the first two-storey Post Hospital, built as a result of a contagious disease outbreak, was located near the site of the current Royal Regina Golf Course Club House. The hospital had "three spacious wards, but the surgeon complained of the earth closets* and closeness of the hospital to the polluted Wascana Creek which flooded every year." (51)

When this building was demolished, a newer building was constructed in 1943. It was the last of several successive hospital facilities constructed at "Depot." "Its construction was prompted by a lack of available civilian hospitals in Regina in 1942-1943. Designed by the Regina architectural firm of Van Egmond and Storey, it was 32 by 90 feet, stone trimmed red brick structure set on a full concrete basement. The Post Hospital contained five wards, doctor's examination rooms, a dispensary and waiting rooms. The rooms were to accommodate patients who were not seriously ill, but who needed isolation and medical attention." (52)

In 1976, a full-time physiotherapist was hired to treat recruit injuries which occurred during training. In addition to some minor interior alterations and renovations in 1978, a link was constructed in 1995 to join the physiotherapy and psychology departments to the treatment area.

MTC as it appears today – on the right is the original section built in 1943. The significant addition was added in 1995

In 1977, in order to accommodate female recruits, extensive renovations to the Medical Treatment Centre (the Post Hospital) were completed. These improvements were long overdue and welcomed enthusiastically by the medical staff at "Depot."

---

* indoor latrines, consisting of a bucket holding earth or straw, placed in a closet on each ward for the comfort and convenience of the infirm

As with any public institution, "Depot" Division is not immune to sickness on a large scale. In the 1885 Commissioner's Annual report, concerning the health and welfare of the Regina Headquarters, Dr. A. Jukes, the senior surgeon of the NWMP, Reg. #0.47, wrote:

"...The barrack accommodation, owing to the suddenly increased force, was, for the time, inadequate, and an additional guardroom had to be erected, in order to accommodate the unusual influx of prisoners. These latter suffered little from the endemic forms of disease to which they were acclimated, but a good deal of sickness, as my annual report of sick shows (105 cases of diarrhea, 20 cases dysenterica-diarrhea and 6 cases dysentery) occurred among the men, and more especially, as I had anticipated, among the new recruits..."

History repeated itself at "Depot" both in 2000 and 2003 when a Norwalk-type virus outbreak occurred. In 2000, 300 cadets, staff and course candidates were affected by a gastro-intestinal illness which was the worst-ever epidemic at "Depot." The base was quarantined and a triage centre was set up in the gymnasium where the ill were treated. Some of the catered food to serve the remaining people at "Depot" included 300 pizzas for the first and last night of the epidemic, 6,000 catered meals over 17 meal periods and 403 dozen cookies. In 2003, a smaller, yet similar, epidemic hit "Depot" with approximately 100 people being treated over the period of one week.

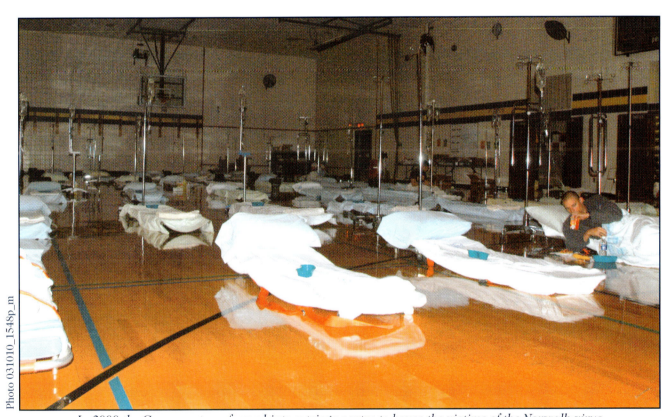

In 2000 the Gym was transformed into a triage centre to house the victims of the Norwalk virus

Today, the hospital is referred to as the Medical Treatment Centre (MTC) and has been expanded to provide space for a full-time doctor, psychologist, nurse, physiotherapist, fitness and lifestyle coordinator and health services clerk. The MTC treats sports injuries, a variety of aliments, provides inoculations and performs minor surgical procedures.

Messes

Division Mess – Building #65

Division Mess – 1936

Division Mess – 1936

The Junior Ranks' Mess was originally situated in what would become the Chapel and remained there until 1895. In 1885, the Mess fed approximately 140 people. Sergeants and officers took their meals separately, according to their rank in their own designated messes. In 1900 the Mess was attached to the rear of "B" Block. This was done to facilitate the easy access to the mess from the men's quarters to avoid the bitter cold winters. This building was demolished in the 1950s and a new mess was built in 1957, where the existing building remains, to accommodate 340 persons per sitting. It has undergone two major renovations and has been expanded since 1957. The Division Mess houses the Saskatchewan General Mess and the Stand Easy Lounge for cadets, which was inaugurated in May of 1975.

"B" Block being built around the Division Mess in 1956

Division Mess under construction during the winter of 1955-1956. "F" Block is located in the top left corner

"The changes in the Mess over the years were simultaneous with the changes in the training environment. In 1942, feminine touches were added to the Division Mess – five waitresses were engaged." (53) Officers dined separately, and until the mid-1990s table assignments placed junior troops at one end of the mess, progressing through until they became senior troops and were assigned tables with tablecloths.

Given that the Mess now prepares approximately 1,500 meals a day, there are plans for new construction to accommodate the large number of cadets, course candidates and employees. It is anticipated that the new Mess will be attached to the north side of the Drill Hall.

The food at Regina was notoriously unpalatable, as I am very sure any former denizen of the "Depot" barracks at that time would testify. On one occasion a mass boycott of the noon meal was organized which resulted in an inquiry, but brought no improvement. At midday the canteen in old "C" Block did a thriving trade and anyone who could scrape together the wherewithal purchased a pint of milk and something like "pigs in a blanket," brought in by local women, thus skipping the mess hall entirely. – ex-Cst. T. Jamieson Quirk, Reg. #11951 – 1932 (54)

Some recruits found the food "plain and rough fare." The main meal in the middle of the day was usually cooked meat and potatoes. Supper consisted of cold meat, bread and tea. The principle dish for breakfast was commonly referred to as "mystery." It was the remains of previous meals fried up into a kind of hash and served with bread and coffee. The menu changed very little from day to day. – S.W. Horrall, RCMP historian (55)

After we finished morning stables, we had to put on a shirt and tie and our riding breeches and boots before we could go into the Mess Hall to eat. The Mess Staff did not care how much toast that you took, but God help you if you tried to take more than one glass of milk. One cook always stood by the trays of milk with a big carving knife in one of his hands. I do not know what would have happened if you were caught taking a second glass of milk. Every so often, a member of the training staff came into the Mess Hall during a meal period and asked if there were any complaints about the food. You would have had to be out of your mind to say anything and no one ever did. – Supt. J. Religa (rtd.), Reg. #O.947, "H" Troop, 1953/54 (56)

Table in Mess reserved for senior troop – circa 1972

Female recruits receiving their meals – circa 1974

Division Mess – 1990

CHAPTER 2 – BUILDINGS 115

Mess Catering – A Diary

I glance over the following extracts from my diary … I have a satisfaction of knowing that I have been able not only to serve my fellow men, but also to serve them at the rate of so much per meal, as per Rules and Regulations, paragraph so and so – and, of course the necessary amendments.

Thursday – Mess waiter complains that there is no hot water and why don't I do something about it. Listen for 15 minutes to member with culinary knowledge explaining proper manner of preparing white sauce.

Friday – Get frantic report from cook that the stove has broken down and it's only an hour to supper time and what'll he do. Save situation by serving cold meat. At supper abused by members who threaten to register complaint if they have to eat cold meat every acidulous day of the week.

Monday – While doing up the books for the day discover that allowance is overdrawn. Decide to serve prunes and beans more frequently.

Tuesday – Informed by the Mess waiter that kitchen orderly has broken plate and two saucers and if this kind of thing is going to continue I had better get some tinplate (sic). Watch recruit consume half bottle of "H.P." sauce at dinner. Decide not to furnish "H.P." in future.

Wednesday – Hear signs of tumult in Mess where breakfast is just starting. Hasten to investigate. Discover cause of uproar to be pot on serving table apparently containing boiled sawdust. Sample same. Tastes like boiled sawdust. And told that this is the edible bran I brought in a fit of economy the other day. Recall that I forgot to tell cook to mix half bran and half with rolled oats. Find it necessary to keep out of sight for the remainder of the day.

Thursday – Receive present of measure of soft feed and neatly tied bundle of hay as reminder of yesterday's breakfast.

Front entrance to Mess – 1990

Current front entrance to the Mess – 2005

Kitchen staff prepare hundreds of meals a day

Sunday – Notified by a member that there was a cockroach in his soup. Tried the old gag about there being no extra charge for meat in the soup. (No success.)

Thursday – Receive demands for shrimp salad and molasses. Promise to see what can be done. Decide that nothing can be done.

Friday – Work to 11 p.m. balancing Mess books. Had figured on surplus of 40 dollars. Discover surplus is only 14 cents. Take 2 aspirins and go to bed. – Cst. A.L. Alsvold, Reg. #11272 – 1936 (57)

Inside the old Division Mess with Mess staff and instructors – December 1955

Interior of the new Mess – January 30, 1957

Familiarization Booklet for Recruits – "Depot" Division 1967

Head dress must be removed immediately upon entering any mess. This rule is not applicable to members on duty in the mess, for example, an Inspection Party or the Mess Senior on duty during meal hours.

A new member should understand from the outset that the mess is "his mess." With this in mind, you can readily recognize the need to observe good economy and avoid waste at every opportunity. At the same time any breach of good manners in a mess reflects the gross ignorance of the member concerned, therefore you should exercise your best manners at all times and maintain a gentlemanly decorum while in "his mess."

The Duty NCO will visit the mess daily. His purpose is to receive complaints and supervise the good conduct of the mess. The Post S/Major is ex-officio president of the Division Mess and may be approached at any time regarding messing and mess functions.

Officers' Mess – Building #80

Deriving from true Military tradition, the Royal Canadian Mounted Police have messes in each Division across the country. "Depot" Division has three messes on the base. These include the Saskatchewan Officers' Mess, the Saskatchewan General Mess and the Stand Easy Lounge for Cadets.

Historically, the messes have played an integral part in business and social activities for the RCMP and Saskatchewan, and have always ensured that communities and charities were involved and benefitted from their existence. These messes were started by Commissioner Herchmer in the late 1800s because he wanted to provide a place of entertainment for troops on the base, and to eliminate the temptation for the men to visit bars and brothels in the City of Regina.

On May 10, 1886 the establishment of an Officers' Mess was sanctioned by the Prime Minister, Sir John A. Macdonald, with an annual mess allowance of $200 from the Police Appropriation. The first Officers' Mess was located in a small building on the Square's east side in the approximate location of the present residence of the Officer Commanding "Depot" Division. It was recommended for replacement in 1893, but with some minor repairs remained until 1912 when it was demolished. In 1912, the mess moved to a three-storey building on the north-east corner of the square. This building had been occupied since 1885 as the Commissioner's Residence, but was made available as a Mess when a new residence was constructed to accommodate the large family of Commissioner Herchmer.

NWMP Officers in Regina – 1895: Standing, left to right – Inspector Scarth, Inspector Constantine, Inspector Gilpin-Brown, Superintendent Perry, Superintendent R. Belcher, Inspector Strickland, Veterinary Surgeon Burnett; Seated, left to right – Inspector Monty Baker, A/Commissioner McIllree, Commissioner Herchmer (evidence in this photo confirms that these two members did not have a good relationship), Inspector Starnes, Inspector Irwin, Surgeon Bell

Considerable renovations were carried out, including the covering of the wooden siding with brick veneer. A verandah was built around the south and west sides of the building. The interior of the building included a large billiard room on the north side, an anteroom, a dining room, a games room, a writing room and a kitchen on the first floor. Six bedrooms were located on the second floor and two bedrooms and a steward's quarters on the third floor.

The Officers' Mess quickly became one of the most prestigious places in Regina and Saskatchewan to entertain and be entertained. Minutes from committee meetings in the early 1900s documented the importance of separating the rank and file in the police force and in society. To ensure their involvement with "Depot," planning meetings with the business leaders of the Hudson's Bay Company, Eaton's, Simpson's and other prominent leaders in society were held every Wednesday morning. Functions ranged from formal dinners to curling events and all functions concluded at the Officers' Mess for social festivities.

Officers' Mess – formerly the Commissioner's Residence

Officers' Mess with summer awnings – circa 1915

The interior of the second Officers' Mess – circa 1925

CHAPTER 2 – BUILDINGS

Reception area – 1959

The Games Room – 1959

Formal gathering in the Officers' Mess – circa 1960

Senior Officers' bedroom – 1959

Officers' Mess – featuring south main entrance – December 1958

Program for the opening of the new Officers' Mess

In 1959, the current Officers' Mess was officially opened. The building covers the area formerly occupied by the Old Officers' Mess and Officers' Residence No. 6. Sergeant James C. Coughlin, Reg. #12511, a master draftsman who designed the Officers' Mess, served the Force for nearly 28 years, his entire service at "Depot" Division. "The exterior of the mess contains a large anteroom, a lounge, library and a dining room. A large kitchen, mess stewards' living quarters and games room containing a large billiard room, leather-covered furniture and a collection of trophies completes the first floor. An oak staircase leads to the second floor with 16 furnished bedrooms." (58)

The Officers' Mess also welcomed its share of dignitaries and VIPs. "Mess Register dates back to first establishment of the Officers' Mess in 1886 and reads like a composite of the pages of the world's 'Who's Who.' Late King George VI and his Queen in 1939, Queen Elizabeth the II and Prince Philip in 1951, Stefansson and Shackelton – explorers, H.R.H. The Prince of Wales, later to become for a short time King Edward VIII, the Rt. Honourable Sir Winston Churchill, William Lyon McKenzie King, Sir Wilfred Laurier. Other notables include Lord Baden Powell, Sir Martin Harvey the great English actor, John McCormack the Irish tenor, John Philip Sousa the band leader and the great soldier Lord Byng of Vimy who have signed the guest book, a time-honoured Mess tradition." (59)

Regina Leader-Post – Churchill's visit – 1929

Signature of Sir Winston Churchill – Officers' guest book – 1929

CHAPTER 2 – BUILDINGS   121

Officers' Mess – 2005

Regimental dinners, formal dinners and social gatherings continue to play a large role in the operation of the Messes.

The Saskatchewan Officers' Mess proudly displays artifacts from its origins, including North-West Mounted Police china and silver, artwork, various Officer kits and uniforms, and historical photographs. Also on display are two armchairs upholstered in royal purple, presented to the Officers' Mess on the occasion of the visit of Their Majesties King George VI and Queen Elizabeth in 1939.

To this day, the annual RCMP Regimental Dinner, held every May to celebrate the anniversary of the Force, attracts Chief Justices, Police Chiefs, military leaders and citizens of Saskatchewan. The Commanding Officer also hosts a regimental dinner for the members of every troop prior to their graduation.

The reception area – 2004

Senior NCOs' Mess

The Senior NCOs' Mess was first built in 1883 on the south side of the Parade Square, situated to the east of the Chapel. The building was 48 feet long and 16 feet wide. It served as the Mess for the Sergeants until 1890 when it moved to the northwest corner of the Parade Square, the present site of the "Depot" Post Garage. This Mess was a much larger two-storey building which contained sleeping quarters for the senior NCOs.

The Senior NCOs' Mess was relocated in 1913, with the completion of the new "A" Block. It was comprised of four rooms on the north end of the main floor.

In 1938, the Mess was further enlarged by the addition of seven bedrooms and a bathroom on the second floor.

Sergeants' Mess members, "Depot" – circa 1890

The Sergeants' Mess – centre background with a peaked roof and a verandah – circa 1890

Members in front of the Sergeants' Mess – circa 1910

Chapter 2 – Buildings

Rules for the Conduct of the Sergeants' Mess

1. All Sergeants' Major, Staff Sergeants, Sergeants and Acting Sergeants stationed at Regina are members of the Sergeants' Mess.
2. The Senior Sergeant Major (in Depot) will be ex-officio President of the Sergeants' Mess.
3. A Secretary-Treasurer will be elected monthly by vote of a general meeting.
4. There will be a committee of the President, the Secretary-Treasurer and one member; this committee will conduct the business of the Mess.
5. A general meeting will be held at 6.30 p.m. the second Wednesday in every month; all members who are present in the Post and not necessarily absent on duty will attend.
6. Any member who is absent from a Mess meeting without reasonable excuse will be reported to the Officer Commanding Depot Division.
7. The Minutes of the meeting will be kept and submitted to the Officer Commanding for approval within forty-eight hours of each meeting.
8. Every member, on joining the Mess, will pay an entrance fee of Two Dollars ($2.00); this will be deposited to the credit of the Mess Property Fund.
9. Honorary Members of the Mess from ex-Members of the Force, and such others to the number of ten (10), may be elected on a two-thirds majority vote at a full meeting. Notice of the proposed honorary membership, signed by proposer and seconder, to be posted in the sitting-room of the Mess at least one month before vote taken.
10. A Monthly subscription of twenty-five cents will be paid by all regular members to the Property Fund.
11. The Property Fund will only be used for the general up-keep of the Mess, apart from the Messing, as may be agreed upon by a majority of the members at a general Mess meeting.
12. There will be a Messing account kept separately from the Property Fund account; this will be made up at the end of each month and all accounts incurred for Messing paid by the dining members concerned.
13. All stoppages for Messing and for the Property Fund will be made through the Monthly Pay-lists.
14. Members of the Mess, who are not regular dining members, will be charged a price to be fixed by the Committee for any meals they may have in the Mess.
15. Members bringing guests into the Mess will be charged the same rate for any meals the guests may have.
16. Before anyone is entertained as a guest of the whole Mess, the matter will be brought up at a General Meeting, and the consent of two-thirds of the members obtained. The cost of such entertainment will be borne by all members equally.
17. The senior N.C.O. present is responsible for the discipline and good order of the Mess.
18. A book will be kept in the Mess in which any member may write suggestions or complaints. The Mess Secretary will deal with these as far as possible; any matter out of the ordinary will be brought up by him at the regular Monthly Meeting.
19. All Sergeants of other Divisions not stationed at Regina are Honorary Members of the Mess, while they are in Regina and are entitled to sleeping accommodation and meals at the same rates as regular dining members. Should all the rooms be occupied, the visitors will share the rooms of the junior Members of the Mess of equal rank as allotted by the Secretary.
20. A Special Mess Meeting may be called at any time by the President of the Mess.
21. A Visitors' Book will be kept in the Mess; all guests are to be requested to sign this.
22. The Mess Secretary-Treasurer will keep the following books, viz.:

    Property Fund Account (Including inventory of Mess property).
    Messing Account.
    Minute Book.

    These books, together with the Proposition Book and Visitors' Book, will be produced by the Secretary-Treasurer at each regular Monthly Meeting.
23. Two Bank Accounts will be kept; one for the Property Fund and the other for the Messing account. All disbursements will be made by cheque, which will be signed by the President and the Secretary-Treasurer.
24. All non-dining members of the Mess resident in Regina may be the guests of the Mess for one meal in each month.

APPROVED

COMMISSIONER.

Rules for the Conduct of the Sergeants' Mess

The Sergeants' Mess – 2005

In the spring of 1962, as a result of presentations made to the Commissioner, the Mess was considerably enlarged and redecorated. The offices previously occupied by the Sergeant Major and the Division Orderly were joined by archways and made part of the Mess, as was the former billiard room and the lounge room. The second-floor living quarters were then reconverted back to offices. (60)

The Senior NCOs' Mess amalgamated with the Corporals' Mess on April 1, 2006, forming the Saskatchewan General Mess, thus allowing for more office space and a boardroom in the A.B. Perry Building. This amalgamation resulted in the closure of the longest-running uninterrupted operational Mess in western Canada.

One of the highlights for all members of "Depot" Messes is the traditional Christmas Mess Levy. Held annually, this event starts with all Mess members in their respective Messes, they then parade to each Mess, joining their peers and superiors. Camaraderie and esprit d'corps continue throughout the evening and end at the Division Mess for an excellent festive meal. This tradition has been in effect since the late 1800s. It was initially created as a morale booster and remains so to this day.

Traditionally, the Officers' Mess served sausages, the Senior NCOs' served chicken drumsticks and the Corporals' Mess served seafood. The reason the highest-paid served the cheapest food and the lowest-paid served the most expensive food was due to the number of members in each Mess, as the funds came out of their own pockets. At one time, the festivities lasted for two days.

All of the Messes at "Depot" are actively involved in fundraising, for "Depot" and communities in Saskatchewan. The Messes have purchased an organ for the Chapel, updated displays at the Cemetery, sponsored palliative-care rooms in local hospitals and supported numerous individual and group causes in the community.

CHAPTER 2 – BUILDINGS

Corporals' Mess

The Royal Canadian Mounted Police Corporals' Mess in Regina has the distinction of being the first Corporals' Mess in the Force.

On November 25, 1943, the Corporals of "Depot," "F" Division and the Regina Laboratory stationed at the barracks met and forwarded a request to the Officer Commanding that a Corporals' Mess be established in the old Post Hospital. Temporary authorization was provided by headquarters provided that, "no actual Mess will be organized therein and furnishings are to be barrack furniture." The Corporals' Mess in essence became a social club, meeting monthly. Due to the inadequate location and access to the fire exit, the Mess required that it remained open to all. (61)

The Corporals' Mess, 1959, situated in the basement of the new "C" Block – the CIBC bank then occupied this area until leaving "Depot" in the early 80s

The Corporals' Mess – 2005

With the construction of the new "C" Block in 1953, space was provided for the Corporals' Mess in the form of a large room in the basement of the east wing. Furnishings were provided as part of the "C" Block furniture with additional items purchased from Mess funds.

In 1976, the Mess was moved to the basement of the "Depot" Division Mess, alongside the Stand Easy Lounge for cadets. In April of 2006, the Corporals' Mess amalgamated with the Sergeants' Mess to become the Saskatchewan General Mess.

Stand Easy Lounge

Stand Easy Lounge – 2005

The Stand Easy Lounge was officially opened by Chief Superintendent H.P. Tadeson on May 8, 1975. Since then, tens of thousands of recruits, cadets and course candidates have passed through these doors to unwind. Over the years, the dress code has gone from shirts and ties to the current casual dress code, including jeans. The Stand Easy Lounge is remembered by all cadets as a place to go to get away from the stressful environment of training, and to share some laughter and tears with troop mates.

Every troop leaves its "mark" on "Depot" by presenting a plaque to the Stand Easy. As the lounge has accumulated hundreds of plaques over the decades, the staff routinely rotates them.

Canteen

"Depot" Division Canteen Regina – 1941

"Commissioner Herchmer established the "Depot" Canteen in 1888 as a means of providing the men with necessary toiletries supplied at reasonable prices and to keep them from the saloons in Regina." (62) The Canteen could be found in the corner of the Junior Non-Commissioned Officers' (NCOs') Mess. Commissioner Herchmer felt that local merchants were gouging recruits and set up a small area to sell toothpaste, hair tonic, toiletries and the like. Profits from the sales were managed by a committee and used for the purchase of books for the Resource Centre and recreational purposes.

The Canteen "sold beer at 5 cents a glass, about half of the price for a similar quantity in town. Commissioner Herchmer hoped that the recruits would remain in barracks to do their drinking, where the Duty NCO would see that they did not over imbibe. It became a lively place in the evening where the men could relax, play cards or dominoes, throw dice for drinks and work off their frustration. It also became the scene of a form of initiation: liberal libation was given to a new recruit who was then hoisted onto the piano where he was expected to entertain his seniors satisfactorily with a song or two. If his performance was less than adequate, he was required to buy a round of drinks." (63)

The Canteen is in very satisfactory condition. Grants amounting to $979.39 have been made during the year to the Division Mess, and for recreation and other purposes. This does not include $300 paid by the Canteen for a first-class English billiard table, which was placed in the recreation room and has afforded considerable pleasure to a number of men devoted to the pastime. – RNWMP Annual Report 1908 – Superintendent G.E. Sanders

The beer sold is 4 percent, and some bottled lager, it is supplied in pewter pint pots at 5 cents a glass, the same beer being sold in town for 15 cents for the same quality. The Canteen enables the men to have an excellent mess at a very small expense, and plenty of amusement of a healthy sort is provided. – NWMP Annual Report 1891

Model Detachment
– Building #42

The model detachment was built in 1941-1942 and was likely one of the wood-frame buildings that was taken over from the Department of National Defence at the end of World War II. A number of these buildings were transported to "Depot" and were known as 14X structures. The buildings were moved to "Depot" in 1946 and 1947 and utilized for various purposes. The model detachment was used to create various crime scenes, providing the recruits with an opportunity to gain hands-on investigational experience.

"Depot" – 1960

CHAPTER 2 – BUILDINGS   129

RCMP Museum
– Building #99

Tunic of Inspector John French – the last member killed in the Riel Rebellion

Recreated NWMP Office – a steer horn chair presented by a native craftsman to Insp. Cunning; a rolltop desk dated 1917 used by A/Commr. J.A. McGibbon; an office chair used in the Regina Crime Lab until 1973; a pastel portrait of Insp. James Walker by Grandmaison; a clock from Lethbridge Detachment circa 1914

Entrance to Museum when situated in "C" Block – the RCMP Beechcraft D18S was mounted circa 1971

The Museum was established in 1933 with the approval and support of Commissioner MacBrien, acting on an idea from the Officer Commanding "Depot" Division, Stuart Wood, to celebrate the Diamond Jubilee of the Force. The Museum prospered in the growth of the collection and in attendance. The Museum was located in various buildings, including the basement of "A" Block and the old "B" and "C" Blocks. The Museum then moved to a dormitory wing of the new "C" Block (the current site of the Tailor Shop) from 1958 until 1973.

To mark the Centennial of the Mounted Police, a new environmentally controlled building was constructed at the present site, directly east of the Chapel. Her Majesty Queen Elizabeth II, the Honorary Commissioner of the Force, opened the Centennial Museum on July 4, 1973.

Sgt. Art Band, pictured here, was replaced by S/Sgt. Jack Chester upon his retirement. A committee continued until the appointment of the first professional museum curator, Civilian Member Malcolm Wake, in 1969. Civilian Member William MacKay, the current director, took over in 1998

Uniform and equipment of Superintendent J.M. Walsh. His photo is hanging in the centre of the display. Sitting Bull described Walsh as an honourable friend and trusted advisor

Display of aboriginal artifacts – circa 1958

CHAPTER 2 – BUILDINGS   131

Museum Entrance – 2006

Museum displays – 2006

Showcase of Female Kit items from 1974 to 2006

132   BEHIND THE BADGE

The Museum collection contains approximately 27,000 artifacts and the library is home to approximately 5,000 documents, 10,000 photographs and 1,500 books, all relating to the history of the Force.

As most artifacts are donated, the Museum's successful development is a tribute to the generosity of the Force's members, former members, relatives, friends and the general public.

The Museum has developed into an international attraction for both the Province of Saskatchewan and the City of Regina. Construction is underway on the new RCMP Heritage Centre, replacing the current Museum.

RCMP film posters in the mini movie theatre

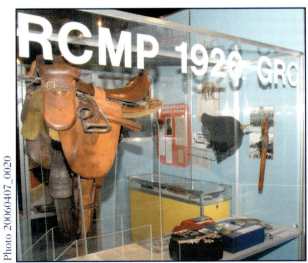
Museum displays – 2006

The Museum with the RCMP Beechcraft D18S in the foreground – 2005

CHAPTER 2 – BUILDINGS   133

The design for the new RCMP Heritage Centre was unveiled November 15, 2005

Heritage Centre Construction – 2006

Collage of men at work on the new RCMP Heritage Centre – April 9, 2006

RCMP Heritage Centre

The RCMP Heritage Centre is one of the largest tourism development projects currently underway in Western Canada. The twelve-acre site will be located on the northeast corner of the Academy grounds, fronted by Dewdney Avenue on the north and Bonner Drive on the east. The sod was turned for the Centre in September of 2002.

It is a 31-million-dollar project that over the next several years will transform the RCMP Academy, "Depot" Division, into one of Canada's major tourist destinations. A national competition awarded world-renowned Canadian architect Arthur Erickson the contract to design the Centre.

The proposed building will contain over 66,000 square feet of exhibition, conservation, administration and public programming space, constructed in two phases over three years.

Phase One will include the construction of the Heritage Centre building; which will offer museum tours and tours of the RCMP Academy Heritage Precinct, RCMP licenced merchandise in the gift shop and visitor hospitality services.

Phase Two will see the completion of the exhibit gallery space.

Visitors to the National Heritage Centre will be able to take guided tours, enjoy the famous Sunset Ceremony or the Sergeant Major's Parade, view film presentations, interactive exhibits, see displays on forensic science, indigenous people and Mountie history. (64)

The Victoria Cross

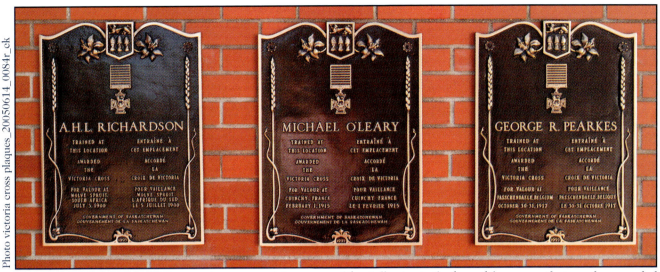

The Victoria Cross is the highest and most prestigious award for gallantry in the face of the enemy that can be awarded to British and Commonwealth forces

One member of the North-West Mounted Police and two members of the Royal Northwest Mounted Police, who trained at the Academy, were subsequent recipients of the Victoria Cross. Three bronze plaques at the entrance to the museum commemorate their heroism.

Arthur Herbert Lindsey Richardson

Arthur Herbert Lindsey Richardson was the first soldier to be awarded the Victoria Cross with a Canadian Unit under British Command. Cst. Richardson joined the North-West Mounted Police and was serving as a sergeant in the Lord Strathcona's Horse during the South African (Boer) War. On July 5, 1900 at Wolve Spruit, Standerton, South Africa, a party of Lord Strathcona's Horse, numbering 38 in total, came into contact at close range with the enemy force, which totaled 80. When the order was given to retire, Sergeant Richardson rode a wounded horse into heavy crossfire and rescued a trooper who had been badly wounded and whose horse had been shot. This act of gallantry and valour resulted in his being awarded the Victoria Cross. His Victoria Cross is currently displayed at the Museum of the Regiments in Calgary, Alberta.

Cst. Richardson (third from left, middle row) at "C" Division, Battleford – 1905

CHAPTER 2 – BUILDINGS

Michael O'Leary

Poster illustrating Lance Corporal O'Leary capturing a machine-gun nest of five German soldiers in 1915

Cst. O'Leary joined the Royal Northwest Mounted Police in 1913. Lance Corporal O'Leary was 26 years old and serving with the Irish Guards, British Army, during the first World War. On February 15, 1915, at Cuinchy, France, Lance Corporal O'Leary was one of the storming party which advanced again enemy barricades. He rushed to the front, killing five Germans who were holding the first barricade. He attacked the second barricade 60 yards further on, killing three additional Germans and taking two more prisoners. His heroic actions prevented his storming party from being fired on. His Victoria Cross is displayed at The Guards Regimental Headquarters in London, England.

George R. Pearkes

Cst. Pearkes in the Yukon – circa 1913

George Pearkes was born in Watford, England and immigrated to Alberta in 1906 with his brother, settling near Red Deer, Alberta. Cst. Pearkes went to Regina and joined the Royal Northwest Mounted Police in 1913. Six weeks after he joined, he was selected to serve in the Yukon on detachment duty. He worked in various areas of the territory. Upon the outbreak of World War 1, Pearkes received his discharge from the RNWMP in February of 1915 and enlisted. Acting Major Pearkes was a member of the 5th Canadian Mounted Rifles Branch Canadian Expeditionary Force. On October 30, 1917, near Passchendaele, Belgium, due to his determination and fearless personality, he maintained his objective with a small number of men against repeated enemy counterattacks. Following the First World War he became a career officer, retiring as the General Officer Commander in the Pacific Command 1945. In 1945, he was elected to the federal government, ultimately becoming the Minister of National Defense from 1957 to 1960. In 1960, he became the Lieutenant Governor of British Columbia and his term was extended to July of 1968. He is buried at Holy Trinity Cemetery in West Saanich, British Columbia and his Victoria Cross is on display at the Canadian War Museum in Ottawa, Ontario.

Officers' and NCOs' Quarters

Throughout the history of "Depot," there have always been residences (quarters) for senior and non-commissioned officers. Given that "Depot" is a city within a city, being self-reliant was critical for the operation of the base. At one time "Depot" also contained its own water supply and Fire Department. There are currently six Officers' Residences and two duplexes on base.

Why do staff reside on base?

1) *Immediate management response to emergency/physical issues – Because this is an Academy environment and there is the possibility of 500-600 cadets being here at one time, there is an operational requirement for an on call person (Regular member) to provide 24/7 coverage for emergencies and other occurrences after hours.*

2) *Constant deportment presence for Cadets – With cadets residing on base, the presence of management reinforces to them that their behaviour and deportment is under scrutiny at all times, just as it will be once they are sworn in as regular members. As members of the Force, our conduct and deportment is answerable under the provisions of the RCMP Act – Code of Conduct*

3) *Numerous ceremonies – Throughout the year, our management personnel are required to attend many ceremonies, social functions and troop graduations. Residing on base is very practical, as many of these ceremonies occur after normal working hours. In order to ensure their success, consideration must be given to the numerous voluntary hours required to participate in these events. With the number of various orders of dress involved with these functions, residing on base reduces the number of constant commutes that would be required if living off base.*

4) *Reduce transfer costs/mobility of personnel – With the incoming/outgoing nature of Force transfers, especially senior management positions, residing on base results in some reduced transfer costs for the Force on moving expenses. From an operational standpoint, it provides quick mobility of those residents when transferred in/rotated out of "Depot." (65)*

Officers' Residences located on the north side of the Parade Square – circa 1920

The brick residences were erected in 1908 to replace the original portable structures and were equipped with all modern conveniences. The residences each contained a total of seven rooms. The cost for all seven Officers' Residences was $38,794.32.

A view of the Officers' Residences looking eastward – the St Roch monument is in the centre foreground – circa 1952

Officers' Quarters building #6 being demolished to make room for the Officers' Mess – March 1958

Building #87 – The Commanding Officer's Residence in 1959 and 1974

Building #82 – Officers' Residence in 1956 and 1974

Building #81 – One of the "Depot" Officers' Residences on Cameron Avenue on the southeast side of Sleigh Square – 2005

Building #11/12 – This unpretentious duplex was erected on the south side of Sleigh Square for married NCOs in 1930-31, and designed to blend in with the seven Officers' Residences that lined the north and east sides of the Square. The main floor contains a living room, dining room and kitchen with three bedrooms and a bathroom on the upper floor. It is the only surviving example of the numerous early married quarters that once faced onto the Barracks Square. The duplex is still utilized to provide accommodation for two married NCOs – 2005

Building #36/37 – NCO's duplex on Moriarty Road – 1956

Building #36/37 – NCO's duplex on Moriarty Road – 1956. The duplex will be moved to the north side of the campground to form part of a rural farmyard scenario complex

Post Garage
– Building #26

View of the Gymnasium, Pool and Post Garage – new "B" Block under construction in the foreground – 1956

"The original Post Garage was built in 1931-1932 at the northwest corner of the Barracks Square by contractor R.M. Reckert for a total outlay of $6,140.80," (66) giving every appearance of having been designed and constructed in the most economical fashion. "It was designed by the Regina firm of Reilly, Warburton and Reilly which replaced Van Egmond and Storey as the Government's architects of choice during the Conservative tenure of power. One of the partners of the firm, Francis B. Reilly, was an apparently prominent Conservative supporter." (67)

The post garage was utilized as a shared facility with "F" Division to end the Force's reliance on Regina civilian garages for the maintenance of its growing automobile fleet by placing the work in the hands of more reliable and less expensive RCMP mechanics. (68)

The building was extended in 1953 to the north, to accommodate equipment and additional parking spaces.

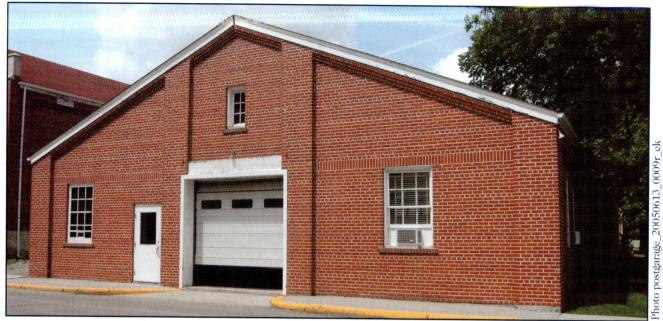

View of the principle south facade of the Post Garage facing Sleigh Square – 2005

The building currently holds the "Depot" Division bus, which transports the cadets to the Firearms Range, and division vehicles. In 2001, renovations were made to the south portion of the garage to equip it with proper ventilation systems and workspace so that the cadets could have an suitable environment in which to clean their firearms after each shoot.

Interior view of the Post Garage. Bicycles are available for cadets' use and workspace is provided on the right for cadets to clean their firearms in a ventilated area – 2005

Recreation Hall
– Building #4

The Hall had a stage, piano and dance floor which was the scene of many popular events. The original Recreation Hall was built in 1883 and was demolished in the early 1920s. The Hall was the home for meetings, dances and community events.

The was likely the first home of the NWMP Masonic Lodge #11, which began in 1894.

Where various forms of entertainment were held – circa 1886

NWMP Masonic Lodge #11, "Depot" – 1895

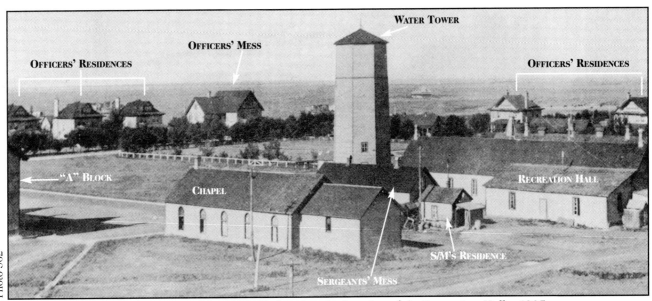

Headquarters of the RNWMP showing the location of the Recreation Hall – 1905

CHAPTER 2 – BUILDINGS

Regina Town Station

"New arrivals were directed to the Regina Town Detachment close by the station. It was connected to the orderly room at the "Depot" barracks. This was a party line and it could take time to get a call through – so there might be some delay before a wagon came to pick them up. The telephone line was shared with the Provincial Government House, and the Lt. Governor's wife spent a lot of time on the phone." (69) This was also the first phone line in Regina.

Regina Town Station – there were holes in the floor, a cracked stove, no storm door and no toilet – circa 1895

One recruit who arrived from the East at this time left his impressions of the scene as he alighted from the train that brought him to Regina:

… all around outside lay a great muddy expanse, with pools of water, while a soaking rain fell from a leaden sky. A few unpainted wooden houses bearing dingy sign boards form Broad Street… . The great prairie stretched away as far as the eye could see, flat and cheerless like a ghostly sea. (70)

Learning Resource Centre
– Building #24

Learning Resource Centre – 2002

Libraries have been part of the RCMP since its very early days. Superintendent Neale felt that libraries would provide relief from the "terrible monotony ... especially during the winter."

Commissioner Irvine pointed to the example of the British Service where regimental libraries and recreation rooms encouraged the men to enjoy their leisure hours in a manner that combined amusement with useful knowledge and taught them the value of sober, regular and moral habits.

In 1893, Commissioner Herchmer established a Central Library in Regina designed to supplement Division Libraries by exchanging books with them. The Parliamentary Librarian in Ottawa also provided acquisition services. By the late 1890s, libraries or reading rooms were established in many posts, including Regina and Battleford.

The reading room at Regina, however, had deteriorated. In the RNWMP Annual Report of 1906, Superintendent Sanders, the C.O. of "Depot" Division, described the reading room as a "bare, inhospitable looking place, with a long table down the middle and a few papers scattered thereon."

By 1907, a substantial grant from the fine fund was made to the library, renewing its original intention. Canteen profits, a monthly loan fee of .25¢ and a late fee of .05¢ per book also contributed to the purchase of new library books and magazine subscriptions. All members who entered the library were required to wear either a serge or stable jacket. (71)

CHAPTER 2 – BUILDINGS 145

RNWMP Annual Report 1908 – Superintendent G.E. Sanders

The library has been substantially increased and a number of appropriate and interesting newspapers and magazines are subscribed for. The subscription of 25 cents per month from everyone living in barracks supplies ample funds for all the requirements. The number of volumes is now about seven hundred and we require more shelving to accommodate future purchases.

On March 21, 1912 the library and contents were destroyed by fire which burnt "A" Block to the ground. Corporal Bennett, the Librarian, reported that except for the few books which were in the hands of members living out of barracks, all 2,300 volumes were destroyed. The Comptroller authorized the expenditure of $200 from the fine fund towards replacing the furnishings and volumes that had been destroyed in the fire. Unexpected help came from Mr. H.A. Kennedy of the Times of London. Through Mr. Kennedy's efforts over 800 books were shipped from England to Regina. The new library opened with a stock of over 1,000 volumes. (72)

The RCMP 1928 Rules and Regulations encouraged the continual use of reading rooms:

#2245 – Division Commanders are expected to take particular interest in post recreation and reading rooms, in order that the men of their commands may have a cheerful and comfortable place in which to spend the hours of the long winter evenings.

In 1939 the library was housed in "C" Block and remained there until it moved to the lower floor of the APS building.

In May of 1977, the library was staffed with a library technician and was renamed the Learning Resource Centre.

December 1995 saw the completion of renovations to the Artisan Building as the future site of the Learning Resource Centre. The current Resource Centre houses on its "main floor the resource collection, the reference desk, study tables and copier. The second floor has been renovated to include office and conference rooms, four internet sites, one multimedia site, the video collection and study carrels." (73)

The Learning Resource Centre continues to provide its services to cadets and members. Over the decades, the building has served as an overflow barrack, Artisan Shop, classrooms, Tailor and Leather Shops.

Riding Schools

"The first riding school, erected in 1886, was the largest structure in Regina. It ensured that foot and mounted drills could continue during the winter, and large enough for recruits to play baseball during the winter." (74) "This riding school held the first performances of the NWMP musical rides. It was completed in May 1886 at a cost of $30,000. The palatial structure was over 60 meters long, 36 meters wide and 12 meters high. It also con-

The first Riding School – 1886

tained a gymnasium, spectators gallery and a band room." (75) The Regina *Leader* described it as "one of the finest in the country." (May 11,1886) It accidentally burned to the ground on November 26, 1887, when the fire hoses froze in sub-zero weather

The second riding school was completed in 1889, almost identical in appearance. The Commissioner deemed such a building a necessity because of the severe low temperatures of the Regina winter. The riding school burnt down in 1920 but was not replaced until 1929 as less (sic) than 100 recruits passed through "Depot." (76)

Interior of the second Riding School – circa 1890

The Riding School in 1920 – before and after the fire

In 1929 the RCMP was finally able to replace the riding school destroyed by fire in 1920 with a large new riding school. This structure, the first new depot building in a decade, was designed in a Gothic-derived style by the Regina architectural firm of Van Egmond and Storey. (77) It was built by Poole Construction of Regina at a cost of $56,968 and was erected at the southwest corner of "Depot," near the site of its predecessor. (78) Its predominant Gothic forms were derived from the styling of the 1912-13 "A" Block and the 1919 "C" Block, but it is effectively isolated from the most historically significant focus of the depot. (79)

"The excavation and footings for the new riding school and stables were erected on the northwest side of the old school in 1953. The building had accommodation for 70 horses and included an exercise ring, tack rooms and forage space. It was constructed in the same style as the "N" Division riding school" (80). "A gallery at the east end of the building provides visitors with a view of activities in the school." (81) This former Riding School had acoustic ceiling tiles and warm heating installed so it could be used as a Drill Hall, alleviating capacity concerns in the gymnasium.

Drill Hall, formerly the third Riding School – 1956

Looking northwest to the Riding School – taken from the roof of the new "C" Block – the large paved area was known as the "Drill Square" – 1959

The Riding School – Building #63, from the rear – circa 1955

Rear of the Riding School – circa 1955

CHAPTER 2 – BUILDINGS   149

Interior of the Riding School – circa 1955

In 1966 riding was phased out of the recruit training program and the building was converted to an indoor sports arena. The O.C. at the time, Supt. A.V. Currie, an avid hockey fan, was able to convince Headquarters that participation in team sports at "Depot" might well be improved if the necessary equipment was installed to serve as an ice rink in the winter and indoor sports arena in the summer. An artificial ice plant was installed in 1970-1971. It was removed in 2000.

The arena is currently used for drill practice, scenarios and floor hockey. A spectators' gallery located at the east end of the arena has been converted into scenario residences – Sam Steele suites #1 and #2, for operational training.

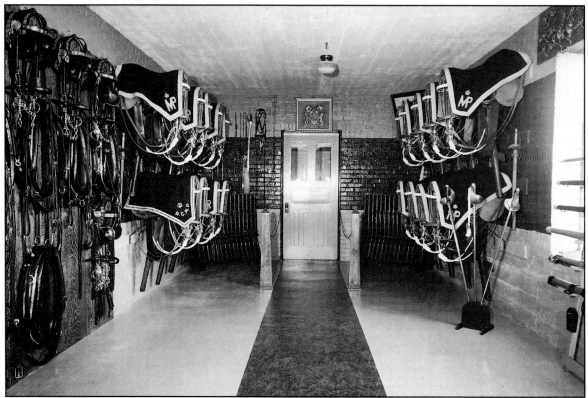

Tack room – Shabracks (Turkish for horse blankets) are mounted along the walls – circa 1950

Stables

NWMP Stables constructed 1890

The original Stables were built in 1890 and were described as wood frame buildings that were kept white by regular paintings and cleanings by recruits and prisoners. Stables 1, 2 and 3 were constructed in 1910/1911. Each of the Stables was divided into thirty-eight stalls, each six feet by ten feet, the partitions being made of two-inch planking with a neat capping. The Stables were lighted by a window in each of the stalls. These Stables were destroyed between 1948 and 1954.

Stables 1, 2, and 3 – 1936

Once the oath of office and the oath of allegiance had been taken, a third class constable led a spartan existence, paced by trumpet calls throughout the day, commencing with reveille at 6:30 a.m. between November 15th and February 15th or at 6:00 a.m. from February 16th to November 14th. Stable parade started a half hour after reveille. During this time, the "dunging out," feeding and grooming of the horses took place. A hasty breakfast followed before changing into boots and breeches and all ranks were off to saddle up for parade.

The daily routine of the barracks was riding in the morning, stable parade, foot drill, physical training and lectures in the afternoon, followed by the final stable parade.
– ex-Cst. T. Jamieson Quirk, Reg. #11951 – 1932 (82)

Cst. Geo. E. McLeod of the RNWMP on stable duty – May 1919

Stable duty – 1931

Cleaning out stalls – circa 1940

Interior of Stables – circa 1940

One of the less delightful features of "Depot," which I recall vividly, were the rats that inhabited all four stables in large numbers. These were rarely evident during the day, but after dark, when the night guard on his hourly round turned on the light, he witnessed hundreds of those unlovely creatures, leaping for cover in every direction, their beady eyes reflecting the overhead glare. – ex-Cst. T. Jamieson Quirk, Reg. #11951 – 1932 (83)

The Home Run

Any member who has been a "stable bitch," will know all about the "home run." This was an exercise that took place shortly after guard mount, or just before the orderly officer was expected to visit your stable to make sure that everything was neat and clean and that all the equine members were happy. Sunday afternoons were crucial times, also, because civilians were often escorted through the stables and droppings in the straw bedding were definitively a no-no. This is when the "home run" came into play, so to speak. The only equipment required was a sharp eye, a scoop shovel and running shoes – not to mention stamina. The players were the stable orderly, scoop in hand and a wheelbarrow nearby, and up to 30 horses. Looking left and right, the orderly would sprint as soon as a tail began to rise: if he was in time to catch it all, it was scored as a "home run." There were times when the hay burners conspired to defeat him. Two or sometimes more would start the action at the same time, at opposite ends of the stable. The orderly had to reach top speed in hope of reaching even partial success. Some horses were known to fake the action just to annoy the orderlies. It was pretty maddening to stand with scoop extended and nothing happening, while farther down the aisle everything was landing in the straw. – S/Sgt. E.C. Parker (rtd.), Reg. #12640 – 1935 (84)

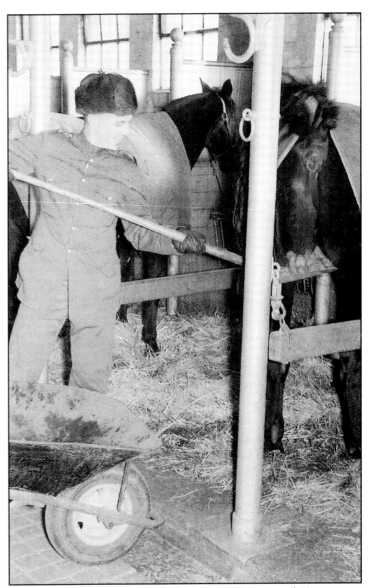

Cst. Doug Mervyn of Troop #26, 1955-1956, successfully executing a home run

Swimming Pool

Preliminary plans for the new gymnasium/swimming pool complex, to be located between the garage and the artisan's shops, were prepared by Reilly, Warburton and Reilly in the spring of 1935. In 1936, Commissioner MacBrien was informed that the approved architectural firm, dating back to 1907-1908, would be restored. The Reilly's design for the gymnasium/pool complex was slightly redrawn by the architect firm of Van Egmond and Storey. (85) The gymnasium/swimming pool building, consisting of two externally identical gabled roof structures linked by a one-storey entry and service facility was erected in two segments. The gymnasium in 1937-38 and the pool in 1940-41. Poole construction built the swimming pool wing at a contract price of $72,100.00. (86)

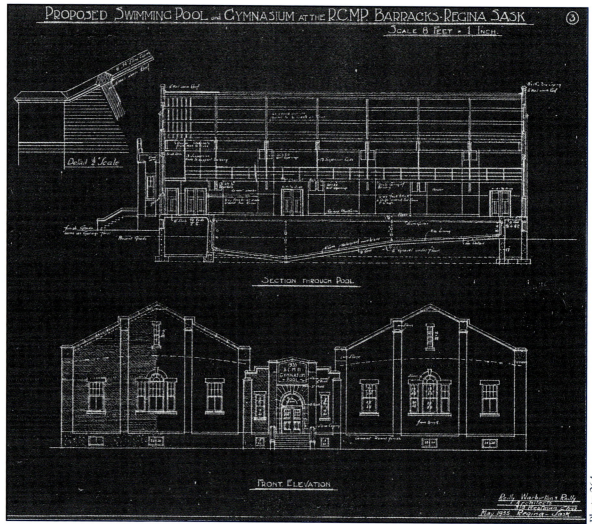

A 1935 front elevation and section of the Gymnasium/Swimming Pool Complex

Construction initiated on the Pool – Building #25 – The Division Mess is located centre left with the Riding School in the centre rear – 1940

Extension to the Gymnasium, looking north – the Lecture Hall can be seen centre right – 1940

A rear view the Gym/Pool Complex with the Post Garage in the background – circa 1956

CHAPTER 2 – BUILDINGS   155

Swimming Pool - Depot Div. Regina - 1955

Members of Troop #26, 1955/56

The completed Pool building with the pool itself laid in yellow, gray and green terrazzo tile, its acoustically excellent battened ceiling and sound deadening wall finish and its upper-level galley with seating for 400 spectators appears to have been an innovative and useful facility. One of the four or five largest swimming pools in Canada when it was constructed, it continued to attract visitors through the 1950s who came "for the express purpose of studying its construction and equipment for their own pool plans." (87)

"In 1941, the Swimming Pool was officially opened and swimming was integrated into the recruit training program. Described as one of the finest indoor swimming pools in Canada, it measures 90 feet long by 40 feet wide and was modeled on the specifications of the pool at the Seigneury Club at Montebello, Quebec." (88) Over three million three-quarter-inch tiles in various colours added to the decor of the pool, walls and walkways. Lifesaving, swimming techniques and sports quickly became a loved or feared aspect of every recruit's training. Diving and boating lessons were also provided to those interested.

The completion of the Gymnasium/Pool Complex was an important component in Commissioner MacBrien's plans for the improvement of the depot training facilities intended to improve barrack life and permit a further broadening of the training syllabus. (89)

Swimming Pool – 2001

Water Tower

Looking northeast onto the Parade Square in 1905, a steepleless Chapel, Water Tower and the Commissioner's Residence in the rear centre can be observed. The original "A" Block on the west side of the Parade Square burnt down in 1912

An adequate water supply was a serious problem from the time headquarters was moved to Regina in 1882. The first water supplies were hauled by cart from Wascana Creek. It became polluted by human and animal waste. As a result, reoccurring outbreaks of typhoid and similar epidemics resulted in fatalities not only with the members, but their families. The 20-meter tower was constructed in 1890, complete with pumps and engine on the Square's southwest corner, directly in front of the present museum site, replacing the well. Although this well brought an adequate supply of safe drinking water to "Depot," its water was very hard and its alkali content had an upsetting effect on the stomachs and bowels of recruits until they became used to it. The tower not only decreased the hazards of fire, it also brought about the greening of the barrack. Trees had been previously sent from the Experimental Farm in Ottawa, but attempts to grow these and start lawns had met with failure because of the lack of water. By 1892, native maples taken from nearly creeks had become firmly rooted, green lawns were in evidence and vegetable gardens had appeared beside the married quarters. Some of the Officers and NCOs began to keep chickens, ducks and even a cow. There was the devil to pay after someone's dog got into Commissioner Herchmer's chicken pen one night. The water tower was demolished in 1910 and the lumber used to build a new bridge over the Wascana. (90)

Without a plumbing system, having a bath could be quite a chore. Each bather had to heat his water in pails on a stove, then pour it into the iron tub. When he finished, he had to empty the tub with a pail to make it ready for the next man. Bath night must have been quite a scramble when you realize that there were only two tubs for up to 100 recruits. It was not until 1907 that the barracks were hooked up to the city's new water system and the difficulties of washing and shaving eased. – S.W. Horrall, RCMP historian (91)

Today, the training academy maintains its own water supply for ground maintenance only.

Prior to the construction of a well, water was collected from Wascana Creek. This photo was used to establish the Mounted Police's water rights to Wascana Creek prior to 1885

CHAPTER 2 – BUILDINGS   157

Chapter 3

CHANGE OF COMMAND CEREMONY

One of the most colourful and traditional ceremonies that occurs at "Depot" Division is the Change of Command ceremony. Each time a new Commanding Officer is appointed to "Depot" Division, an old European military tradition takes place. This affords the rank and file an opportunity to give a last farewell to the departing Commanding Officer and acknowledge the new command for the Division.

In the past 120 years, there have been 52 Commanding Officers at "Depot." All regular-member staff and all cadets in training participate in the pomp and ceremony each time there is a change of command at "Depot" Division.

The most recent Change of Command occurred on May 4, 2005 when C/Supt. Tugnum turned over his command to C/Supt. Ménard.

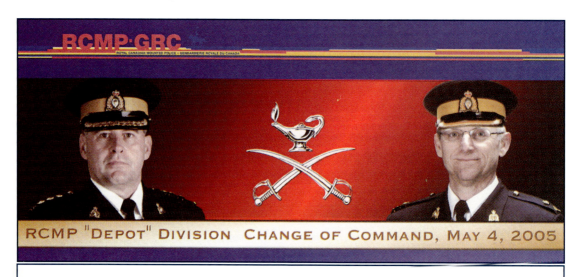

Invitation to Parade and Reception marking the occasion of the Change of Command Ceremony

158   Behind the Badge

C/Supt. Pierre Ménard, the 52ND Commanding Officer

C/Supt. Tugnum being thanked by Commissioner G. Zaccardelli

Change of Command Ceremony – May 4, 2005

Chapter 3 – Personnel

Commissioners/ Commanding Officers

As the Commanding Officer, you have a hand in creating each and every member of the RCMP that trains here during your tenure. It is a formidable responsibility.
– Commissioner G. Zaccardelli (1)

NWMP Headquarters Regina 1891 – Officers of "Depot" Division
Standing, left to right – Inspectors Routledge, Burnett, Macdonell, Howard.
Seated, left to right – Inspector Wilson, Surgeon Jukes, Commissioner Herchmer,
Superintendent Gagnon, Superintendent Moffat. Sitting – Inspector Starnes

Throughout the history of the Royal Canadian Mounted Police the role of Commanding Officer of "Depot" has been deemed to be one of the most critical positions in the RCMP. Being in charge of the Training Academy and forming the future of the membership for the Force are high-profile positions. Several Commanding Officers have accomplished noteworthy achievements in their service with the RCMP.

E.W. Jarvis, Reg. #O.73, was the Commanding Officer of "Depot" between 1886 and 1887. In 1871, at age 24, he was a location engineer who journeyed by dog sled from Prince George to locate a suitable pass for the future transcontinental railway. He endured much hardship, returning with no food or dogs, and almost barefoot, to Lac Ste. Anne in March of 1873. Mount Jarvis, 175 km ENE of Prince George was named after him.

Richard Deane, Reg. #O.49, was Commanding Officer from 1887/88 and has authored two books about policing, *Pioneer Policing in Southern Alberta* and *Mounted Police Life in Canada*.

A.B. Perry, Reg. #O.44, was Commanding Officer from 1890/91 and 1895/96. He was also the Commissioner for the North-West Mounted Police, Royal Northwest Mounted Police and Royal Canadian Mounted Police. "A" Block at "Depot" is now named after him.

William Morris, Reg. #O.51, was Commanding Officer from 1900/02. He suffered a stroke and fell off a roof while trying to extinguish a fire at a member's residence.

Walton Routledge, Reg. #O.85, was Commanding Officer from 1909-1912. He authored the first book of Rules, Regulations and Orders.

Arthur Duffus, Reg. #O.133, was Commanding Officer from 1922-1925 and is believed to have used the first car on duty. He was a grand nephew of Sir Samuel Cunard, founder of the Cunard Steamship Line.

James Spalding, Reg. #O.166, had a lake named after him – Spalding Lake, Saskatchewan.

Theodore Sandys-Wunsch, Reg. #O.195, was Commanding Officer in 1941. He won the gold medal as the best shot in the Force in 1923.

Cecil Hill, Reg. #O.189, was Commanding Officer from 1931-1937, and was in the official party when Lord Bessborough presented the Guidon at "Depot" in 1935.

Several Commanding Officers are buried in the RCMP Cemetery at "Depot."

With regard to this list of Commanding Officers of "Depot," record keeping was not always meticulous. This "final" list was prepared based on intensive research and taking into account some conflicting historical records.

Irvine, Acheson Gosford, Reg. #O.30

- Born Lower Canada (Quebec), 7 December 1837; died Quebec City, Quebec, 9 January 1916
- Engaged Winnipeg October 1873; Resigned Regina, North-West Territories, 31 March 1886
- Commanded "Depot" Division: 1 November 1885 to 31 March 1886

Commr. A.G. Irvine

Herchmer, Lawrence William – Reg. #O.72

- Born Oxfordshire, England, 25 April 1840; died Vancouver, British Columbia, 17 February 1915
- Appointed Regina 31 March 1886; Resigned, Regina, North-West Territories 31 July 1900
- Commanded "Depot" Division: 1 April 1886 to 14 April 1886

Commr. L.W. Herchmer

Jarvis, Edward Worrell – Reg. #O.73

- Born Prince Edward Island, 1847; died of apoplexy Calgary, North-West Territories (Alberta), 27 November 1894
- Appointed Superintendent April 10, 1886
- Commanded "Depot" Division: 14 April 1886 to 30 April 1886
- Commanded "Depot" Division: 19 July 1887 to 1 August 1887

Supt. E.W. Jarvis

Insp. F. Norman

Norman, Frank – Reg. #O.46

- Born Dublin, Ireland, 19 November 1846; died Toronto, Ontario, 7 October 1906
- Engaged 6 May 1874 as Sub. Cst.; retired to pension 30 April 1895
- Commanded "Depot" Division: 1 May 1886 to 29 July 1886

Insp. J.B. Allan

Allan, Joseph Beresford – Reg. #O.55

- Born Armagh, Ireland, November 1840; died Vancouver, British Columbia, 10 October 1927
- Engaged 1 August 1885; retired to pension 01 January 1900
- Commanded "Depot" Division: July 1886

Supt. S. Gagnon

Gagnon, Severe – Reg. #O.20

- Born Montreal, Canada East (Quebec), 1845; died Regina, Saskatchewan, 9 May 1909
- Appointed Sub Inspector 3 April 1874; retired to pension 1 April 1901
- Commanded "Depot" Division: 1 August 1886 to 12 May 1887
- Commanded "Depot" Division: 12 May 1888 to 31 July 1890
- Commanded "Depot" Division: 19 September 1891 to 15 February 1895

Supt. R.B. Deane

Deane, Richard Burton – Reg. #O.49

- Born Ootacomund, India, 30 April 1848; died Mariana, Italy, 13 December 1930
- Appointed Inspector 1 July 1883; retired to pension 31 March 1915
- Commanded "Depot" Division: 1 August 1887 to 11 May 1888

Supt. A.B. Perry

Perry, Aylesworth Bowen – Reg. #O.44

- Born Violet, Canada East (Ontario), 21 August 1860; died Ottawa, Ontario, 14 February 1956
- Appointed Inspector 24 January 1882; Retired to pension 31 March 1923
- Commanded "Depot" Division: 1 August 1890 to 18 September 1891
- Commanded "Depot" Division: 15 February 1895 to 31 July 1896

Supt. J. Howe

Howe, Joseph – Reg. #O.48

- Born Saint John, New Brunswick, 1856; died suddenly while on duty Fort MacLeod, North-West Territories (Alberta), 17 August 1902
- Engaged Fort Walsh 4 July 1879
- Commanded "Depot" Division: 1 August 1896 to 30 June 1899

Constantine, Charles – Reg. #O.79

- Born Bradford, Yorkshire, England, 1849; died while on leave Long Beach, California, 5 May 1912
- Appointed Inspector 20 October 1886
- Commanded "Depot" Division: 1 July 1899 to 31 July 1900

Supt. C. Constantine

Morris, William Springfield – Reg. #O.51

- Born New Brunswick, 1860; died Regina, North-West Territories, 4 April 1905
- Appointed Inspector 1 May 1884
- Commanded "Depot" Division: 1 August 1900 to 19 October 1902

Supt. W.S. Morris

MacDonnell, Sir Archibald Cameron, K.C.B., C.M.G., D.S.O. – Reg. #O.95

- Born Windsor, Canada West (Ontario), November 1863; died Kingston, Ontario, 23 December 1941
- Appointed Inspector 28 September 1889; retired to pension 31 March 1915
- Commanded "Depot" Division: 20 October 1902 to 3 January 1905

Supt. A.C. MacDonnell

Wilson, James Osgoode – Reg. #O.64

- Born Dundas, Canada West (Ontario), September 1856; died Victoria, British Columbia, 29 April 1927
- Engaged at Fort Walsh Reg. #392 9 June 1879; retired to pension 16 January 1919
- Commanded "Depot" Division: 3 January 1905 to 31 July 1906

Supt. J.O. Wilson

Sanders, George Edward – Reg. #O.52

- Born Yale, British Columbia, 25 December 1863; died Calgary, Alberta, 19 April 1955
- Appointed Inspector 1 September 1884; retired to pension 1 March 1912
- Commanded "Depot" Division: 1 August 1906 to 31 September 1909

Supt. G.E. Sanders

Routledge, Walton Harrison – Reg. #O.85

- Born Durham, England, 20 January 1863; died while on leave prior to pension, Regina, Saskatchewan, 6 November 1919
- Engaged as Constable Reg. #465 on 21 August 1880;
- Commanded "Depot" Division: 1 October 1909 to 31 May 1912

Supt. W.H. Routledge

CHAPTER 3 – PERSONNEL

A/Commr. R.S. Knight

A/Commr. G.S. Worsley

Supt. A.W. Duffus

Supt. W.P. Lindsay

Supt. C.H. Hill

Knight, Reginald Spencer – Reg. #O.130

- Born Surrey, England, 16 May 1864; died of heart attack while on duty, Regina, Saskatchewan, 4 November 1927
- Engaged as Constable Reg. #2441 on 1 May 1890
- Commanded "Depot" Division: 1 June 1912 to 31 July 1914
- Commanded "Depot" Division: 1 January 1925 to 4 November 1927

Worsley, George Stanley – Reg. #O.123

- Born Baddeck, Nova Scotia, 1865; died Victoria, British Columbia, 19 December 1945
- Appointed Inspector 1 April 1900; retired to pension 15 June 1931
- Commanded "Depot" Division: 1 October 1914 to 30 June 1922
- Commanded "Depot" Division: 19 April 1928 to 31 December 1930

Duffus, Arthur William – Reg. #O.133

- Born Halifax, Nova Scotia, 29 May 1872; died Vancouver, British Columbia, 6 September 1933
- Engaged as Constable 24 October 1895, Reg #3159; retired to pension 1 September 1931
- Commanded "Depot" Division: 1 July 1922 to 1 January 1925

Lindsay, William Pentland – Reg. #O.153

- Born Quebec City, Quebec, 15 December 1879; died on duty Regina, Saskatchewan, 4 August 1929
- Appointed Inspector 1 January 1910
- Commanded "Depot" Division: 1 September 1927 to 18 April 1928

Hill, Cecil Henry – Reg. #O.189

- Born Australia 1884; died Vancouver, British Columbia, 12 May 1953
- Engaged as Reg. #4750, 1 September 1908; retired to pension 1 April 1944
- Commanded "Depot" Division: 1 January 1931 to 31 May 1937

Cooper, Arthur Stafford – Reg. #O.226

- Born Ashbourne, Derby, England, 19 January 1881; died Victoria, British Columbia, 1 October 1969
- Engaged as Reg. #4878, 13 May 1909; retired to pension 30 September 1946
- Commanded "Depot" Division: April to October 1935 – acting capacity
- Commanded "Depot" Division: 16 October 1941 to 30 September 1943

Supt. A.S. Cooper

Irvine, Thomas Hill – Reg. #O.191

- Born England, 28 February 1880; died Victoria, British Columbia, 15 July 1970
- Engaged as Reg. #4793, 11 November 1908, retired to pension 30 November 1941
- Commanded "Depot" Division: 1 June 1937 to 31 May 1941

Supt. T.H. Irvine

Sandys-Wunsch, Theodore Vincent – Reg. #O.195

- Born Cheshire, England, 9 January 1892; died Duncan, British Columbia, 25 July 1966
- Engaged as trumpeter Reg.#5185, 1 April 1911; retired to pension 28 February 1947
- Commanded "Depot" Division: 1 June to 15 October 1941

Supt. T.V. Sandys-Wunsch

Radcliffe, Edward Walker – Reg. #O.258

- Born Sussex, England, 26 November 1887; died Toronto, Ontario, 26 August 1975
- Engaged Reg. #6325, 30 September 1914; retired 14 January 1946
- Commanded "Depot" Division: 1 October 1943 to 31 January 1945

Supt. E.W. Radcliffe

Day, William Richard – Reg. #O.262

- Born Georgetown, British Guiana, 10 September 1896; died Vernon, British Columbia, 6 February 1971
- Engaged 9 November 1920 Manitoba Provincial Police; retired 9 February 1946
- Commanded "Depot" Division: 1 February 1945 to 9 February 1946

Supt. W.R. Day

Armitage, Robson – Reg. #O.283

- Born Toronto, Ontario, 1891; died 18 January 1956
- Engaged Reg. #6369, 1 December 1914; retired 31 December 1950
- Commanded "Depot" Division: 10 February 1946 to 31 August 1947

Supt. R. Armitage

Michelson, Robert Thomas – Reg. #O.297

- Born Dublin, Ireland, 24 May 1899; died Dartmouth, Nova Scotia 9 February 1971
- Engaged Reg. #8915 25 November 1919; retired to pension 31 March 1949
- Commanded "Depot" Division: 1 September 1947 to 31 December 1947

Supt. R.T. Michelson

Supt. E.H. Perlson

Perlson, Edward. H. — Reg. #O.319

- Born Montreal, Quebec, 27 December 1906; died Kelowna, British Columbia, 07 June 2003
- Engaged Reg. #11977, 2 March 1933; retired to pension 29 March 1968
- Commanded "Depot" Division: 1 January 1948 to 1 January 1950

Supt. J.C. Story

Story, John Copland — Reg. #O.336

- Born Largo, Scotland, 1 November 1893; died Dartmouth, Nova Scotia, 18 June 1980
- Engaged Reg. #10183, 27 April 1926; retired 31 January 1954
- Commanded "Depot" Division: 1 January 1950 to 01 February 1954

Supt. J.F. Thrasher

Thrasher, John Francis — Reg. #O.318

- Born Sarnia, Ontario, 23 September 1905; died Toronto, Ontario, 25 June 1990
- Engaged Reg. #11963, 30 December 1932; retired 31 December 1959
- Commanded "Depot" Division: 1 February 1954 to 30 April 1955

Supt. C.N.K. Kirk

Kirk, Cyril Nordheimer Kenny — Reg. #O.326

- Born Toronto, Ontario, 16 September 1911; died Ottawa, Ontario, 26 May 1981
- Engaged Reg. #12503, 27 November 1934; retired to pension 12 May 1970
- Commanded "Depot" Division: 1 May 1955 to 31 July 1956

Supt. H.O. Maxted

Maxted, Harry Amos — Reg. #O.344

- Born Toronto, Ontario, 18 May 1911; died Edmonton, Alberta 19, November 1996
- Engaged Reg. #12041, 5 August 1933; retired to pension 29 April 1970
- Commanded "Depot" Division: 1 August 1956 to 30 June 1959

Porter, Eric – Reg. #O.381

Supt. E. Porter

- Born Grand Junction, Colorado, USA, 18 October 1907; died Calgary, Alberta, 26 August 1979
- Engaged Reg. #12073, 1 November 1933; retired to pension 1 November 1968
- Commanded "Depot" Division: 1 July 1959 to 27 December 1961

Forbes, Henry Christopher – Reg. #O.384

Supt. H.C. Forbes

- Born 1908; died Kelowna, British Columbia, 12 June 1999
- Engaged Reg. #11849, 16 November 1932; retired to pension 16 November 1967
- Commanded "Depot" Division: 28 December 1961 to 30 June 1964

Mudge, Gerald W. – Reg. #O.424

Supt. G.W. Mudge

- Born Vancouver, British Columbia, 13 September 1912; died Mill Bay, British Columbia, 5 November 1999
- Engaged Reg. #12918, 3 September 1937; retired to pension 2 September 1972
- Commanded "Depot" Division: 1 July 1964 to 7 December 1966

Currie, Raymond Victor – Reg. #O.476

Supt. R.V. Currie

- Born Fredericton, New Brunswick, 2 February 1913; died Regina, Saskatchewan, 27 December 1982
- Engaged Reg. #12502, 27 November 1934; retired to pension 24 April 1970
- Commanded "Depot" Division: 8 December 1966 to 24 October 1969

Stone, Richard Percy – Reg. #O.471

Supt. R.P. Stone

- Born Toronto, Ontario, 16 April 1913; died Kelowna, British Columbia, 7 December 1982
- Engaged Reg. #16471, 15 August 1950; retired to pension 8 May 1973
- Commanded "Depot" Division: 1 October 1969 to 8 May 1973

C/Supt. H.P. Tadeson

Tadeson, Henry. P.   Reg. #O.313

- Born Fredericton, New Brunswick, 2 February 1913; died Toronto, Ontario, 27 December 1982
- Engaged Reg. #14596, 27 November 1934; retired to pension 24 April 1970
- Commanded "Depot" Division: 9 May 1973 to 9 July 1975

C/Supt. R.J. Mills

Mills, Robert J. – Reg. #O.574

- Born Fort Pitt, Saskatchewan, 12 May 1927
- Engaged Reg. #15075, 4 August 1948; retired to pension 20 August 1981
- Commanded "Depot" Division: 14 September 1975 to 9 August 1978

C/Supt. D.A. Whyte

Whyte, David A. – Reg. #O.655

- Born 14 November 1933
- Engaged Reg. #17573, 25 February 1952; retired to pension 10 April 1987
- Commanded "Depot" Division: 1 August 1978 to 26 September 1980

C/Supt. G.C Caldbick

Caldbick, George C. – Reg. #O.614

- Born southwestern Manitoba, 28 August 1926
- Engaged Reg. #14966, 5 May 1947; retired to pension 5 May 1982
- Commanded "Depot" Division: 27 September 1980 to 5 January 1982

C/Supt. J.L.D. Ling

Ling, J.L. Denis – Reg. #O.720

- Engaged Reg. #18701, 22 August 1954; retired to pension 1 September 1986
- Commanded "Depot" Division: 1 April 1982 to 11 August 1983

Supt. R.L. Fletcher

Fletcher, Robert Lorne – Reg. #O.633

- Born Killarney, Manitoba, 23 January 1928; died Vancouver, British Columbia, 29 May 1993
- Engaged Reg. #15969, 2 November 1949; retired to pension 1 November 1984
- Commanded "Depot" Division: 11 August 1983 to 31 October 1984

Lagasse, J.A.D. – Reg. #O.935

- Born Manitoba, 20 January 1939
- Engaged Reg. #20635, 3 July 1958; retired to pension 2 July 1993
- Commanded "Depot" Division: 1 November 1984 to 8 January 1988

C/Supt. J.A.D. Lagasse

Bell, Robert G. – Reg. #O.905

- Engaged Reg. #19184, 25 November 1955; retired to pension 4 July 1989
- Commanded "Depot" Division: 9 January 1988 to 31 May 1989

C/Supt. R.G. Bell

Spring, William Ronald – Reg. #O.1103

- Born Moose Jaw, Saskatchewan, 5 February 1941
- Engaged Reg. #21451, 7 May 1960; retired to pension 22 January 1993
- Commanded "Depot" Division: 1 June 1989 to 31 October 1992

C/Supt. W.R. Spring

Matchim, Ford – Reg. #O.1165

- Born Bonavista Bay, Newfoundland
- Engaged Reg. #21919, 3 April 1961
- Commanded "Depot" Division: 1 November 1992 to 19 June 1994

C/Supt. F. Matchim

Gauthier, J.R. Andre – Reg. #O.1333

- Born LaTuque, Quebec 1950
- Engaged Reg. #29099, 9 July 1971
- Commanded "Depot" Division: 20 June 1994 to 09 March 1998

C/Supt. Gauthier was Commanding Officer during a period of tremendous changes, changes with major historical significance. He oversaw: the start of the transition from the old recruit program to the new cadet program; the regaining of "Depot" Division status from the RCMP Training Academy in 1995; the addition of responsibility of the C.O. "Depot" to include the Centralized/Regionalized In-Service Training in Ottawa; the Police Dog Service Training Centre in Innisfail, Alberta; the Field Coaching Program and Centennial Museum. C/Supt. Gauthier also oversaw the creation of the Canadian Law Enforcement Training (CLET) Unit and the start of the planning for the new RCMP Heritage Building.

C/Supt. J.R.A. Gauthier

C/Supt. Harper Boucher

Boucher, Harper – Reg. #O.1555

- Born Bathurst, New Brunswick, 8 December 1949
- Engaged Reg. #29897, 21 June 1972
- Commanded "Depot" Division: 9 March 1998 to 18 June 1999

C/Supt. Lynn Twardosky

Twardosky, Lynn, Reg. #O.1713

- Born Melville, Saskatchewan
- Engaged Reg. #33496, 20 January 1975
- Commanded "Depot" Division: 18 June 1999 to 10 September 2002

C/Supt. Curt Tugnum

Tugnum, Curt, Reg. #O.1688

- Born Smithers, British Columbia
- Engaged Reg. #30802, 15 August 1973
- Commanded "Depot" Division: 10 September 2002 – 4 May 2005

C/Supt. Pierre Ménard

Ménard, Pierre – Reg. #O.2100

- Born St.-Isidore de Prescott, Ontario, 18 November 1956
- Engaged Reg. #33327, 20 April 1976
- Commanded "Depot" Division: 4 May 2005 –

Reflections of "Depot" Commanding Officers

Commanding Officer A/Commr. Robert J. (Bob) Mills

- 14 September 1975 to 9 August 1978

As C.O., the 1970s at "Depot" were a time of considerable changes in the training programs. In 1974 the first female troop was formed. This was followed by combined troops, male and female.

For the first time, combined special courses were held for other agencies. Federal Fisheries and the Dakota Ojibway Tribal Council of Manitoba started training at "Depot." Special Constable courses were held for airport policing and other Force branches, as well as courses for Aboriginal members and for Inuit members from the north.

There was also some facility activity – the opening of the new "D" block, Drill Hall renovations, completion of the first driver-training track, indoor range renovations due to lead accumulation, and the building of the campground. The campground was the initiative of Insp. Jim Maloney, the F.S.S. officer, with funding from the "Carden Estate."

A/Commr. Mills enjoyed his three-year posting to "Depot," which, he stated, "is a unique command." The main frustration for him, much as at present time, was troop load. It was either "feast or famine," i.e., going with a full house or down to one troop. He is still an active participant in all "Depot"-related activities through the Veterans Association.

A/Commr. Robert J. (Bob) Mills

Commanding Officer C/Supt. Harper Boucher

- 9 March 1998 to 18 June 1999

Like so many other members who left basic training, Chief Superintendent Harper Boucher had a dream to one day return as an instructor. From Boucher's perspective, as a recruit, as an instructor and as the Commanding Officer "Depot," it was those duties which had the most positive impact on him as an individual, and that instilled values which he tries to exemplify in his daily life.

As a recruit in 1972, Boucher was proud to have passed all the criteria to become a member of the RCMP. He was also proud of the people in his troop, their high ideals and their genuine willingness to help others. He enjoyed training and the camaraderie it provided. His time as Commanding Officer "Depot" helped him realize the power of the history and ongoing traditions of the Force.

C/Supt. Boucher knew from the beginning that he wanted to return to "Depot" as an instructor. He prepared himself for that eventual day, firmly believing that returning would allow him to have an impact on the organization. He loved every minute of his duties at "Depot" Division.

C/Supt. Boucher returned to "Depot" after a tour as an Instructor. He was assigned to implement the new Cadet Training Program in 1994. Moving away from the old recruit training model was perhaps the greatest fundamental change the RCMP had ever made in its training program at "Depot." Boucher noted this as one of the most significant contributions of his years at "Depot" Division.

C/Supt. Boucher was promoted to Commanding Officer, "F" Division (Saskatchewan) and then to Deputy Commissioner, Atlantic Region.

C/Supt. Harper Boucher

Commanding Officer C/Supt. Lynn Twardosky

C/Supt. Lynn Twardosky

• 18 June 1999 to 10 September 2002

As a recruit, C/Supt. Twardosky arrived at "Depot" on January 21, 1975, immediately after having been sworn in at the Headquarters building in downtown Regina. She had been given just one day's notice to report from her hometown of Melville, Saskatchewan. Twardosky was given the opportunity to attend RCMP training with the promise of returning to Toronto, where she had originally applied to the Force and would return to perform special duties at Toronto International Airport. At the time, these positions were designated as "Special Constables."

Twenty-seven women from across Canada formed "J" Troop, the second all-female troop. As the female members' uniform had not yet been approved, these first two troops participated in the uniform design discussions led by a female Major from the Canadian Forces, Major D.E. Toole. Although issued Sam Brownes, they were accompanied by purses that had been originally intended to hold revolvers.

In August 1976, Twardosky returned to "Depot" to complete the training required to perform regular member duties and was posted to Surrey, British Columbia. In 1999, Twardosky returned as the Commanding Officer.

Upon her returning to "Depot," the base appeared to be deserted. There were only three troops, one of which was composed of only ten cadets from Nunavut. In less than a year "Depot" was at full capacity, with new troops arriving weekly and biweekly. Staff was required for every facet of training as well as for the general operation of the Academy. Additional classrooms were constructed in an annex to the Academic Building and the Arena was transformed into a multi-purpose training facility. This ramp up did allow unprecedented numbers to move through the Academy, notwithstanding the strain on the infrastructure.

Twardosky was instrumental in the development and establishment of the RCMP Academy Site Development Plan. She also oversaw the inauguration of the "Depot" Sweat Lodge with the C.O.'s Aboriginal Advisory Committee.

In one of the most unique incidents outside of training at "Depot," Twardosky was in command when the Norwalk virus struck the Academy. Hundreds of staff and cadets fell ill and, as a result, a contingency plan was structured. Twardosky also takes pride in having watched the challenges of a troop which included two members from the United Arab Emirates, reinforcing the C.O.'s Diversity Management Committee mandate.

Having been born and raised in Saskatchewan, C/Supt. Lynn Twardosky was especially proud of her service as Commanding Officer, "Depot" Division.

Cst. Twardosky in training – Troop #6 – 1976

Commanding Officer C/Supt. Curt Tugnum

- 10 September 2002 – 4 May 2005

At his first staffing interview as a recruit, then Constable Tugnum was asked what his goals were in the Force. Tugnum looked out of the staffing office window, across Sleigh Square, and stated, "I would like to live in one of those houses some day." In 2002, Tugnum assumed Commanding Officer responsibilities for "Depot" Division, fulfilling the dream he had had since he was a recruit.

His main mandate was to prepare "Depot" for the expected large increase in the number of cadets arriving at "Depot" to handle the anticipated staffing requirements of the Force.

C/Supt. Curt Tugnum retired in 2005, and one of his final duties was to present a badge to his son Mark at his graduation. Mark was stationed to Kamloops, British Columbia.

C/Supt. Curt Tugnum

C/Supt. Curt Tugnum at his son Mark's (Reg. #51986) graduation in March 2005

CHAPTER 3 – PERSONNEL

Commanding Officer C/Supt. Pierre Ménard

Cst. Pierre Ménard

C/Supt. Pierre Ménard

• 4 May 2005 –

When I arrived at "Depot" as a 19 year old in April of 1976, a few of us on the flight from Ottawa were picked up at the airport by the constable assigned duty driver detail. He then whisked us to the guardroom in the basement of "A" Block. There, we were issued our bedding, towels and other essential items. Since it was after 22:45 hours, we had to find our way to our dorm, make our beds and put our things away without turning on the lights. It wasn't until the next morning at daylight that we became aware of our new surroundings and realized that we had just started a whole new life.

While I was somewhat intimated by the new environment at first, it did not take very long before I began to enjoy living in a dorm with 31 other characters from all parts of Canada.

Even though training provided many challenges along the way, it proved to be the most rewarding experience that I had enjoyed to that point in my life. So much so that I left training with a goal of returning to "Depot" as an instructor. In December of 1988, I was able to attain that goal when I was transferred from "E" Division to "Depot's" Academic Section. During this time, I had the opportunity to work in several aspects of the training program, from instructing to program development, to standards and evaluation. The experience was again a most rewarding one and, for the second time, I set a further goal of returning one day in some capacity to the "Cradle of the Force."

In March of 2005, I was appointed as the 52nd C.O. of "Depot" Division. This opportunity by far exceeded any goal I ever had and I was honoured to be given such an important responsibility.

In addition to having the opportunity to meet some of the most influential "Depot" personalities, such as Supt. Bill MacRae and A/Commr. Bob Mills, who were my training officer and C.O. respectively when I was a recruit, I had the great honour of meeting Queen Elizabeth II during Her Majesty's visit to "Depot" within a few weeks of my arrival. While it would hardly seem possible to experience anything more significant than such a visit, I am sure that there are many more memorable events that lie ahead.

The current training programs are without a doubt the best that we have ever had. However, the demand for cadets in numbers beyond anything ever experienced before will provide our existing infrastructure with major challenges. It is my sincere intention to contribute to the development of the facilities to meet these demands head on while ensuring that the integrity of the existing infrastructure is maintained and that new structures are compatible with the existing buildings on site. In that way, we can ensure that within the walls of this venerable institution, we will carry on with the great traditions of this Force and maintain our reputation as the greatest police force in the world.

Officers

Under the command of Commissioner Herchmer in 1886, all recently commissioned officers were posted to "Depot" under the watchful eye of the Commissioner.

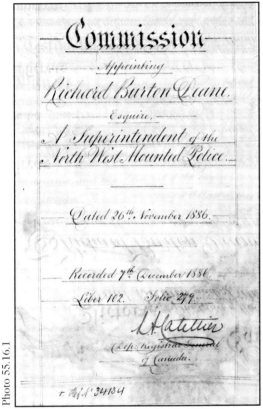
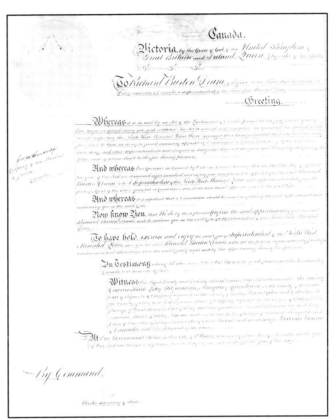

Officer's Commission issued to Supt. Richard Burton Deane in 1886

Advanced training for officers and senior NCOs started soon after "Depot's" formation. From its very beginning, all new officers were required to report there and there they would remain until the Commissioner felt they were ready for duty. Courses for sergeants began as early as 1887. Among the subjects they took were riding, foot drill, musketry, horse care, cypher reading, signaling and police duties. The course concluded with examinations and the understanding that the results would determine future promotions. Similar courses for corporals began a few years later. By 1904 the annual corporals' class concluded with a pass out parade before the Commissioner with the band as accompaniment. – S.W. Horrall, Force historian (2)

S/M MacRae and Sub Inspector Tadeson conducting firearms' inspection and review of troops – circa early 1960s

Chapter 3 – Personnel   175

Officers' course at "Depot" – circa early 1960s

Upon obtaining the commissioned rank of Inspector, members of the RCMP continue to attend "Depot" Division for the Officer Orientation and Development course. The two-week training course covers managerial topics, Force policies, procedures, governmental issues and budgets.

Officers McGibbon (left) and R.H. Simmonds (right)

By attending "Depot" Division and interacting with cadets, junior officers are provided with the opportunity to learn about changes in the Cadet Training Program and are exposed to a second opportunity to attend "Depot" and reflect on their own basic training.

Since 1989, Officers attending "Depot" have participated in the Sergeant Major's Noon Parade. To demonstrate full integration, Civilian Members and Public Service officers attending the course also are "on parade."

New officers on parade during the officer Orientation and Development Course – fall 2002

Sergeants Major

R/S/M Robert Belcher – Reg. #3 – By a General Order of April 1886, the sergeant major of "Depot" Division became the Force's first ex-officio Regimental Sergeant Major. He had served in the 9th Lancers before coming to Canada and joined the Force as an "original" in 1873. The R.S.M. was to be a key figure in the maintenance of discipline and the smooth running of the training program.
– S.W. Horrall, Force historian (3)

Standing Orders 1909

Division Sergeant Major #1471

He should set an example of orderly, and moral conduct and of zeal, promptitude and fidelity in the execution of every duty.

R/S/M Robert Belcher, Reg. #3

SERGEANT MAJOR

The Sergeant Major is the Senior NCO in the Division and it is his responsibility to see that barrack routine duties are arranged for and fulfilled and that regulations and orders governing conduct, discipline, dress and the performance of duties are strictly adhered to.

When the Sergeant Major is being addressed by NCO's and Constables, he will be addressed as Sir, NCO's and Constables will stand at attention while doing so.

– *Prelude to Duty*, 1950

The role of the Sergeant Major is a long-standing tradition in the Force. It was originally established to provide a direct link between the Commanding Officer and the NCOs and other members of a Division. This reporting relationship reflected the unique nature of the rank and of the role played by the incumbent. The S/M position existed in each division, with functions similar to that of the S/M at "Depot," as late as 1972. It is significant that in 1975, when the decision was made to remove the positions of Sergeants Major from active use throughout the Force, the sole position retained was that of the S/M at "Depot." The position continues to be synonymous with the daily operation of the Training Academy.

Over the years, with the changing times at "Depot," through the RCMP Act and now the Cadet Training Program, the role of the Sergeant Major changed. In the past the S/M was looked upon as the disciplinarian who handed out the punishments for minor infractions of dress, deportment and minor breeches of the Code of Conduct. As Cadets are no longer members, the RCMP Act Code of Conduct regulations don't apply to them, but they are bound by similar regulations under their Cadet Training Agreement/Contract.

A Sergeant Major has the responsibility to maintain the integrity of the RCMP institutional memory and provides interpretative direction on the history, regimental customs, traditions of the RCMP and their appropriate place in today's Force.

By virtue of the RCMP Act, the rank of Sergeant Major is the second-highest ranking non-commissioned regular member of the Force, and is an appointment made by the Commissioner. This position carries the responsibility of bringing a consistent focus and direction to dress, deportment, protocol and ceremonial matters. A Sergeant Major must be loyal to the Force and the Commissioner. He/she must take pride in personal appearance, be disciplined and prepared to use his/her appointment in this position to influence others and promote high standards of dress, deportment and self-discipline. In 2000, the rank of Sergeant Major was reintegrated into the RCMP countrywide.

S/M H.M. Gilbey, Reg. #15427, on parade in the spring of 1967

The position and rank of Sergeant Major and Corps Sergeant Major have played a significant role at "Depot" Division. Indeed, other than the Training Officer and Commanding Officer, most recruits best remember the Sergeant Major during their time of training as the member whose office was visited after class as a result of an unkept pit, behavioural issue, or other event that a staff member deemed significant enough to be punishable.

Traditionally, the Sergeant Major was responsible only to the Commanding Officer of a regiment or battalion and played, mostly, an administrative role. He was the person who ran interference for the C.O. by being stationed outside the C.O.'s door and determined who and for what reason someone was allowed to approach the Commanding Officer. During those times the C.O. was the person responsible for handing out the punishment to fit the crime. This usually ranged from a fine to time spent in the stockade. Over the years, the C.O.s enlarged the role of the S/M by giving him the power to dispense the penalties for minor offenses. The S/M then gave an individual the choice of taking his punishment or being sent to the "big office" where, he assured him, the punishment would be greater. As such, the individual usually took the S/M's punishment with pleasure.

As well, the Sergeant Major is responsible for all parades and is highly versed on traditions, protocol and ceremonies. It was he who advised the C.O. on what protocols were to be used in various situations. The S/M was also responsible for the C.O.'s batman, who assured that the C.O.'s kit was always kept in exemplary condition. To the men of a regiment or battalion, the S/M had a mystique. He seemed always to appear out of nowhere and catch them in situations where they deserved and received a good "chewing out." For this reason, the deportment of the unit was usually at its best. It was little known that the actual role of the Sergeant Major was as an administrative assistant to the Commanding Officer, and that his job had been expanded to make him appear to be the chief disciplinarian.

One of the foremost Sergeants Major was S/M Bill MacRae. His role as Sergeant Major and the story of the MacRae family at "Depot" starts on page 282.

Corps Sergeant Major William Pomfret "Depot" Division from 1968-1976

S/M Roger Tardif "Depot" Sergeant Major from 1997-2005

S/M Jas Breton "Depot" Sergeant Major September 2005

CHAPTER 3 – PERSONNEL

Sergeant Major's Parade

The Sergeant Major's Parade, also known as Noon Parade, is held every weekday, Monday to Friday, at 12:50 p.m. on Sleigh Square. In the event of inclement weather, it is held in the Drill Hall.

Sergeant Major's Parade – circa 1946

The parade has its origins in the history and tradition of the North-West Mounted Police. This is one of two scheduled parades held throughout the day. The objective was to ensure that all men were accounted for, as deserters were the responsibility of the Sergeant Major.

"Push ups" completed during Noon Parade – circa 1985

Noon Parade in the Drill Hall – 1973

180   BEHIND THE BADGE

Noon Parade – circa 1980

The troops are arranged in order of seniority, with the most senior troop at the beginning of the parade. The troop commander's role is to conduct a roll call and uniform inspection. The outcome of this task is then reported to the Sergeant Major, after which the parade will complete a march past before carrying on to their afternoon duties or classes.

Roll call is also taken at 6:30 a.m., where cadets are inspected before they attend their respective classes for the day.

The type of drill performed by the cadets is known as dismounted cavalry drill. The RCMP is the only regiment in Canada still to perform this type of drill, in which the formation and movements are the same as those done with horses or mounts.

Sergeant Major's Parade in the Drill Hall – circa 1990

Insp. Dale Sheehan on parade – 2003

CHAPTER 3 – PERSONNEL 181

Church Parade

The most disliked parade was the Sunday morning Church Parade. The Church Parade became a regular weekly event after the canteen building was converted into a chapel in 1895. There was no sleeping in that morning after a Saturday night out. The Commissioner himself carried out the inspection and everything had to be spotless and gilded like a lily. It was no wonder that most recruits looked forward to the end of their training and a transfer to another division. – S.W. Horrall, Force historian (4)

Periodically, the Division held Church Parades. Everyone formed up in full dress uniform with his squad on the Parade Square. After being inspected, we had to go to church. I might be wrong when I say, "had to." The statement might not be true. I never found out, because I never heard anyone say he did not want to go to Church. An instructor marched the Protestant members to the service that was being held in the RCMP Chapel on the Division. The Roman Catholic members were given bus tickets, broken off and told to go to mass in the nearest Catholic Church. – Supt. J. Religa (rtd.), Reg. #O.947, "H" Troop – 1953/54 (5)

NWMP, Regina, NWT – Church Parade, 1895 – The members were led by the band twice around the Square and then into the Chapel. The Sergeants' Mess is located in the top left corner of the photo

Church Parade in full-dress uniform at "Depot" Division in the 1890s. In the top left corner is the new "B" Block barrack, completed in 1887

Sunset Ceremonies

One of the most popular tourism events in the City of Regina is the Royal Canadian Mounted Police Sunset Ceremonies. It attracts tourists from around the world, commencing with a Canada Day show on July 1 and followed by a show every Tuesday night throughout the summer. The Sunset Ceremony includes a cadet dismounted marching display, the firing of the original canon brought west in 1873, and the lowering of the Canadian flag at sunset.

Troop of cadets displaying dismounted cavalry drill during Sunset Ceremonies – 2002

Rifle Drill demonstration at the Sunset Ceremony – 2003

Her Honour Lieutenant Governor Lynda Haverstock of Saskatchewan accepts the "Salute" from members on the march past of the Sunset Parade. C/Supt. Curt Tugnum returns the salute. Insp. Sheehan, the Lieutenant Governor's aide-de-camp, accompanies Her Honour – July 1, 2003

In the early 1960s Sgt./Major MacRae and Cpl. Perry were requested to reinstate the recruit band, which was no longer in existence. As the band developed, so did the Commanding Officer's desire for public shows. The drill staff began began working on this new project immediately. In keeping with custom and tradition, it didn't take long to assemble volunteers, including the band. A variety of formations were brought to the square, made up of two of the more senior Recruit Troops, those who had some rifle drill and would be issued with their red serge tunics. In a very short time the parade plan began to take shape and rehearsals started during the evening hours. A/Commissioner Perlson was very much a part of the planning process. It was decided that one or two trial parades would be offered to invited guests. Two such parades were organized, each closing in darkness with the square lit from the floodlights on "A" Block.

184   BEHIND THE BADGE

Photo 020701

Cadets demonstrating the nine-pounder – 2002

Lowering of the Canadian flag just prior to the conclusion of the Sunset Ceremony – 2002

Photo 020716

Cst. Matt Smith served with the mounted section of the London Metropolitan Police and knew Burmese, the horse given to Her Majesty Queen Elizabeth II by the RCMP in 1969

Drill Cpl. Roger Ferland oversees the Parade – 2002

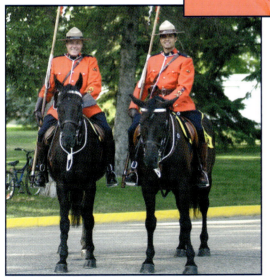

Cst. Matt Smith and Cpl. Raj Gill on horseback

CHAPTER 3 – PERSONNEL   185

Members of Troop #4, 2002/03, Cpl. Redd Oosten (fourth from left) and Safety Bear volunteering their time during Sunset Ceremonies – summer 2002

The critique following the parade indicated an earlier start, at a time which would see the flag lowered as the sun was setting. After one more practice parade it was concluded, by the A/Commissioner, that the performance was suitable for public display. During this discussion the C.O. asked Sgt./Major MacRae which day of the week would be best. The Sgt./Major thought this over and replied that since the stores in Regina were closed on Mondays that other options be considered. He went on to say that the stores are open late on Thursdays and, of course, a lot of people will be leaving town early on Fridays to get a start on the weekend, MacRae suggested that we should try Tuesdays and see how that turns out. The C.O. agreed and the Sunset Parades were scheduled for Tuesday evenings.

That was over 42 years ago, and to this day the parades remain a Tuesday demonstration. "Depot" Division is located within a wedge shot of the Royal Regina Golf Course. And while the Sergeant Major was an avid golfer, he would not play on Tuesdays – Ladies Day – and he rejects the speculation that there is any truth in the rumour that "Ladies Day" had anything to do with the sound advice he offered the Commanding Officer.

To this day, Sunset Ceremonies has remained on Tuesday nights and it is still Ladies night at the Royal Regina Golf Course. (6)

The departure of the band from Sleigh Square marks the conclusion of the Sunset Ceremonies – 1997

RCMP Memorial Service Parade

On the second Sunday of September, each year, the Royal Canadian Mounted Police conduct their Annual Memorial Parade and Chapel Service. This event honours those members of the Force who have died in the line of duty. Since the inception of the Force in 1873, 209 names have been added to the Cenotaph that records the names of fallen members. The Commissioner of the Force, Deputy Commissioners and Division Commanders place wreaths to recognize these members who sacrificed their lives in the line of duty. During the laying of the wreaths all names are read aloud. Family members of those honoured are invited to attend and be part of this special event.

Memorial Day Parades – 2003 and 2004

CHAPTER 3 – PERSONNEL

*Memorial Day Parades
– 2003 and 2005*

188   Behind the Badge

Commissioner G. Zaccardelli and Deputy Commissioner B. Busson lay wreaths – 2005

View of the Cenotaph from the roof of the A.B. Perry Building – 2005

Chapter 3 – Personnel

Musical Ride

The Musical Ride practicing maneuvers at "Depot" Division – 1919

The Musical Ride on the Parade Square – 1936

The Musical Ride was developed from a desire by early members of the North-West Mounted Police to display their riding ability and entertain both themselves and the local community. Considering that the original Mounted Police members had a British military background, it was inevitable that the series of figures they performed were traditional cavalry drill movements. These movements form the basis of the Musical Ride. Although legend has it that the first Musical Ride was performed as early as 1876, the first officially recorded Musical ride was performed in Regina under Inspector George Matthews, former Riding Master and Adjutant of the 3rd (King's Own) Hussars on January 16th, 1887 before His Honour the Lieutenant Governor of the North-West Territories, Edgar Dewdney, and his official party. The Musical Ride, consisting of twenty men, was put on public display for the first time in 1901. In 1904, the Ride was performed at the Winnipeg and Regina fairs.

Today's members of the musical ride are police officers who, after a minimum of two years of active police work, volunteer for duty with the musical ride. Most members are non-riders prior to the equestrian training with the RCMP. Members of the ride remain for three years ensuring an annual rotation of approximately one-third of the riders.

A full troop of 32 men and women participate in the Musical Ride, which is composed of a variety of intricate movements executed to music at the trot and canter by individual horses and riders, in two's, four's and eighth's. These include The Bridal Arch, the X, the Turnstiles, the Diamond, the Shanghai Cross, the Gates, the Star, the Cloverleaf and Wagon Wheel. The Maze, the Dome and the Charge are derived from cavalry drill and demand the utmost control, timing and coordination. The Charge is the highlight of the Musical Ride, when lances, with their red and white pennons, are lowered and the riders and their mounts launch into the gallop.

Horses used for the ride are black and are specially bred in Packenham, Ontario. They are equipped with saddles of Colonial pattern, bridles and white browbands and rosettes bearing the badge of the Force, blue saddle blankets with yellow borders and martingales with a breastplate also bearing the badge of the Force.

The RCMP Musical Ride tours throughout Canada, as well as international venues, performing at approximately forty to fifty locations a year between the months of May and October. Thirty-six riders, thirty-six horses, a farrier, a technical production manager and three NCOs travel with the musical ride. (7)

Musical Ride during the 125th Anniversary – 1998

The Musical Ride practicing maneuvers at "Depot" Division 1998

The Musical Ride at "Depot" – 1998

Chapter 3 – Personnel 193

Musical Ride Horses

Mounted troops on the Parade Square – 1920

In 1937, Assistant Commissioner S.T. Wood headed the RCMP contingent at the coronation of King George VI. Assistant Commissioner Wood was impressed with how the red tunics were more significantly emphasized on the riders in the Household Calvary who were on black horses. When Wood became Commissioner in 1938, he ordered the RCMP to purchase only black horses, however, it soon became apparent that the RCMP would need to establish their own breeding program.(8)

As only five percent of all horses worldwide are truly black, the RCMP realized that there was an inadequate supply of black horses with the necessary conformation and temperament to meet the needs of the Musical Ride. Consequently the RCMP launched its breeding program in 1939.

The RCMP horse breeding program began at "Depot" Division and was subsequently moved to Fort Walsh in 1942, the site of the North-West Mounted Police fort built in 1875 in the Cypress Hills of south Saskatchewan. Fort Walsh was the home of the breeding program until 1968 when the operation was moved to Pakenham, Ontario, about 50 kms west of Ottawa.

The Thoroughbred/Hanoverian cross has been the most dominant in the breeding program in attempts to produce elegant, athletic, black mounts to withstand the rigor and strain of the Musical Ride.

RCMP horses are identified by a regimental number and each is given a name. Each year, children across Canada are invited to suggest names for four to six of the foals in a "Name the Foal" contest. The remaining foals are named by the Pakenham Farm Manager. The names of the foals born in the same year begin with the same letter to assist in the record keeping on the horses.

Horses that do not meet the requirements of the Musical Ride are turned over to the Mounted Police Foundation for sale at public auction. The proceeds from the sale of surplus RCMP horses are reinvested into the breeding program to help sustain the program into the future.

Remounts spend the first three years of their life, growing, developing and maturing into future Musical Ride horses. (9)

Lance Drill – circa 1920

194   BEHIND THE BADGE

Chapter 4

"DEPOT" GROUNDS

Carden Estates Campground

Carden Estates Campground – spring of 1976

The campsite was opened on May 24, 1976, containing 16 fully serviced trailer sites, washroom and laundry facilities. Each site has its own barbecue pit and picnic table. The campsite is available for use by employees of the Force at the cost of $15.00 a night.

The campground was funded by a legacy "bequeathed to the Force by Miss Audrey Carden, an English woman who died in London on December 26, 1936, leaving her estate of £70,000 to her two close friends, the Professional Fire Brigades Association of England and the RCMP. No reason has ever been established for Miss Carden's generosity." (1)

Carden Estates Campground – 2005

RCMP Cemetery at "Depot" Division

– by S/Sgt. W.K. (Kenn) Barker (retired) Reg. #14375

On September 12, 1882, on instructions from the Commissioner, Inspector Samuel B. Steele commenced laying out the grounds for a relocated Headquarters of the North-West Mounted Police. While not his choice, the land selected was along Pile-of-Bones Creek, N.W.T. Only three months later, on December 6, 1882, Commissioner A.G. Irvine occupied the new headquarters about two miles west of the settlement which, a year later, in December, became the Town of Regina, not to be incorporated until twenty years later on June 19, 1903.

Early sketches of the NWMP Barrack show locations of buildings, but do not indicate a cemetery. One of the unsolved mysteries of the NWMP is why the cemetery was established and developed at its present site. Like the Regina Cemetery, "Depot's" is now like an oasis nestled close to the present barrack buildings: a mini model town site used for training, "F" Division Headquarters and the Regina RCMP Forensic Laboratory, all of which crept closer to the cemetery boundary. The encroachment and magnitude of future development was, no doubt, not envisioned by the planners when the cemetery was positioned on the near edge of a horse pasture which, at the time, was quite remote from the existing buildings.

A need for a nearby gravesite came about with the death, on February 28, 1884, of Constable W. Armstrong, Reg. #843, age 20 years. His grave marker shows the earliest date in the cemetery. He died of typhoid fever, which he contracted in Winnipeg. The Commissioner's Annual Report for the period ending November 1884 states that Constable Armstrong's death was the only one in the Force that year.

If there had been a plan to show the intended placement of future graves it was not available for those attempting to set out an orderly system years later. Several old lists, some with beautiful penmanship, attempted to designate a plot number system, but all seem to have been abandoned in frustration.

Cst. Armstrong's tombstone – he was the first member to be buried in the "Depot" Cemetery in 1884

From Constable Armstrong's death in February 1884 until 1900, there were twenty-five plots used, but the order in which they were chosen revealed no hint as to the reason for their placement.

The oldest section of the cemetery, known as Block A, has one hundred and twenty-five plots with grave markers of different styles. After 115 years, two plain wooden grave markers, bearing initials and the date 1890, were identified for twins born May 11, 1890 – Isabel Eleanor Cotton, who died August 6, 1890, and Frank John Cotton, who died June 16, 1890. It is believed that, due to misinterpretation of flamboyant penmanship, Isabel's gravestone bears the initials J.E.C. These twins were born at the NWMP Barracks in Regina to Isabella Cotton, the wife of Supt. John Cotton. Mrs. Cotton died in childbirth. Supt. Cotton was on duty at Fort MacLeod, arriving too late to comfort his wife

Funeral procession past the Chapel – circa 1920

Funeral at "Depot" Division – circa 1920s

"Depot" Cemetery – 1937

Regimental tombstones in section A of the Cemetery

Onward from 1950, families of members and pensioned retired members were using the facilities more frequently. Land immediately adjacent to the two blocks that comprised the cemetery had been suitably prepared by 1973 and was able to receive its first burial in July 1974. This was an opportune time to designate the Blocks alphabetically, with the plots numbered in sequence. The oldest section became Block A with plots 1 to 125, Block B has plots 126 to 269 and Block C with plots 270 to 449.

In June 1996 the cemetery was extended by refining and developing a high grassy area with a paved access laneway and perimeter roadway. This new area is centred around a large paved circular concourse. A columbarium was added in 1997, with a second one added in 2000. Consideration is being given for a third columbarium in the future.

Butting up to the concourse is a special area of plots prepared to accept urns or containers of ash. This area, designated as Block D, received its first burial in August 1998. Block E is set out for traditional casket burials and was first used in November 1998.

Entrance to the "Depot" Cemetery – circa 1950

Entrance to the "Depot" Cemetery – 2004

The cemetery entrance is flanked on each side by Memorial Walls bearing black polished marble plaques with the names of members whose lives were lost in the performance of their duty. While the members may have been buried elsewhere, these walls, in addition to the Cenotaph on Sleigh Square, are the focal point of the RCMP Memorial Service and Parade held each September at "Depot." Inside the gates, on a slightly raised grass mound, the Canadian flag and RCMP Corps Ensign fly on brushed aluminum poles. On the base of the mound is the inscription "They rest in the peace that passes all understanding." Presented by the Regina Area Corporals' Mess in 1999, it attests to the pride and respect serving members have for those who have passed on and signifies their commitment to the history and heritage of the Royal Canadian Mounted Police.

Entrance to the "Depot" Cemetery – March 2006

CHAPTER 4 – GROUNDS

"Depot" Columbarium – 2004

Here, in this historic cemetery, everyone regardless of rank or station in life, be it Commissioner or tiny newborn baby, is of equal status and receives the same loving care in their final resting place.

To date, five former Commissioners of the Force are interned in the cemetery at "Depot."

* *S.T. Wood (1938-1951), Mrs Wood (1994) and their son, Cst. Hershel Wood (1950), lie at rest beside the Commissioner who died in January 1966. A telling inscription on Commissioner Wood's headstone reads, "The Force was his life."*

* *L.H. Nicholson (1951-1959), a man deeply respected and held in much affection, and who made all members feel proud when he chose to resign on a point of principle following a disagreement with the Diefenbaker government. He died in March 1983.*

* *C.E. Rivett-Carnac (1959-1960), who in 1944 was posted to "A" Division to take charge of the intelligence section of CID. He was involved in the Gouzenko defection/espionage affair. In 1947, he returned to "F" Division as the Officer Commanding. He was interred in the cemetery at "Depot" in July 1980 beside his wife who predeceased him.*

* *G.B. McClellan (1963-1967) came from Moose Jaw. He was a graduate of the Royal Military College in Kingston, Ontario. He joined the force in 1932. He was laid to rest in July 1982. Mrs. McClellan, who died in June 1984, rests beside him.*

* *W.L Higgitt (1969-1974) was born in Saskatchewan. He was Commissioner during the FLQ crisis and in office when the Force celebrated its 100th Anniversary. He died in April 1989."* (2)

Commissioner W.L. Higgitt and his grave marker

BEHIND THE BADGE

Unmarked Graves

Aerial of "Depot" – 1970

On June 26, 1883 a telegram was received at NWMP headquarters that a murder had been committed at Qu'Appelle. A party of police under Superintendent L.W. Herchmer, then stationed at Regina, was sent to investigate, and it was found that a respectable settler, John McCarthy, had been done to death in the vicinity of his shanty. Convincing evidence supported the murder theory, especially as the victim was known to have a considerable sum of money in his possession. Commissioner Irvine, upon receiving a preliminary report, went to the scene of the crime himself, and in short order two Métis were arrested and committed for trial. On October 3, 1883, Stipendiary Magistrate Richardson at Regina found both men guilty and sentenced them to death. The death sentence was carried into effect on April 3, 1884 at the NWMP Guardroom. The bodies of John and George Stevenson were buried in unmarked graves near the CPR main line, approximately 500 meters west of the original Riding School.

In the mid-1970s failed attempts were made to find these unmarked graves. It was believed that the gravesites should be on the southwestern extremities of the Royal Regina Golf Course or on the property of the CPR main line right-of-way. The academics of the day were unable to locate these graves. Also, the possibility exists that the Stevenson family, in 1887, received approval from the Commissioner to repatriate the bodies.

Cenotaph

I expect to pass through this world but once. Any good thing, therefore, that I can do or any kindness I can show to any fellow human being let me do it now. Let me not defer nor neglect it, for I shall not pass this way again. – Stephen Grellet – 1773-1885 (American Quaker)

On September 8, 1935, Reverend A.E.G. Hendy, RCMP Chaplain, presided over an unveiling ceremony for the Cenotaph, which majestically sits in the centre of the west side of Sleigh Square. The Cenotaph had 48 names when unveiled and, as of 2005, now contains 209 names of those killed in the line of duty.

Rev. A.E.G. Hendy, RCMP Chaplain, unveiling the Cenotaph which bore 48 names – Cpl. Robertson and Sgt. Rathbone assist – September 8, 1935

Cenotaph – September 8, 1935

Looking westward at the Cenotaph from Sleigh Square – circa 1940

The Cenotaph in 1977

As part of the "Depot" "125" initiative, an eternal flame was mounted at the Cenotaph. Martin Castle designed and coordinated the installation of the flame which was dedicated during the memorial service held in September as a tribute to those members of the Force who lost their lives in the line of duty

CHAPTER 4 – GROUNDS

The Cenotaph received an update in 2005 with the addition of the Force's Ensigns and lattice fencing prior to the Queen's visit in May of 2005

Each September "Depot" Division holds a Memorial Service to honour RCMP officers who have died in the line of duty. Since its inception in the mid-1930s, the Memorial Weekend has become a "Depot" and Force tradition.

Since the 1930s, a Memorial Parade has been held every year on Sleigh Square. A ceremony follows in which the names of all those who have been killed in the line of duty are read aloud, as well as any additional names from the preceding year, to acknowledge the ultimate sacrifice of the RCMP members.

The names of the fallen members are inscribed on the Cenotaph, which is located on the west side of Sleigh Square.

Following the Memorial Parade there is a service in the RCMP Chapel. A Page of Honour is unveiled in the Chapel detailing the member's name, regimental number and circumstances of death. This page is turned every Sunday so that all Honour Roll members are honoured. Their names are listed on page 400.

After the service, families of the fallen officers, members of the Force and visiting public walk to the "Depot" Cemetery to unveil Memorial Wall Plaques for each of the members who have died in the line of duty during the previous year.

A scroll of the Honour Roll is kept in the mace carried by the Drum Major so the Members on the Honour Roll are remembered and are with the Force on Parade every day.

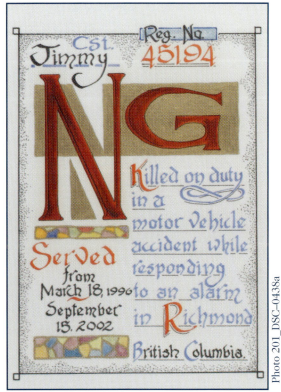

Roll of Honour – Constable J. Ng, Reg. #45194

204   BEHIND THE BADGE

Entrances to "Depot"

Former entrance to "Depot" – Sgt. Walker on "Nell" – 1941

The main entrance to the Barracks, the South Gate off 11th Avenue, has now assumed a very smart appearance. The roadway has been improved, large cement pillars erected, double iron gates constructed and hung, and the whole is surmounted by ornamental iron work with a crown above. These gates were made by the staff and look very well; they embody the initials of the Force from its inception; NWMP, RNWMP, RCMP – the motto is also worked in. A bronze buffalo head has been placed in the centre of each gate; they were presented by Mr. J.B. Cross of Calgary, a grandson of the late Commissioner MacLeod. (3)

The south gate – when recruits were told, "Go to the south gate and a cab will pick you up," they knew their career with the Force had been terminated – circa late 1950s

CHAPTER 4 – GROUNDS

The broadening of the turn from Dewdney Avenue, onto Bonner Drive, into the north entrance of "Depot" looking north – circa 1950

The main entrance to "Depot" off Dewdney Avenue – 2003

Entrance to "Depot" – 2005

* South entrance to "Depot" – the main entrance into "Depot" was located off 11 Avenue – circa 1957

206   BEHIND THE BADGE

Footbridge

*G*iven the fact that "Depot" Division was built on the outskirts of Regina, it was quite an achievement each time the base was "connected" to the town. At first, wood from buildings that were torn down at "Depot" Division was utilized to build a sidewalk "connecting the base to the town."

Cst. Bill Moffatt on the footbridge – winter of 1955/56

In 1889, the boardwalk from "Depot" was extended to meet the one coming from Regina, along what is now 11th Avenue.

Over the years, vast improvements have been made. In 1940, the Regina City Parks Development Scheme improved the appearance of Wascana Creek and the flats to the northeast of the barracks. Laborers made islands, improved the landscape, planted trees and shrubs and built a dam by the Dewdney Bridge.

Today, the base can be accessed by both Dewdney and 11th Avenues. The bridge adjacent to the Royal Regina Golf Course on 11th Avenue is sometimes rendered inoperable in the spring given the flooding that occurs.

Looking south toward "Depot" – 1965

St Roch Memorial

Henry Larsen

Already a seasoned seaman by his early 20s, Sergeant Larsen, a Norwegian-Canadian, joined the RCMP as a constable specifically to navigate the St Roch, which made the first west to east journey through the Northwest Passage in 1942. For twelve years the ship's presence reinforced Canadian sovereignty in the Arctic and her crew of nine served as administrators for the Northwest Territories Council.

In 1944, the vessel made a return voyage through the Northwest Passage, the first both ways. Later, in traveling from Vancouver to Halifax via the Panama Canal, it became the first ship to circumnavigate the continent of North America. The St Roch became a part of the Vancouver Centennial Maritime Museum in 1954.

Carefully constructed to the RCMP specifications to withstand the rigors of winter weather in remote Arctic waters, the St Roch was launched in 1928. A supply ship for northern posts, she was destined to become the first vessel to sail through the Passage both ways and the first to circumnavigate the continent. An unassuming vessel, she was 104 feet long, her beam was 25 feet and she had a draft of thirteen feet when fully loaded. Diesel-powered, she also carried sails in case of engine failure.

In the spring of 1940, Sergeant Larsen received a command to "Proceed to Halifax by way of the Arctic." Thus began one of the most incredible sea journeys of all time – a saga of human endurance, and skill. Ice locked for two winters in succession, the ship made painfully slow progress. When one of the crew died during the second winter, Larsen trekked 500 miles to arrange funeral services.

Finally, after a voyage of 10,000 miles over a period of 28 months, the ship sailed into Halifax on October 11th, 1942. Two years later, Larsen set off on the return voyage, which was accomplished in only three months. (4)

"Depot" Division Final History Exam January 1974

Question 46. A monument stands at the northeast corner of the square. What event in the Force's history does this stone commemorate?
1. March West
2. Journey of the St Roch
3. Founding of "Depot"
4. Queen's Visit
5. Centennial of the Force

The St Roch was built at North Vancouver by the Burrard Dry Dock Company to serve as a supply vessel and floating detachment in the Arctic. The St Roch was named after a parish in the Quebec City constituency of the Honourable E. Lapointe, Minister of Justice, responsible for the RCMP

Sleigh Square

Looking southward over Sleigh Square – circa 1930

The square is named after Cpl. Ralph Bateman Sleigh who was killed on May 2, 1885 during the battle at Cut Knife Hill, North-West Territories.

On May 1st, 1885, Lt. Col. Otter led a force of 319 men including 74 NWMP towards the Cut Knife Reserve. The next morning the column reached Cut Knife Hill, and a furious six hour battle began. Predictably, the Indians proved to be a valiant foe. They surrounded Otter's troops and drove them into retreat.

From the beginning of the battle, the NWMP were in the vanguard of the column. Consequently they drew a great deal of fire. The first Mountie to fall was Cpl. Sleigh. He was shot through the mouth while repulsing an attack on the field guns. Moments later NWMP Cpl. W.H. Lowry and NWMP trumpeter Paddy Burke were mortally wounded, dying the following day. (5)

Commissioner Irvine and General Middleton joined forces in attacking Batoche, which fell on May 12, 1885.

Cpl. Sleigh was born in Matlock, England, where his father still resided at the time of his death. A former farmer, the Corporal was single and had been a member of the NWMP for four years. He was awarded the North West Canada medal, which went unclaimed and is now on display at the RCMP Centennial Museum at "Depot." The auction sale of his kit and personal belongings, including his prized shotgun, brought $31.25. (6)

The death of King Edward VII on May 6, 1910 was acknowledged on Sleigh Square with the use of the nine-pounder

Sleigh Square with the nine-pounder in the foreground – circa 1945

CHAPTER 4 – GROUNDS

Troops on Sleigh Square – circa 1940

Exiting Sleigh Square at the completion of Noon Parade – circa 1990

The origin and significance respecting the protocol of the Parade Square is in keeping with the British military tradition. After a battle, when retreat was sounded and the unit had assembled to "call the roll," and count the dead, a hollow square was formed. The dead were placed within the square and no one used the area as a thoroughfare. The Cenotaph, which represents our fallen comrades in the RCMP, further reinforces this sense of hallowed ground and thus traffic, whether vehicular or by foot, is completely prohibited from crossing the Parade Square. (7)

Stripes of gold and blue were painted on the perimeter of Sleigh Square in 2005 to reinforce the historical significance of this hallowed area.

Sleigh Square – 2005

Street Names of "Depot"

During the reign of Commissioner A.B. Perry, a decision was made by the Royal Canadian Mounted Police to name the streets and roadways at "Depot" Division and "N" Division in Rockcliffe, Ontario. A recommendation was made that names of members on the Honour Role would be utilized as street names. The Honour Role of the RCMP was divided into two parts, those who have been killed due to violence encountered in the line of duty and those who have perished due to accident or other hazards while on duty. (8)

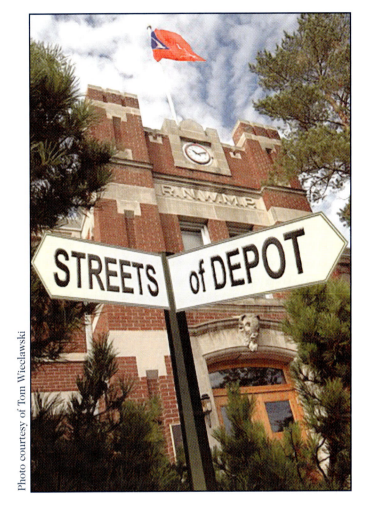

Photo courtesy of Tom Wieclawski

Unfortunately, there were more names on the Honour Role than streets, so it was decided that, for fairness, a draw of names would be made.

Until 1944, twenty streets at "Depot" Division were named after members who had died in the line of duty. Since then, "Depot" has undergone many physical changes, including the official opening of "F" Division (Saskatchewan) Headquarters in 1983, a Forensic Laboratory in 1994, which resulted in an increase of street names to 54. The street names are official names registered with the City of Regina and pay homage to members of the Force who died in the line of duty.

The following criteria were taken into consideration when selecting names:
- there would be no conflict with street names in the City of Regina
- each decade of the Force's history and as many ranks and divisions as possible be represented (9)

Abel St. – Aux/Cst. Frederick Allan Abel, Reg. #A/3512, Age 23 – On April 4, 1986, A/Cst. Abel and his partner Cpl. Budd Johanson were travelling west on Highway #3, approximately six miles east of Lethbridge, when their marked RCMP car struck a half-ton truck travelling east in the westbound lane without its headlights on. The occupants of both vehicles perished.

Agar Lane – Cst. Thomas J. Agar, Reg. #33580, Age 26 – On September 19, 1980, Cst. Agar was working the front desk of Richmond Detachment when Steve Leclair entered, intent on killing a policeman. Leclair removed a .45 calibre revolver from his pants and shot Cst. Agar in the chest.

Amey St. – Cst. Robert W. Amey, Reg. #22240, Age 24 – Cst. Amey joined the RCMP in January 1962 at Sydney, Nova Scotia. On December 17, 1964, four escapees from Her Majesty's Penitentiary in St John's, Newfoundland ran a roadblock manned by Cst. Amey and Cst. David Keith near Whitbourne. A chase ensued and the escapees abandoned their vehicle. They became cornered and refused to surrender. Cst. Keith kept the escapees in his gunsight while Cst. Amey returned to his car to call for assistance. Cst. Amey returned to find that Cst. Keith had been severely beaten and his service revolver was in the possession of Melvin Young. Cst. Amey attempted to hold the escapees, but was shot three times.

Arnold Mews – Cst. George P. Arnold, Reg. #1065, Age 25 – Cst. Arnold died on March 27, 1885 from wounds received during a skirmish at Duck Lake, North-West Territories, the previous day. Cst. Arnold was originally from Georgia and had served previously in the US Cavalry as a scout.

Bailey Court – Cpl. Maxwell G. Bailey, Reg. #4968, Age 28 – On April 23, 1913, Cpl. Bailey, Csts. S.C. Whitley, R.W. Tetley, and L. Stad approached the residence of Oscar Fonberg at Grassy Lake, Alberta, to arrest Oscar on a warrant of insanity as his neighbours alleged he had taken a shot at them. When the RCMP arrived, Oscar situated himself in a dugout stating, "Go away or I'll shoot." The members refused to leave and Oscar's first shot hit Cpl. Bailey in the head. Cst. Whitley was seriously wounded in the groin and Cst. Stad was hit.

Barker Avenue – Sgt. Arthur Julian Barker, Reg. #7606, Age 50 – Sgt. Barker served the Force from April 10, 1919 to February 1, 1921. He rejoined the Force on June 1, 1928. On March 16, 1940, he was shot and killed in the lobby of Shaunavon's Grand Hotel by Victor Greenlay, who was mentally troubled. He claimed that Barker was a devil.

Bonner Drive – Lt. Commander J. Willard Bonner, Reg. #12130, Age 44 – In 1929 Lt. Commander Bonner joined the preventive service, which was absorbed into the marine section of the RCMP. In July 1942, he was promoted to the rank of Lieutenant Commander of the corvette HMCS Charlottetown. On September 7, the Charlottetown was struck by two torpedoes from U-517 of the German fleet. The corvette began to sink, and it is believed that Lt. Commander Bonner was killed by several violent underwater explosions while swimming from the Charlottetown.

Buday Crescent – Cst. Michael Joseph Buday, Reg. #33631, Age 27 – On March 19, 1985, Cst. Michael Buday was in pursuit of trapper Michael Oros with the backing of his dog, Trooper, and the ERT with relation to a break and enter at a vacant cabin near Teslin Lake. Oros managed to circle the ERT team and shot Buday with one hit to his head.

Cameron Avenue – Cst. Edison A. Cameron, Reg. #12856, Age 26 – Cst. Cameron served with the Force from April 16, 1937 to December 28, 1943. He was killed in action while serving in Ortona, Italy with the No. 1 Provost Company, RCMP.

Carroll Court – Cst. Thomas P. Carroll, Reg. #20388, Age 28 – Cst. Carroll joined the Force in April 1958. Cst. Carroll was killed in the crash of a Beaver aircraft at Cyril Lake in Manitoba on February 11, 1966. The plane was making its way back to Ilford from Shamattawa when it stopped at Cyril Lake for refueling. As the plane left Cyril Lake, it suddenly stalled and spiraled nose first into the frozen lake. Cst. Carroll, the pilot, Alex Lazaruk, and an Indian agent, Donald McEwen, perished in the crash.

Chandler Court – Cst. Henry C. A. Chandler, Reg. #18656, Age 20 – Cst. Chandler was operating a RCMP motorcycle on the Bedford Road from Bedford to Halifax on June 14, 1956. A large truck filled with logs backed out in front of him, sudden braking caused his motorcycle to skid, striking the rear of the truck and crashing into a metal guard rail. Cst. Chandler died the following morning as a result of severe head injuries.

Colebrook Place – Sgt. Colin C. Colebrook, Reg. #605, Age 33 – Sgt. Colebrook was killed by Almighty Voice, an escaped Cree Indian prisoner near Kinistino, NWT, while trying to arrest him on October 29, 1895.

Cormier Lane – S/Cst. Joseph E.R. Cormier, Reg. #10410, Age 39 – S/Cst. Cormier was serving as an air engineer, as a member of the RCMP Air Section, since 1949. On August 4, 1958, a naked female body was located in a fruit picker's cabin near Kaleden, British Columbia. While conducting a follow-up investigation, Cpl. George R. Browne stopped a vehicle on a country road for questioning. The driver, Donald Stevens, shot Cpl. Browne three times, but Browne survived the attack. A massive manhunt was initiated and air services from Vancouver were called out. The RCMP de Havilland Beaver, CF-FHW, holding S/Sgt. Stanley Rothwell, S/Cst. Cormier and Cst. Green, while on a low-altitude reconnaissance, on August 6, 1958, crashed into an unnamed mountain, killing everyone on board.

Counsell Street – Cst. F. Gordon Counsell, Reg. #11298, Age 31 – Cst. Counsell joined the RCMP in Ottawa in 1932. On May 21, 1940, members of Claresholm Detachment in Alberta were notified of the murder of George Hanson. The suspect, George's father, Charles, had returned to his residence where he opened fire upon the arrival of the police. The mounties called in reinforcements and ordered tear gas to flush out Hanson. A small group of members cautiously entered the residence on May 22. The gas remained dense on the second floor as Cst. Counsell and a second member approached. Charles Hanson flung open the attic door and fired at Cst. Counsell, striking him in the forehead.

D'Albenas Walk – Cst. Kenneth L. D'Albenas, Reg. #13678, Age 27 – Cst. D'Albenas served with the Force from September 6, 1940 to May 15, 1944. While preparing for the battle of Monte Cassino in Italy, Cst. D'Albenas was with a reconnaissance party traveling in a jeep that hit a Teller mine. Cst. D'Albenas was with the No. 1 Provost Company RCMP.

DeBeaujeu Crescent – Cst. George Q.R.S. DeBeaujeu, Reg. #2439, Age 18 – Cst. DeBeaujeu had just turned 18 when he joined the Force at Regina in April of 1890. Cst. DeBeaujeu was aboard the Keewatin, a small sailing vessel, with Cpl. Harry Morphy and Captain Matthew Watts on Lake Winnipeg to curb the influx of illegal liquor. On September 7, 1890, a fierce storm which included high winds caused the Keewatin to strike a reef, destroying its centreboard and forcing the crewmen to climb onto its side to remain afloat. The crew, Cst. DeBeaujen and Cpl. Morph, were unable to hang on due to fatigue. They slipped off the boat on September 10. Captain Watts was rescued on September 20 and died a few days later. Cst. DeBeaujeu had five months of service at the time of his death.

Doak Court – Cpl. William A. Doak, Reg. #4396, Age 39 – Cpl. Doak was serving in the Arctic detachment of Tree River, Northwest Territories. In February 1922, Tatamagama and his nephew Alikomiak were arrested by Cpl. Doak and Cst. D.H. Woolams for the murder of five Cogmollock natives in the northern Arctic. While in custody, Tatamagama managed to escape from his cell on April 1, 1922. Locating a rifle in an adjacent shed, Tatamagama shot and killed Cpl. Doak as he lay sleeping.

Dubuc Crescent – Sgt. Louis R. Dubuc, Reg. #10982, Age 34 – On September 26, 1941, Sgt. Dubuc left Newfoundland to fly an RCAF bomber to England. While enroute he encountered a severe storm and thick fog over the Atlantic Ocean. He attempted to land near Dundalk County, Louth, Eire, on September 27 when he hit an obstruction. It is unknown if the plane ran out of gas or if Sgt. Dubuc miscalculated the runway. All three crewmen on board were killed.

Elliot Avenue – Cst. Frank O. Elliott, Reg. #973, Age 37 – Cst. Elliot was killed by Indians near Battleford, North-West Territories on May 14, 1885 while on scouting duty.

Fitzgerald Lane – Inspector Francis J. Fitzgerald, Reg. #2218, Age 41 – Inspector Fitzgerald, Constable George Kinney, Special Constable Sam Carter and Constable Richard Taylor lost their lives on the ill-fated dog sled patrol from Fort MacPherson, NWT to Dawson City, Yukon on February 14, 1911. This incident is more commonly known as the "Lost Patrol."

Flanagan Crescent – Cpl. Derek J. Flanagan, Reg. #31162, Age 36 – While conducting a drug deal in Chang Mia, Thailand, on February 21, 1989, Cpl. Flanagan boarded a pickup truck to exchange his flash roll for a quantity of heroin. The driver of the pickup became suspicious when the cover team approached to effect the arrest, and placed the vehicle in motion. Cpl. Flanagan was thrown from the truck as a result of a struggle and died of severe head and spinal injuries.

Garrett Avenue – Cst. George Knox Garrett, Reg. #852, Age 24 – Cst. Garret served from July 4, 1881 to March 27, 1885. He died from wounds received during the previous day's skirmish at Duck Lake, North-West Territories.

Graburn Walk – Cst. Marmaduke Graburn, Reg. #155, Age 19 – Cst. Graburn enlisted in Ottawa and was sworn into the Force on June 9, 1879 in Fort Walsh. He was the first member of the NWMP to be murdered. He was found with a gunshot through the back of his head, after his horse arrived back at Fort Walsh, bridled and saddled, on November 17, 1879. The person(s) responsible for his death is not known.

Hockin Avenue – Cpl Charles H.S. Hockin, Reg. #3106, Age 37 – Cst. Hockin served with the Force from October 12, 1894 to May 29, 1897. He was killed at Minchinass Hills, near Duck Lake, NWT, while attempting to apprehend Almighty Voice, who was also responsible for Sgt. Colebrook's murder.

King Boulevard – Cst. T. Brian King, Reg. #31915, Age 40 – On April 25, 1978, Cst. King was overpowered at a vehicle stop just north of Saskatoon and taken hostage. He was driven to the banks of the Saskatchewan River and shot twice in the head. The two culprits then dragged his body further down the bank and threw him into the river.

Laughland Place – Sgt. K. Morley Laughland, Reg. #17368, Age 31 – Sgt. Laughland joined the RCMP at Winnipeg at the age of 19. On July 13, 1963, Sgt. Laughland was piloting a float plane, RCMP Beaver CF-MPO, with Cpl. Robert Asbil, Cst. Proctor Malcolm, Cst. William Annand and an 56-year-old prisoner on board. While attempting to land at Carmacks, Yukon Territory, the aircraft suddenly lost power, plummeting straight down into a ditch, killing all aboard.

Lowry Place – Cpl. William H.T. Lowry, Reg. #907, Age 28 – Cpl. Lowry was a member of the Galway Militia prior to the joining the NWMP. He was born in County Galway, Ireland. Lowry had been a member of the Force for two years when he died from a gunshot wound to his head on May 3, 1885, at the battle of Cut Knife Hill.

Millen Lane – Cst. Edgar Millen, Reg. #9669, Age 31 – Cst. Millen served the Force from November 22, 1920 to January 30, 1932. Cst. Millen was shot by Albert Johnson, the "Mad Trapper of Rat river," near Rat River, NWT, while attempting to apprehend him.

Moriarity Road – Cpl. Michael Moriarity, Reg. #6352, Age 48 – Cst. Moriarity joined the Force on October 20, 1914, and then left in 1917 to join the Alberta Provincial Police. The RCMP absorbed the Provincial Police in 1932, re-engaging Moriarity. Cpl. Moriarity was murdered on April 26, 1935, while attempting to serve a summons on David Knox, a farmer in Alberta's Rosebud district. The summons was for the unlawful use of a firearm in relation to threats towards a bailiff who had approached Knox earlier with an eviction notice.

Nash Field – Sub Constable John Nash, Reg. #135, Age 27 – S/Cst. Nash joined the Force on October 18, 1873. He was accidentally killed while on duty near Fort MacLeod, Alberta, on March 11, 1876. He was returning to the fort with a load of firewood. S/Cst. Nash was sitting on top of the load when he fell off, the load of logs following and instantly killing him. Nash was the first member of the North-West Mounted Police to be entered into the Honour Roll.

Nicholson Field – Sgt. Richard H. Nicholson, Reg. #5611, Age 34 – On December 31, 1928, Sgt. Nicholson and a Manitoba Provincial Police Officer were conducting a search for an illegal still at the residence of William Eppinger near Molson, Manitoba. The two officers separated, advancing through the thick bush towards the still. Sgt. Nicholson was already speaking with Mr. Eppinger when the provincial police officer arrived. The conversation became heated, Mr. Eppinger grabbed a rifle and a struggle between Sgt. Nicholson and Mr. Eppinger ensued. During the struggle for control of the rifle it went off, striking Nicholson at the knee and traveling up his thigh. Nicholson went into shock and died that afternoon.

Oliver Crescent – Cst. Peter S. Oliver, Reg. #12572, Age 29 – Cst. Oliver served the Force from June 22, 1935 to August 19, 1942. Cst. Oliver was killed in action at Dieppe, France while serving second in command as a Lieutenant of the No. 2 Provost Company RCMP. He was killed on the beach near Dieppe, France during the ill-advised attack where 900 others died and 1,900 were taken prisoner.

Pedersen St. – Cst. Gordon E. Pedersen, Reg. #20865, Age 23 – On June 18, 1962, Kamloops RCMP received a complaint from a provincial game warden that George Booth was walking near the Provincial Government Administration Building carrying a rifle. Mr. Booth had recently been released from Essondale Mental Hospital, believing that the Mounties had placed him there. Constables Keck, Pedersen and Weisgerber (off duty and unarmed) responded and became involved in a foot chase with Mr. Booth, into a wooded area. All three members were shot and killed by Booth. Reinforcements were brought in and George Booth was subsequently shot.

Pierlet Avenue – Cst. Roger Emile Pierlet, Reg. #29984, Age 23 – Cst. Pierlet was on shift during the early hours of March 29, 1974, while on patrol in Surrey, British Columbia. John Miller and Vincent Cockriell had been drinking heavily that night and decided that they would kill a policemen, as Miller felt the police had caused his brother's death by chasing him at a high speed. Miller and Cockriell headed out in Miller's '64 Dodge, trying to attract the attention of the police. Cst. Pierlet stopped the Dodge and, as he approached, the passenger, Cockriell, raised his rifle from the passenger side and hit Pierlet in his chest, the shot tearing through his heart.

Ralls Avenue – Cpl. Leonard V. Ralls, Reg. #6177, Age 44 – On July 5, 1932, Cpl. Ralls, of Foam Lake Detachment in Saskatchewan, received a request at 1:40 a.m. from Yorkton Detachment to intercept a dark-blue Plymouth believed responsible for break-ins and store robberies in the area. Cpl. Ralls signaled the vehicle to stop as it approached. As Cpl. Ralls started towards the Plymouth he was fired on, hit and subsequently died at the doctor's office the next day.

Schrader Anson Sports Field – Sgt. Robert J. Schrader, Reg. #15445, Age 41
– Cst. Douglas Bernard Anson , Reg. #21129, Age 30 – On October 9, 1970, Sgt. Schrader and Cst. Anson responded to a domestic dispute at the Wilfred Robertson farm just outside of Prince Albert, Saskatchewan. Prior to this complaint, Mr. Robertson had seen his wife sitting with her neighbor in a car on a deserted country road. Robertson confronted the two with his rifle, throwing his wife in the cab of his pickup and taking a shot at the neighbour. Cst. Anson approached the residence while Sgt. Schrader checked the truck for evidence. Cst. Anson entered the residence, requesting to speak with Robertson. Robertson responded with a single shot to Anson's chest. Sgt. Schrader had left his revolver in the police car, and found himself in a precarious position. The cruiser was too far from the residence to retrieve his gun and he didn't want to leave his comrade behind. Due to the thin brush cover, the yellow stripe on Schrader's pants gave away his position. Robertson took three shots at Schrader, leaving him to bleed to death.

Shaw Street – Cst. John George Shaw, Reg. #11582, Age 38 – Cst. Shaw served the Force from April 1, 1932 to October 4, 1935. Cst. Shaw was murdered near Benito, Manitoba, by three young Russian Doukhobors while transferring them to Pelly Detachment in Saskatchewan on suspicion of recent crimes in that area.

Shwaykowski Track – Cst. Dennis Shwaykowski, Reg. #25308, Age 31 – Cst. Shwaykowski joined the RCMP in 1967 in Swan River, Manitoba. On April 6, 1977 the RCMP in Red Deer received a complaint of a male about to enter a lounge with a rifle. Cst. Shwaykowski and Cst. Dave Guy responded and located the suspect in a pickup driven by a Stanley Hicks. Cst. Shwaykowski ordered Hicks out of the vehicle, Hicks refused and an argument ensued. As Hicks began to pull away, Shwaykowski jumped on the running board. Hicks had reached speeds of 50 miles per hour in the mall parking lot when Shwaykowski was thrown from the pickup. His head struck some boulders and he was killed.

Street Sign – 2006

CHAPTER 4 – GROUNDS

Usher Street – Cpl. Ernest Usher, Reg. #6096, Age 25 – Cst. Usher served the Force from September 4, 1914 to August 7, 1920. Cpl. Usher was killed while attempting to arrest train bandits at Bellevue, Alberta. The bandits had held up CPR train No. 63.

Wallace Avenue – Sgt. Thomas Sellar Wallace, Reg. #11326, Age 39 – Sgt. Wallace served from March 29, 1932 to October 8, 1935. Sgt. Wallace was killed near the Eastern Gate of Banff National Park while attempting to apprehend three young Russian Doukhobors suspected in the murder of Cst. Shaw.

Wilde Lane – Sgt. William Brock Wilde, Reg. #857, Age 42 – Sgt. Wilde joined the Force on July 13, 1882. On November 10, 1896, he was killed while attempting to arrest Charcoal (alias Bad Young Man) near Dry Forks, Kootenay River, North-West Territories. Charcoal was responsible for the murder of Medicine Pipe Stem, who was having an affair with Charcoal's wife, Pretty Wolverine Woman.

Willmett Crescent – Cst. George E. Willmett, Reg. #4584, Age 25 – On April 12, 1908, Cst. Willmett was on night duty, patrolling Frank, Alberta, due to a series of break-ins. He was found dead in an alley behind the Imperial Hotel with shotgun blasts to his neck and face. Three years later, the RNWMP arrested and convicted a man who was sentenced to hang on June 1, 1912 for the murder of Cst. Willmett. Two reprieves, which allowed for appeals, resulted in his sentence being commuted to life imprisonment at Stony Mountain Penitentiary in Manitoba.

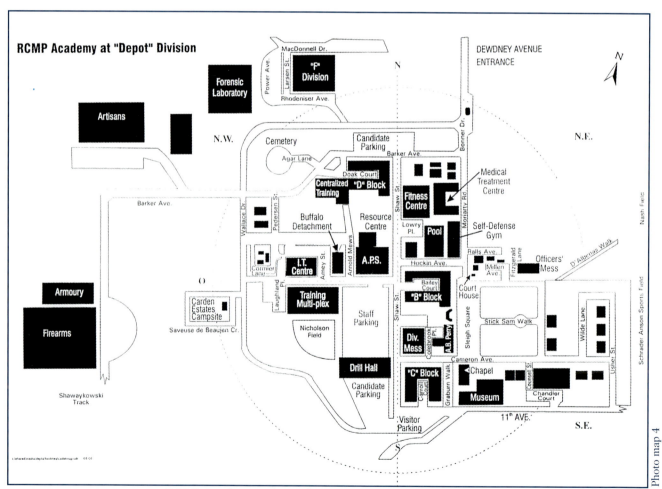

RCMP Academy at "Depot" Division, showing street names

Gardening

The Works department is responsible for the immaculately cut, lush green lawns, the floral beds that light up Sleigh Square, and ensuring that the heritage trees are kept well trimmed.

It did not come easy. As the infrastructure of roads and buildings grew, so too did the greenery evolve. Trees, shrubs and flowers are planted regularly. The Force played a pivotal role in pioneering the growing of trees on the Prairies, and responding annually in the Annual Report about their growth. The trees were supplied by the Department of Agriculture. In 1942 alone, 30,000 carragana seedlings, 800 young trees and 25,000 plants were set at "Depot."

Two greenhouses are utilized extensively to ensure that the flowers, plants and shrubs are maintained and that flowers are available year round. Often, the color scheme in the main beds includes scarlet (geraniums) and gold (marigolds)

Gardening will be a major undertaking this year at "Depot." The Division Mess is to have the garden behind the stables, while the married personnel will be hoeing and weeding north of the gymnasium. (10)

"In 1952, 1,000 trees were planted around the sports field, which was utilized as a soccer field by the City of Regina. A nursery of 1,500 seedling trees, elm, Siberian elm, ash and maple was started to ensure future growth could be maintained." (11) Many of those same trees are now fully grown and adorn the roadways on and around the base.

The South Saskatchewan Lily Society approached "Depot" around 1994. They requested and received permission to start a plot on the base to preserve old historical bulbs. The plot is marked with a sign and is visible when entering the base via the Dewdney Avenue entrance. In full bloom it is extraordinarily beautiful.

Interior view of the greenhouse – circa 1970

Front entrance to "Depot" on Dewdney Avenue – 2004

The barren prairie landscape that greeted the settlers of "Depot" is in stark contrast to the RCMP base today – winter 1936

218 BEHIND THE BADGE

Weather at "Depot"

NWMP Annual Report 1883 – Superintendent R.B. Deane

In my last year's Annual Report, I called your attention to the fact, that the ... buildings had suffered very much, through the severity of the climate, and ... been erected in the mid winter they received much rougher treatment than otherwise would have done. The sections of which the buildings are composed ... roofs leaked, especially in the Logan and O'Doherty buildings, and floors ... and twisted. (12)

The Dominion Meteorological Station for Regina was established at the NWMP Barracks in 1884. Readings were taken at 7 a.m. and 7 p.m. and phoned from the Guardroom to the CPR Telegraph in Regina. They were then relayed to the Weather Bureau head office in Toronto.

William A. Cunning, a regular member, was the observer from 1904 until his retirement in 1932. The wind gauge was situated on the roof of the Guardroom and the rain gauge about 30 feet west of the flagpole.

Members of Troop #26 enroute to sandbagging – spring 1956

Members of Troop #26 assisting with sandbagging as Wascana Creek flooded along Dewdney Avenue – the red coats in the foreground are actually peacoats turned inside out to keep them clean – 1956

Members of Troop #26 enroute to sandbagging – spring 1956

Spring flood of 1971

Flood of 1971 looking northwest

March 9, 1900

The weather has not been enjoyable as it has gone from one extreme to the other without any warning. A terrific wind squall from the northwest set in for a few minutes between 8:30 and 9 p.m. March 9. It blew a brick chimney off one of the officer's quarters, it blew in a large window in No. 1 stable, it blew in and demolished the doors of the paint shop. The posts of the pasture and corral fences were broken off in several places, and one of the hay stacks was thrown over and an estimated 15 tons of hay scattered on the prairie. We gathered this up and rebuilt the stack. (13)

"In 1971, a record spring runoff from Lake Regina (sic) resulted in major flooding of Wascana Creek. In excess of 200 homes were affected and several families had to be rescued by boat. 'Depot' was inaccessible at one time as both 11th avenue and Dewdney were flooded. The RCMP provided recruits and staff to assist in the deployment of 190,000 sandbags." (14) It was possible to reach "Depot" by driving past the airport as Museum Director Malcolm Wake had to do when ordered by the C.O. to photograph the rising water using the Museum's new 35mm camera.

Regina was boiling hot in the summer and freezing in the winter, and I remember times when it was so cold at night that we went to bed wearing our woolen toques. I am reasonably sure that I went through a bout of penumonia (sic), but sick bay was such an unpleasant prospect that I remained on duty, as desperately ill as I felt. – ex-Cst. T. Jamieson Quirk, Reg. #11951 – 1932 (15)

Regina Weather – the Extremes

The coldest day on record:	January 1, 1885	-50°C
The hottest day on record:	July 5, 1937	43.3°C
Record rainfall in a day:	June 15, 1887	160.3 mm
Record snowfall in a day:	October 16, 1984	26.4 cm (16)

CHAPTER 5
TRAINING

Curriculum

The training curriculum at "Depot" Division has evolved since 1885, as did the Royal Canadian Mounted Police and the nature of police work in Canada.

Recruits at "Depot" – 1894

Training in the early years of "Depot" was little different from that given in a military regiment. It was deemed to have two general purposes. The first was to instill self discipline, the by-product of which was obedience.

It was widely accepted in military circles that the most efficient force was that in which orders given by all levels of command were obeyed to the letter, promptly and without question. The attainment of efficiency promoted self confidence, high morale and esprit de corps. The means of instilling discipline was drill and more drill coupled with a strict adherence to all regulations with punishment a certainty for the transgressor. In 1887 the "General Rules for Recruit Drill" was printed. They provided for individual rather than group progress. The recruit advanced from one drill, or mounted squad, to another as he attained the necessary proficiency. The object was to reach No. 1 Squad from which he would be posted to the field.

Training included practical objectives. It was essential that a recruit know the basics of horse management. He received lectures in elementary veterinary principles, and practiced shoeing horses. There were also weekly lectures on police work, criminal procedure, the powers and duties of a peace officer. After he took command of "Depot" in August, 1886, these latter courses were given by Supt. S. Gagnon, who was a qualified lawyer. The training does not sound very professional, but it should be understood that only a minority of members would actually be engaged directly in police work. At the time, the Force provided almost all of its support services from the ranks: most members would be employed full time as clerks, bakers, tinsmiths, saddlers, tailors, farriers, teamsters, carpenters, prison guards, stokers, hospital orderlies, and the like.

Advanced training for officers and senior NCOs started soon after "Depot's" formation. From its very beginning, all new officers were required to report there, and there they would remain until the Commissioner felt they were ready for duty. Courses for sergeants began early as 1887. Among the subjects they took were riding, foot drill, musketry, horse care, cypher reading, signalling and police duties. The course concluded with examinations and the understanding that the results would determine future promotions. Similar courses for corporals began a few years later. By 1904, the annual corporals' class concluded with a pass out parade before the Commissioner, with the band as accompaniment.

"Depot" of course, from its earliest days, had those lasting but less tangible effects upon most recruits who passed through it. For training was also intended to be a crucible which would build character and intensify feelings of loyalty towards the Force. It aimed at toughening recruits not only physically, but mentally as well, to separate the men from the boys, as they would have said. It was a process, which for most, resulted in a new sense of maturity, pride, self confidence, and the development of friendships which would last a lifetime.

"Depot" lived up to everything that Irvine had hoped for it. Its success as a training centre was recognized outside the Force quite early. In the House of Commons in 1887 Sir John A. Macdonald praised the training commenting that there was not "a finer force in the world." (Debates House of Commons June 17, 1887) In Scribners, a prestigious American magazine, the training at "Depot" was described as complete and thoroughly "professional." (Creighton, J.G.A. The Northwest Mounted Police Scribners Magazine October 1893) After a visit from some British journalists in 1889, it received "unqualified praise from the English press," which compared the Force as equal to the Royal Irish Constabulary, the Dublin and the London Metropolitan Police. – Regina Leader August 20, 1889 – S.W. Horrall – Force historian (1)

Superintendent Sanders in his Sessional Paper No. 28 of 1907 wrote: "A class of two sergeants and twelve constables gathered from the different divisions of the force was formed in January 1907 for a three months course and to undergo an examination at its expiration. The course consisted of drill (mounted and foot), criminal law, Dominion and provincial statutes, first aid (medical), veterinary duties, shoeing, stable management, harnessing, driving, packing and interior economy. The result was most satisfactory and a high percentage of marks in the examination was obtained by all."

The Annual Report of 1908 stated: "the training of the recruits has been carried out under difficulties. In order to replace the excessive wastage in different divisions, recruits were hurried through, and drafted out of the 'Depot.' This is not satisfactory as it affects the efficiency of the force but, with the present strength and the ever growing demands, it cannot be avoided. The usual class for qualifying constables for promotion was held at Regina during the winter. It is now impossible to train the divisions annually because there is no time and the strength is too widely distributed."

One of the first and fundamental changes of the training standards to bring the Force into modern day policing and training occurred in 1932. Previous to this, the training concentrated on military drill, discipline and riding. The new training program was now six months and included operational police training which included classes such as first aid, self-defence, mounted drill, physical training, firearms training and concluded with academic work including Criminal

Code, federal statutes, criminal investigation, auto theft, cattle branding, typing, public relations, fingerprinting and, when vehicles were introduced to the Force, maintenance of motor vehicles.

Continuous learning began in the Force with the intent to ensure that policing was a career. Progressive steps were taken to send members to university and promotional exams were introduced. Pay deductions of $2 per month were instituted to purchase textbook and library materials. The Force also began to assume provincial policing duties in some provinces and the training began to include municipal and related duties.

In 1937, a new training syllabus was commenced at "Depot" to reflect changes in the curriculum. One of the largest challenges for the Force was to replace the depleted membership, given a wartime ban on recruiting during World War II.

The O.C. "Depot" Division Regina, A/Commissioner T.H. Irvine commented, "The work began in 1938 had been continued most successfully and it can now be stated that the "Depot" is a training centre which will compare favourably with that of any police force in the world."

Police driving and traffic duty training was implemented and equestrian training was ultimately eliminated from the program in 1966.

Recruits were placed into a troop of 32 members and attended all of their training as such. Roll call was taken at the start of each class or function and, if a recruit was absent, it was documented with an explanation. This method ensured that all recruits met the standards of each course by the end of training.

The history of the RCMP, and indeed Canada, was always front and centre in RCMP training, up to and including a final history exam at the completion of training with questions on issues such as prime ministers, the British North America Act and the March West. History lessons also included the evolution of policing in the world and in Canada.

"In the 1960s, training included boxing, equitation, stable management, foot drill, physical training, police holds and small arms and musketry. The intention was to bring out any undesirable traits in the recruits so that they could be dealt with, and properly develop the recruit." (3) Training days commenced with morning parade (roll call) at 0600 hours, followed by breakfast. The official syllabus program commenced at 0800 and concluded at 1630. Evenings were utilized for extra training or studying as deemed required or assigned.

All recruits were required to meet a minimum standard. If they did not, they were subsequently back trooped into a junior troop and made to study the same lectures and material over again until standards were met.

Aerobics and weights were introduced into the program to ensure that recruits were fit. Swimming and life-saving programs were also incorporated. Crisis intervention and role-playing commenced and there began a swing in the ratio between fitness and related skills to academia. Guidance NCOs were implemented to assist the recruits as they made the transformation from civilian life to a paramilitary lifestyle.

As the Force evolved, computer training – Canadian Police Information Centre (CPIC) and Police Information Retrieval Systems (PIRS) – was implemented. A new Police Driving Unit track was constructed in 1982 and added onto in 2002 with a skid pad and high-speed lane-change facilities completed. A second track was completed in 2004.

Training, through the generations of Members, is often referred to as "soft" by those who have passed through the gates at an earlier time. Despite these claims of "superiority," one thing has always been certain, training at "Depot" has always been challenging and a major adjustment from civilian life.

Cadet Training Program

The Cadet Training Program was initiated at "Depot" on April 1, 1994, replacing the traditional system of engagement into the Force. Under this program cadets sign a contract making them sponsored students until they graduate from the RCMP Training Academy at "Depot" Division. Further to this, instructor-led classes were replaced with facilitation and adult-based learning.

Collision Investigation on Barker Avenue at Pedersen Street – 2004

The Cadet Training Program was designed to:

1. Provide cadets with a clear understanding of their roles and responsibilities in Canadian society and
2. Enable cadets to realize and further the objectives of community policing.

The Cadet Training Program is an extensive 24-week basic training course, offered in both official languages. The cadet is part of a 30-member troop which is diverse in composition. Upon successfully completing the Cadet Training Program, cadets may be offered employment. Cadets are then sent to selected training detachments where they are involved in the Field Coaching Program under the supervision of a detachment coach. (4)

The Cadet Training Program consists of 821.5 hours broken down as follows:

Applied Police Sciences	403 hours
Police Defensive Tactics	75 hours
Fitness	45 hours
Firearms	62 hours
Police Driving	63 hours
Drill, Deportment and Tactical Exercises	44 hours
Detachment visits, exams	129.5 hours (5)

A troop run along Wallace Drive – 2005

Objectives of the Cadet Training Program

To succeed in the program cadets are expected to:
- demonstrate a level of deportment – personal, professional and social – consistent with the core values of the RCMP and pride in self;
- work effectively as part of a policing team with your colleagues, supervisors, clients and partners in policing;
- work with diverse communities and participate in creative and collaborative problem solving;
- demonstrate sensitivity to and respect for the diverse individuals and groups you encounter;
- take responsibility for your own learning and development;
- know the law, RCMP policy and code of conduct sufficiently to ensure that you exercise discretion responsibly and lawfully;
- communicate effectively orally, in writing and electronically by being comfortable with electronic communications technology and RCMP information systems;
- gather information and evidence necessary for effective policing;
- create and maintain good records and present information effectively and appropriately in a court setting;
- manage evidence, exhibits and crime scenes safely and effectively;
- drive safely and competently;
- handle firearms responsibly and proficiently;
- demonstrate fitness, healthy lifestyle and proficiency in self-defence;
- avoid and manage incidents, crises and conflicts and apply appropriate intervention techniques and levels of force, and
- understand policing as a career, vocation and service for self and family. (6)

Police Defence Tactics class – handcuffing session

WHO ARE WE?

Computer module class in Applied Police Services – 2004

Who are we ... Troop 3
and we love PT
The P.A.R.E three times is good enough
maybe the fourth won't be so tough
Pumping iron and running to save lives
and PDT dodging knives
Driving fast with push and pull,
leave the tank nice and full
Shooting guns at the paper men
hoping to score the perfect ten
Awake in mods is the ultimate test,
stand against the wall and do our best
Saluting the people we know we should,
and raising the flag so it looks good
Keeping in step on the drill hall floor,
march, march, march until feet are sore
Stand tall, stand proud of who we are,
our troop is strong, we'll all go far
We all work hard our final days ...
As CONSTABLES we'll go our separate ways!

– Cdt. L.K. Bristow, Troop #3, 1998

Forming up for class – 2003

Statement taking – 2003

Weekly Syllabus for Troop #16

Troop 16-05/06 - November 21 - 25, 2005

Day	Time	Finish	Grp	Module	Grp	Room
Mon	06:30	06:45		Parade		
	07:00	07:30		Breakfast		
	08:00	08:50		Module 9	Mod 9-Sess 1	Hall 21
	09:05	09:55		Fitness	Fitness(27)	Fitness Gym
	10:10	12:05		Module 9	Mod 9-Sess 2	Hall 21
	12:25	13:00		Lunch		
	13:30	15:25		PDT	PDT(40-41)	PDT Gym
	15:40	16:30		Self-Directed Learning		
Tue	06:30	06:45		Parade		
	07:10	07:40		Breakfast		
	08:00	11:00		Module 9	Mod 9-Sess 3	Hall 21
	11:15	12:05		Module 9	Mod 9-Sess 4A	Hall 21
	12:05	12:40		Lunch		
	12:50	13:20		Parade		
	13:30	14:20		Drill	Drill(20)	Drill Hall
	14:35	15:25		PDT	PDT(42)Lecture	Hall 16
	15:40	16:30		Module 9	Mod 9-Sess 4B	Hall 16
Wed	06:30	06:45		Parade		
	07:20	07:50		Breakfast		
	08:00	09:55		Module 9	Mod 9-Sess 5A	Hall 21
	10:10	12:05		FTU	Firearms(15)	Range-25,Range-100
	12:25	13:00		Lunch		
	13:30	14:20		Fitness	Fitness(28)	Weight Room,Fitness Gym
	14:35	15:25		Module 9	Mod 9-Sess 5B	Hall 21
	15:40	16:30		Drill	Drill(21)	Drill Hall
Thu	06:30	07:00		Breakfast		
	08:00	09:55		Miscellaneous	TO Inspection	Dormitory
	10:10	12:05		Module 9	Mod 9-Sess 6-PROS	Hall 21
	12:05	12:40		Lunch		
	12:50	13:20		Parade		
	13:30	14:20		Fitness	Fitness(29)	Fitness Gym
	14:35	16:30		Module 9	Mod 9-Sess 7	Hall 6
Fri	06:30	06:45		Parade		
	07:20	07:50		Breakfast		
	08:00	08:50		Exam	Exam Review	Hall 5
	09:05	12:05	Group A	Progress Reports		
	09:05	12:05	Group B	Police Driving	BOLF	City of Regina
	12:35	13:10		Lunch		
	13:30	16:30	Group B	Progress Reports		
	13:30	16:30	Group A	Police Driving	DOLF	City of Regina

Aboriginal Heritage Room in "D" Block – Aboriginal Elders provide information to cadets on culture, tradition and beliefs during an awareness session

Actors
– Scenario-Based Training

Informal scenario training was initiated as early as 1969, when staff were specifically told to be as difficult as possible when questioned by recruits. Scenario-based training has been in existence at "Depot" since the early '70s, with volunteers from the Globe theatre whose staff felt that it was a great opportunity for their actors to improve their abilities. The volunteers took part in crisis intervention and domestic dispute scenarios, and this program continues to this day with the assistance of community volunteers. Scenario-based training came into prominence in 1994 with the introduction of the Cadet Training Program.

The RCMP recruited volunteer actors and high-school students to give the cadets a realistic portrayal of their future duties. Currently, volunteer actors come to "Depot" to role play in anger management scenarios, domestic disputes and final testing. Many of the 200 volunteer actors have been volunteering for over five years and put in hundreds of hours a year. Utilizing actors greatly enhances the Cadet Training Program, permitting the cadets to apply the skills and knowledge they are taught during their training at "Depot."

Roleplaying with fellow recruits to reinforce skills and knowledge – 1990

Interviewing fellow recruits during scenarios – 1990

Search of a vehicle during an impaired driving scenario – 1990

Practicing arrest procedures outside of the MTC – 2005

Theft of hubcap scenario – 1990

Cpl. Bob Smart monitoring a scenario – Cst. Andre Paradis is effecting the arrest on Cst. Guy Belley – Cst. M. Hustins looks on – 1992/93

High-risk officer violator contact scenario – 2004

Scenario-based training involving the valuable assistance of volunteer actors at the Mall – 2004

Canadian Law Enforcement Training (CLET)

In order to meet the training needs of other government agencies and police departments, the Canada Law Enforcement Training (CLET) Unit was established at "Depot." The Canadian Law Enforcement Training Unit's mission is to provide the highest quality of training via experienced professionals, as well as state-of-the-art methodology, facilities and technology.

The Canadian Law Enforcement Training Unit is the RCMP section that specializes in providing training to outside (non-RCMP) agency clients.

CLET offers basic and advanced law enforcement and investigative techniques courses, as well as specialized courses in driver training, firearms, police defensive tactics, drill, deportment and tactical training. CLET course candidates must be employed and sponsored by a federal, provincial, municipal or tribal government or police force.

External Training has been provided to over sixty agencies, including:

Canada Customs and Revenue Agency/Canadian Border Services Agency, CN Police, CP Police, Dakota Ojibway Police Service, Department of Fisheries & Oceans, Department of Natural Resources & Energy, Department of National Defence, Environment Canada, Industry Canada, Opaskwayak Cree Nation Police Service, Parks Canada, The Senate of Canada, Alberta Justice.

In 2006 the Department of Fisheries and Oceans celebrated 29 years of partnership training at "Depot" Division.

Experiencing pepper spray

Department of Fisheries on Parade – 1990s

Cst. Kristen Tompsett graduating with the Dakota Ojibway Police Service on March 6, 2006

CHAPTER 5 – TRAINING

Dress/Deportment

... you may never become a commissioned officer, but you will be a gentleman at all times or else ... Sgt. Bill Poole (rtd.) Memories – of the Way We Were (7)

Cst. "Wahoo" Hanson, "Depot" – 1936

Prelude to Duty 1947

Keep your uniforms clean. There is no excuse for dirty shoes or dusty clothes. Pay attention to your equipment and beds. A few minutes a day will keep them all in tip top shape. Get into the habit of doing a little each day and soon you will be doing it as a matter of course. Before going on Parade have the other fellow check you and do the same for him.

There are mirrors on each floor. Use them to inspect your personal appearance before leaving your room.

Prelude to Duty 1951

Always walk smartly about the grounds of your training establishment. Be properly dressed whenever you leave your barrack room or the building in which you live. Do not wear part civilian clothing and part uniform. Always see to it that you are properly clad, particularly in the summertime when you think the wearing of certain apparel is unnecessary.

When in the barrack room, refrain from discussing politics, religion, races or any contentious matters. You are all Canadians and, in the eyes of the Force, you are all looked upon equally. There is no room in this organization for bigotry in any form. Respect the other man's view.

Photo 989.66

Dress and Deportment – General

1) Appearance in both dress and behaviour has become synonymous with the position as a member of the Force, and primarily, the basis on which he/she is judged and accepted by the public. It is therefore imperative that we continue to strive towards maintaining this professional image at all times.

2) Slouching, sauntering, hands in pockets, smoking on the street, holding hands or walking arm in arm while in uniform, all detract from the image of the RCMP and will not be tolerated. – RCMP Academy at "Depot" Division Basic Recruit Training Course 1988 (8)

Familiarization Booklet for Recruits – "Depot" Division 1967

Members hanging off the fire escape at "B" Block – circa 1950

Discipline means "orderly conduct," and "subjection to rules of conduct or behaviour." One of the prime aims of your training will be to teach you discipline – that is – how you should behave in accordance with the RCMP rules of conduct or behaviour. All of this in the hope that you will learn self-discipline – which means you do not act according to your likes or dislikes, but according to the principles of right and wrong.

Attention Area:

While specific boundaries are set in Post Orders for the Attention Area, it is better to describe it as being any area of the barracks open to public view. All ranks are considered "on parade" whenever they move about outdoors. This regulation is in effect 24 hours a day, therefore everyone is expected to move around the barracks smartly at all times. Recruits in training must swing their arms shoulder high and, whether moving singly or in pairs, will march smartly on the sidewalk only, as cutting corners and walking across the lawns is prohibited. Talking, whistling and horse-play, generally, is strictly forbidden in the Attention Area.

Drill and Tactical Unit

"Depot" 1912 – Looking eastward from "A" Block onto Parade Square – an Officer's Residence prominent in the rear

The term "discipline" should not be related to the notion of punishment but to the positive and desirable elements of self-control, strength of character and the will to overcome adversity. – The Drill Manual – Function of Drill (9)

Having been formed as a para-military Force, foot drill played a large part of the discipline, deportment and training at "Depot" Division. In annual reports, Drill was given a separate heading to report on. In 1887, it was noted that "recruits have had a great deal of drill, and have been well instructed in police duties, and with very few exceptions, all the force are good riders. The horses have been well trained to lead and stand fire in addition to regular drill movements." – NWMP Annual Report 1887 – Commissioner L.W. Herchmer (10)

One recruit in 1886 received one month's hard labour for being "inattentive while at drill" and stubbornly persisting in moving his arms awkwardly, contrary to the directions of the Drill Instructor. – S.W. Horrall – RCMP historian (11)

The component of the current Cadet Training Program is designed to develop a sense of pride in self through professional deportment. Cadets are taught how to care for and maintain their kit and proper turn out in uniform and mufti.

Cadets are taught the importance of maintaining a clean and orderly dormitory out of respect to those who share their environment with them. They also learn etiquette and proper protocol in formal settings.

Troop formation, "eyes right" – 1978

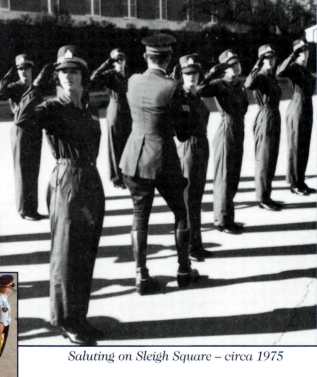

Saluting on Sleigh Square – circa 1975

Squad formation on Sleigh Square – circa 2000

This program aims also at developing esprit de corps through precision teamwork in ceremonies and tactical related exercises. Cadets learn to listen and respond to orders as would be required in situations of celebration, where the RCMP represents Canada on formal occasions, or in situations where public safety may be threatened by potential crowd violence. The skills are essential to professional client service. – Overview of the Cadet Training Program – 2005 (12)

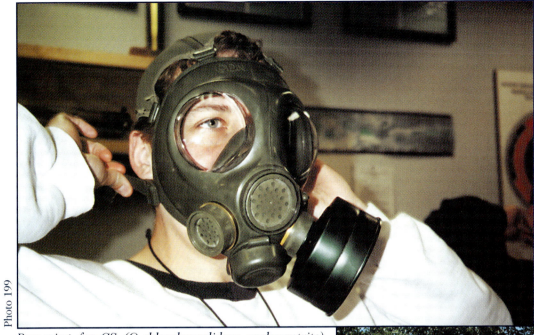

Preparing for CS (O-chlorobenzylidene malonontrite) gas exposure

Tactical practice – 2001

Double time – cadets are required to double time until they earn their right to march

CHAPTER 5 – TRAINING 235

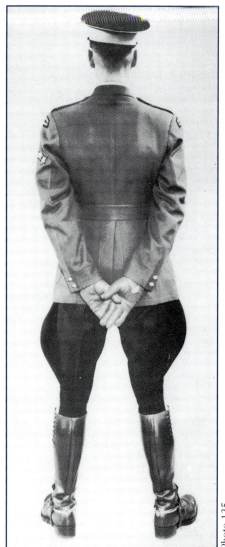

Drill Manual Section 3 – Stand at Ease

"Stand at Ease" – Keeping the right foot still and leg braced back, "bend the left knee" and carry the left foot to the side so that the feet are 12 inches apart; at the same time force the arms by the nearest way behind the back, keeping them straight, and place the back of the right hand in the palm of the left, thumbs crossed, fingers and hands straight and pointing towards the ground: at the same time transfer the weight of the body slightly to the left, so as to be evenly balanced.

Common faults:
(i)   Failure to carry the foot off 12 inches and not square to the left.
(ii) Bending the arms when bending the knee.
(iii) Movement of the right foot with consequent loss of dressing.
(iv) Bending at the waist when picking the foot up.

– The Drill Manual – Cavalry Drill – 1956 (13)

Troop inspection conducted by Cpl. G. Warkentine in Drill Hall – 2003

236   BEHIND THE BADGE

Duties

Training and Duties in the Force – The Quarterly, April 1947

He'll learn to wear his red serge and not be self conscious about it – not to blush when he hears a feminine tourist's gasp of admiration, not to scowl at the facial or verbal sneer of those who, for reason, hate his uniform. He'll learn to be a diplomat, father confessor, friend in need, amateur doctor and lawyer of parts. He'll learn to go without sleep for two or three nights, to travel cross country, without the benefits of roads. By car, to paddle a canoe, drive a dog team or motorsled, even perhaps a pilot of a plane. He will, if found suitable, spend a year at a time in the solitude of an Arctic outpost or fight his part of the war against crime with microscope or typewriter. He will, after 20 years, have the opportunity to retire on pension, with enough of his life left to earn a useful living and to look back with satisfaction on his days in the Force, days and nights of hard work, good comradeship, of contrasting adventure and routine.

Yes, it's still something, this being a "Mountie."

A Guide to Success – 1960

During your stay in this Training Division, you will be required to do certain fatigues, guard duties, etc. These duties are necessary and they should be done cheerfully. Unless you have the proper attitude toward these duties, you cannot be expected to have the proper attitude toward duties you will be required to do in the field. Develop the faculty of doing a job pleasantly, even if it is something which you do not care to do. Don't be a grumbler. Always try to see the bright side. Develop a sense of humour. You'll need this to get along with the public.

RCMP Academy at "Depot" Division Basic Recruit Training Course – 1987

With undergoing the Basic Recruit Training (BRT) at "Depot" Division, trainees will be required, from time to time, to perform certain duties and assume specific responsibilities.

Additional duties as follows:
a) Duty Constable
b) Duty Driver
c) Security Guard
d) Lifeguard
e) Orderlies

Photo 190

Cst. Normand Dupuis, Troop #22, performing guard duty at the south gate – 11th Avenue – 1989/90

Members of Troop #13 perform security duties at the entrance of the APS building – 1988/89

Trainees will be selected on a rotational basis and will be informed of their pending assignments through the distribution of a "Duty Roster," which is prepared by the Division Orderly. These duties must be performed in a mature and sincere manner, and are included in the overall assessment process, utilized to determine the performance level of each respective trainee.

Familiarization Booklet for Recruits – "Depot" Division 1967

EQUITATION

The course in equitation is made up of 140 periods of instruction. The first two times at the stables are set aside for the teaching of stable routine, familiarization of stables, saddling and unsaddling, care and cleaning of equipment, grooming, etc. Fatigue dress will be worn on both of these parades.

Troops detailed for equitation in the morning will be in the stables by 7:55 a.m., troops detailed in the afternoon will be in the stables by 12:55 p.m.

DRESS

Summer: Cloth cap
Khaki shirt with tie and tie clip
Blue breeches
Long boots (no spurs)
Belt
Gloves
Above to be worn when in shirt sleeve order. At other times, the fatigue tunic will be worn to the Riding School.

Winter: As above, with the addition of fur cap, blue sweater, pea jacket and mitts. Cloth cap will be carried to the riding school. Orders will be given daily, as to the wearing of felt boots, mitts, etc., depending on the daily temperature.

When the members' breeches and boots are being altered at the tailors and saddlers the orders of dress will be as follows:
- when members do not have breeches and long boots they will wear long underwear under fatigue pants, black boots.
- when they only have long boots, they will wear long underwear under fatigue pants and long boots.
- when they only have breeches, they will wear breeches under the fatigue pants and black boots.

GENERAL INSTRUCTIONS

Horses will be assigned to the members of troops riding each day, and will be posted on the notice board in the west saddle room the afternoon before. All saddlery is numbered and is fitted to each horse. This saddlery is not to be exchanged except by a member of the riding staff. It will be the responsibility of the member to clean his saddlery after 5:00 p.m. of the day before he is detailed to ride.

Each troop is assigned one instructor who is responsible for the progress of the troop. All members of the Riding Staff are present in the Riding School to assist the instructor taking the class and are available for individual instruction if required.

The course of equitation consists of the following:

Stable management	Elementary veterinary first aid
Care of horses and equipment	Feeding of horses
Rudiments of equitation	Mounted sports

This is all which can be taught in the time allotted, the remaining time being taken up with practice of the various phases.

Troops detailed to ride in the morning will be saddled up ready to turn out in the Riding School at 8:10 a.m. In the afternoon, troops will be ready to turn out at 1:20 p.m.

STABLE ORDERLIES

Members will be detailed as stable orderlies from the troops that are taking equitation in the a.m. and p.m. of that day, two men from each troop. Members detailed for the a.m. will not go on the Reveille parade; will proceed to breakfast and report to the Staff members I/C Reveille stables at 6:55 a.m. for instructions.

The duties of the stable orderlies are laid down in Permanent Orders #S.56. A copy of these are posted on the notice board in the stables and will be explained in the first periods. It is essential that they be followed to the letter.

Particular attention must be paid to horses in box stalls and especially the stallions. If any of these horses roll over on their back against the wall, and are not helped, they will die in a short period, this is known as cast.

The Stable Orderly detail for Monday to Saturday is posted on the bulletin board in the stables in the west tack room.

Stable orderlies for Sunday are detailed on the fatigue detail.

Facilitators/Instructors

Rules and Regulations for the Government and Guidance of the Royal Canadian Mounted Police Force – 1936

728. Officers and others who have the ability and knowledge to instruct will be employed in Training and must be given every encouragement and facility to produce the best result in the interests of the Force.

Troop performing rifle drill under the close scrutiny of a drill instructor – circa 1936

731. The following books will be used in connection with instruction and training:
- Rules and Regulations of the Force
- Constables' Manual
- *Cavalry Training (Imperial) latest edition*
- *Criminal Code*
- *Federal Statutes*
- *Any Provincial or Territorial Statutes or Ordinances for which the Force may be called upon to enforce.*
- First Aid to the Injured *as used by the St. John Ambulance Association*
- *Such other books as the Commissioner may direct.*

Additional books recommended for study are:
- Crankshaw's Criminal Code
- Tremeer's Criminal Code
- Justice's and Police Manual *by Popple*
- Boys on Coroners

732. It is necessary that members of the Force be fully instructed in police duties, lecturers will therefore thoroughly prepare their subjects beforehand.

733. The "Depot" has been established at Regina, Saskatchewan for the instruction and training of members of the Force generally and particularly for the training of Officers on appointment and recruits. (14)

Prelude to Duty – 1947

Your instructors have been chosen for their jobs because of some special skill. They are practical men and are charged with your development along some special line. Cooperate with your instructors and pay attention to what they tell you. If you have some knowledge of a subject, don't think you know it all. There is no place in this or any organization for a know-it-all or a smart aleck.

The notion of facilitation over instruction came into play in 1994 when the Cadet Training Program, with an emphasis on adult-based learning, became instrumental. Currently, facilitators are serving members of the RCMP who have demonstrated an ability to instruct and have successfully completed the Instructor Facilitator Techniques Course. Due to the vastness of Canada, the facilitators come to "Depot" with a wide range of experiences and expertise that have a very positive impact on the program.

The facilitator is responsible for facilitating the cadet training program, monitoring and documenting cadet performance, providing first line supervision, leadership and direction to an assigned troop and acting as a team coordinator on a rotational basis. (15)

Class in Applied Police Sciences – circa late 1970s

Facilitators at "Depot," left to right – Cpls. G. Warkentine, J. White, R. Baalim, S. Bourassa-Muise – in front of the Drill Hall – 2003

Police Driving Unit (PDU) instructors on the track – 2005

Chapter 5 – Training

Female Recruits

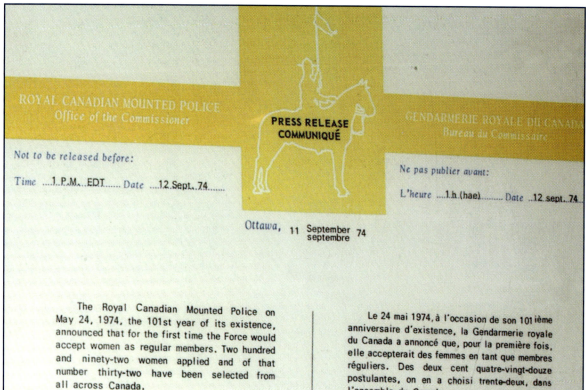

Women Recruits – press release – 12 September 1974

On May 24, 1974, Commissioner M.J. Nadon announced that, for the first time in its history, the Force would accept applications from women to perform regular police duties in uniform. This announcement opened up positions in areas which had previously been reserved for males.

In what was a major transition for the RCMP, simultaneously across Canada, on September 16, 1974, 32 women were engaged as female members of the RCMP and sent to "Depot" for Recruit Training. They arrived at "Depot" on September 18 and 19, 1974 to commence training. The newest troop ranged in ages from 19 to 29 and represented all provinces except for Prince Edward Island. The simultaneous engagement ceremony and the issuance of random regimental numbers was to ensure that no one could claim to be the first female to join the Force.

First female recruit arrivals in front of the Guardroom – September 1974

Female troop marching off Sleigh Square – 1974

For Troop 17, training required some modifications in regard to physical abilities, but other than that the training received was identical to that received by the male troops. For "Depot" Division, other changes were experienced. It was the first time recruits had dated each other, Force-issue brassieres were handed out, separate dorms were required and hairdryers were installed in the pool changing room. On March 3, 1975, the first female troop graduated and the members were deployed across the country to join their counterparts in the field of policing, breaking the all-male-orientated tradition of the Force. A second troop began training immediately afterwards.

Address to Troop 17 at their Graduation Parade
by Commissioner M.J. Nadon 1975-03-03

Commissioner M.J. Nadon

Royal Canadian Mounted Police, "Depot" Division, Regina, Saskatchewan

Recruit Training - Troop 17 -74/75
September 23, 1974 to March 3, 1975

Front Row: J.L. Graham; S/M W.D. Pomfret; Supt. E.R. Madill; C/Supt. H. Tadeson; Supt.W.F. MacRae; Major D.E. Toole; Cpl. K.F.G. Wilkens; H.A. Phyllis
Second Row: C.M.Lafosse; S.E. MacNeil; B.A. MacDonald; J.M. Whidden; D.G. Courtney; P.R. Painter; S.E. Lowden; R.M. Russell; K.L. Somers
Third Row: S.A. Merinuk; C.J. Smith; C.A. Marshall; J.P.M. Potvin; D.I. Burns; T.G. Kivissoo; M.I.L.D. Wright; P.S. Moisse; S.H. Sullivan; D.L. Pohorelic
Fourth Row: J.E. Giergon; G.E. Mortensen; C.L. Joyce; A.V. Pritchard; B.J. Woods; M.L.D.Pilotte; B.A. Glassman; B.K. Hosker; B.J. Morris

Troop 17, 1974-1975 – First females to graduate from the RCMP Academy

It is a real pleasure for me, both as Commissioner and personally, to be here today to witness your graduation. I am impressed with what I have seen today, and with the reports I have received on your progress during your training. You have done well and I have every reason to expect you will continue to do well.

I must admit that these occasions always give me a great feeling of pride – pride in you and in the fact that the Force continues to attract such fine young people to its ranks. And I think it is quite in order for you to share my pride in how well you have done.

Women have always been an important part of the Force, but never before in the role for which you have been prepared. In the past women were hired for specific duties, such as special constable matrons, civilian member scientists and as clerks and stenos. Wives of members stationed on detachments were in many cases unofficial, unpaid and all too often unrecognized but always appreciated members of the Force.

Troop 17 is the first troop of female regular constables to graduate. I know your uniqueness in that regard has not been hidden from you. Perhaps you have heard more about it than you cared to. But that is the only thing different about Troop 17. In all other respects you are like every other troop that graduated in the past, and considering the high standards our recruits have maintained over the years you can be justly proud of that.

Your long months of basic training are now at an end. You are being posted to the field where you will have to mold the basic skills you acquired here with the realities of police work in a world where problems are not unknown. I can assure you, on the basis of long experience, that you will find the tasks before you challenging, to say the least. And I hasten to add that I have every confidence that you will be equal to the challenge.

The end of your basic training is not the signal that you are finished learning about being peace officers. Quite the contrary. The learning process for you, as for me and all peace officers, continues for as long as you serve.

Police work is a profession like no other. You will be confronted by situations and face demands that will tax your every resource. We have provided you with a sound basic training, a framework. You will have to finish the building by your own efforts. Throughout your service the Force will continue to provide you with training to help you meet the demands of new responsibilities as you progress up the ladder of promotion. How much value you get from this additional training will depend, as it did during your basic training, on how much effort you put forth.

There is one kind of training, however, that will depend entirely on you – the training of experience. There is always something to learn form experience. It is up to you to find and profit from the lessons it holds. Learn from your mistakes and failures as well as from your successes.

The profession of police work is a people profession – a profession of service. You will do well to always remember that. Remember, also, that the police – you – are a part of the mainstream of society, not an entity set part from it. Get involved in the communities you work in, communicate with the people you serve. Get to know and let them get to know you.

There is a lot more I would like to say to you, but time does not permit. So I would like to leave you with the thought that since you are a part of one of society's control mechanisms, you have a heavy responsibility to be sensitive to the legitimate needs and aspirations of the people you serve.

The efforts you make will not go unnoticed. They will earn you respect, advancement and the satisfaction of knowing you are doing a worthwhile job well. I and the Force, join your parents, relatives and friends in wishing you well as you begin your new career. Good luck.

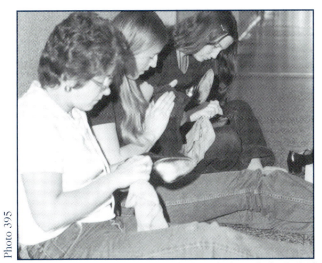

Polish, polish, polish, "B" Block barracks – circa 1975 and 1988

Over the years the RCMP experimented with shared dormitories, separate rooms, and inclusive troops. Today, troops are assigned male and female cadets randomly and the integration into the day-to-day training is a regular occurrence. All cadets must achieve the same benchmarks in academic, physical and skills training to graduate from "Depot" Division.

CHAPTER 5 – TRAINING   245

Recruit Identification, Cst. Janet Steel, Reg. #38837, Troop #3, 1986/87

Recruits looking over assignments – circa 1978

Females on Noon Parade – "Flanks of sections prove!" – circa 1980

Formation of a pyramid – circa 1980

Members of Troop #22, 1987/88, on Sleigh Square – the last all-female French-speaking troop. The bicycles were used on weekends and evenings as an aid to physical training

Cst. K.D. Messer #42994, Troop 2, 1991/92 (centre) – preparing for Physical Training demonstration as part of the graduation exercises

Revolver practice – kneeling position – circa 1990

CHAPTER 5 – TRAINING 247

All-female troop marching on Sleigh Square – circa 1990

In 1999, The RCMP again made history as Chief Superintendent Lynn Twardosky became the first female Commanding Officer of "Depot" Division.

Women have made significant contributions to the RCMP over the decades, serving as police matrons, public servants, civilian and regular members. In the past, RCMP members' wives had often been the unpaid members of a detachment, manning the phone and feeding the prisoners in the cells while their husbands were on patrol. Today, women are full-fledged members of the RCMP, sharing the duties and responsibilities of service equally with their male counterparts.

Members of the RCMP

As of 2006-02-01	Men	Women
Special Constables	76	6
Constables	7834	2430
Corporals	2532	417
Sergeants	1540	126
Staff Sergeants	761*	30*
Inspectors	312	35
Superintendents	144	5
Chief Superintendents	51	4
Assistant Commissioners	23	2
Deputy Commissioners	7	1

Total 16,115

* includes Corps Sergeant Major, Staff Sergeant Major, Sergeant Major

Firearms

Old "Depot" range north of Dewdney Avenue near current site of Paul Dojak Youth Centre – circa 1935. It was last used as a driver-training range for the Haitian police in 4WD vehicles

Shooting for cross rifles, Sgt. Paton in charge – 1936 – to obtain "cross rifle" designation a score of 80/100 is required

"Depot" Division, Rifle Range, Sgt. Camm and Cst. Hudon – June 1936. Sgt. Camm was the father of RCMP member Bob Camm, who was pictured on the "Career in Scarlet" booklet and recruiting poster

CHAPTER 5 – TRAINING   249

Shooting for cross rifles, Csts. Lunkie and "Goose" Gosselin in the rifle range pit – June 1936

Constable attempting revolver qualification, "Depot" – 1936

A fine new rifle range has been built in the basement of the new gymnasium. It is well lighted, with firing points from ten to twenty-five yards and has target accommodation for eight firers (sic) at one time. With this great improvement in the facilities, keen interest has been aroused in shooting and every member of this Division in training now has the opportunity to practice from two to three hours a week. (16)

The original weapon of issue was a short .577 Snider Enfield carbine and a .450 calibre Deane and Adams revolver. Later, the Force introduced the Smith and Wesson which, over the years, was replaced by a .455 Enfield and Colt .45. In 1954, the Force switched to a .38 Smith and Wesson which was utilized until replaced with a Smith and Wesson 9mm in the mid-nineties. Regardless of the type of firearm utilized by the Force, all induction firearm training occurs at "Depot." For a large majority of the cadets, it is their first exposure to handling and training with a firearm.

Ammunition Magazine, Building 39, located at the rear of the Officers' Residences and to the east of the Heating Plant – built in 1949, this photo was taken in 1956

Construction of the Revolver Range on the north side of the Heating Plant – circa 1958

BEHIND THE BADGE

The Firearms' Complex experienced considerable expansion in 1998. The complex now includes an armorer's shop, with its own test firing range, and two indoor ranges – one being 100 meters and the other 25 meters. The indoor ranges received a 25-year facelift with the installation of clear cubicle dividers and new carriers to transport the targets out to the designated distance. In addition, there is a 50-meter outdoor range, and four simulator rooms available for the use of the interactive program "FATS" (Fire Arms Training System).

Firearms class on the upper floor of "D" Block – 1936, currently the Resource Centre

The firearms curriculum covers handling firearms with safety and precision for public and police safety within the provisions of law and policy. Cadets must gain competency with the semi automatic 9mm pistol, the bolt action .308 caliber rifle and the pump action 12-gauge shotgun. Cadets are also trained in decision making, in situations where firearms use may be warranted, using firearms training simulators. Safe practices, accuracy and judgement making applying the RCMP Incident Management Intervention Model are assessed. (17)

Firearms instructions – 1974/75

AIM

- **A** – ability – does the suspect have or reasonably appear to have the physical ability, capability or mobility to cause death or grievous bodily harm? What abilities do you have to counter their threat?

- **I** – intent – does/did the suspect's words and/or actions lead you to believe they had the intent to cause death or grievous bodily harm?

- **M** – means – did/does the suspect have the means, medium or mechanism to deliver the known or perceived threat?

Use of Force to Prevent Commission of Offence – Section 27 – Criminal Code of Canada

27. Everyone is justified in using as much force as is reasonably necessary

(a) to prevent the commission of an offence

　(i) for which, if it were committed, the person who committed it might be arrested without warrant, and

　(ii) that would be likely to cause immediate and serious injury to the person or property of anyone: or

(b) to prevent anything being done that, on reasonable grounds, he believes would, if it were done, be an offence mentioned in paragraph (a). (18)

Shotgun qualification – circa 1990

Cpl. Brent Bennett oversees a phase of firearm qualification – 2003

FATS "firearms training simulator" room – 2004

Recording of firearms' scores – 2003

Qualifying on the outdoor range – 2004

Front entrance to Firearms Training Complex – 2005

Legal Articulation is the ability to recount the events that transpired, relating continually to use of force outlined in Force policy, procedures and the Criminal Code of Canada.

Cadet firearm records – June 2005

CHAPTER 5 – TRAINING   253

Connaught Cup

The Connaught Cup was donated to the Royal Northwest Mounted Police in 1912 by Field Marshall H.R.H. The Duke of Connaught, Governor General of Canada. The cup is awarded on an annual basis to the best handgun marksman in the RCMP. From 1971 to 2004, the shoot was held at "Depot." Prior to this, the best revolver shots met in Ottawa for the Connaught Cup competition. The Competition has been held since 1913, with the exception of the war years 1915, 1917, 1940 and in 1985. Reg. #5199, Cst. L.J. Collins, was the first winner of the cup in 1913. The name A. Ford appears on the Cup seven times, R.A.O. Gomes appears six times, E. W. Plitz, P.E. Forsland and J.R. Zavitz each appear four times.

The Connaught Cup is one of Canada's oldest trophies and brings out the true spirit of competition and marksmanship excellence. The Connaught Cup has been recently refurbished with three additional tiers to allow for the continual placement of silver plates for future winners. In 2004, the competition moved back to the Connaught Range in Ottawa.

The Connaught Cup for the best RCMP handgun marksman

Connaught Cup participants – 2002

Connaught Competition at "Depot" – 2002

Behind the Badge

Forming Up

A daily reality at "Depot" is forming up. Regardless of the troop's destination, the requirement to form up and depart as a unit is mandatory. This often causes frustration to members of the troop who constantly wait for the same late troop mates. Learning assistance in the form of an early morning inspection can result, where the entire troop is punished for the actions of a few.

Marching in troop formation to class – circa 1945

The more things change ...

In William Kelly's book *Policing the Fringe*, he makes reference to several things he experienced while training in 1937. Sixty-nine years later, the following still hold true:

- The troops had 15 minutes to travel between classes. Every troop had at least one recruit who always asked a question at the end of class, making the troop late for their next class.
- The Drill staff were asked to watch their language when visitors were present.
- Recruits' transfers were delayed while waiting for Ottawa (or divisions) to fill vacancies, and funding for the positions was a problem.
- Upon leaving training, the recruit discovered that to progress in the RCMP, one had to study.

Forming up on Shaw Street across from the Drill Hall – 1990

Forming up in front of the Resource Centre – 1990

256   BEHIND THE BADGE

G8 Summit
Kananaskis, Alberta – 2002

Cpl. Jennifer Carroll (centre) – scribe for the Tact Troop – 2002

Given national priorities and events, it often occurs that "Depot" Division is called upon to assist. As all facilitators at "Depot" are regular members of the Force, and there is always a troop or two ready to graduate, it is not uncommon to have the facilitators and new members seconded to a major event prior to returning to "Depot" for their regular duties or the new members reporting to their first posting.

From Expo 1967 to the Olympics in 1976 and 1988, recruits were often transferred from "Depot" en masse.

In 2002, Canada was hosting the G8 Summit in Kananaskis, Alberta. "Depot" Division was asked to contribute Tactical and Emergency Response Teams comprised of regular members (facilitators). Given that Canada was hosting the first large international event since September 2001, the commitment was made to supply two Tactical Troops and Emergency Response Teams. Three troops of thirty cadets were also "gated" at the front end to graduate and remain at "Depot" for additional training in this field of policing. The new members were blended in with senior members.

Members of "Depot" Tact Troop practice maneuvers on Sleigh Square – 2002

CHAPTER 5 – TRAINING   257

Extensive training was held around the cadet training program to take advantage of the time allotted to prepare for the G8.

Practice sessions were conducted with Tactical Troops from Alberta, Saskatchewan and Manitoba. By the time the G8 arrived, "Depot" Division members were completely trained and qualified to take on any duties assigned to them at the G8 summit.

Left to right – members of "Depot's" Tact Troop, Cpl. Dave Doncaster, Sgt. Roger Plamondon and Sgt. Mike Boyer

Civilian Member Bob Aulie adjusting the uniform of a Tact Troop member

Members of "Depot" Tact Troop on Sleigh Square – left to right – Insp. Dale Sheehan Troop Commander, S/Sgt. Dan Pooler, Cpl. Joe Marando

Graduation Ceremonies

The cumulation of a cadet's efforts, sweat and exhaustion is celebrated with family and friends on graduation day. Graduation is a two-day event beginning on Sunday morning at the Chapel for a non-denominational service. Often cadets, families and friends then meet at the Division Mess for brunch prior to attending a family workshop on Sunday afternoon. On Monday morning the Drill Hall is overflowing with very proud family and friends who witness the cadets complete documents relating to engagement, secrecy and allegiance. Upon the conclusion of this ceremony cadets become regular members of the Royal Canadian Mounted Police as Constables, and as such are placed on the payroll. The highlight of the graduation occurs during "Pass Out," after the Noon Parade on Monday, when each member is presented with his or her badge. The graduation concludes with a formal dinner in the Drill Hall. Members then leave the following morning for their respective new posts.

Graduation Invitation – 1940

Graduation troop in the Drill Hall during Sgt. Major's Parade prior to their "Pass Out" – 2003

Chapter 5 – Training

Graduation of an all-female troop – circa 1987

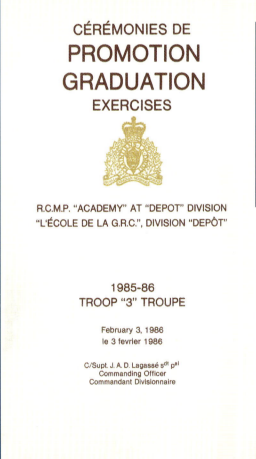

Cst. Redd Oosten, Troop #3, 1985/86

Cst. Candace Pichach, Reg. #51035, Troop #19, 2003/04 on her graduation, March 22, 2004

Cst. T. Maybee, Reg. #51661, Troop #6, 2004/05, standing in front of his troop board – November 8, 2004 – posted to Duncan, British Columbia

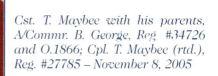

Cst. T. Maybee with his parents, A/Commr. B. George, Reg #34726 and O.1866; Cpl. T. Maybee (rtd.), Reg. #27785 – November 8, 2005

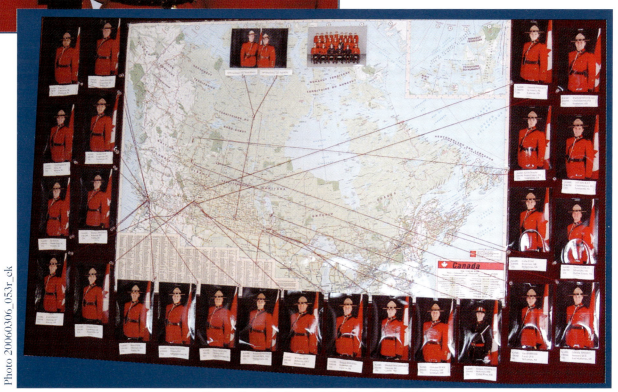

Troop Board – Troop #20, March 6, 2006

CHAPTER 5 – TRAINING

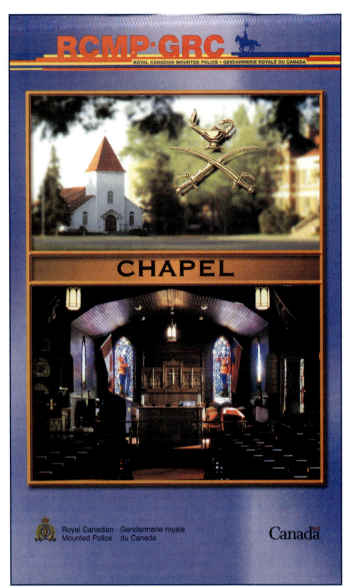

Chapel program for the graduating troop's departing service

Royal Canadian Mounted Police
Graduation

Troop #19
Sunday, March 21st and Monday, March 22nd, 2004

Due to your dedication and commitment to our success at the Royal Canadian Mounted Police Training Academy, Troop 19 requests the honour of your presence as we celebrate in our achievement in becoming newly engaged members of the Force on Monday, March 22nd, 2004.

Schedule of Events

Sunday, March 21st, 2004

9:00 - 10:00 am	Ecumenical Church Service - to be held at the Depot Division Chapel.
10:00 - 11:30 am	Family Brunch - to be held in the Mess.
11:30 - 1:00 pm	Family Workshop - to be held at the Drill Hall. Family and friends will view a short video highlighting training at Depot. Refreshments will be served.
7:30 - 10:30 pm	Wine and Cheese Social - Business Casual

Monday, March 22nd, 2004

10:30 - 11:30 am	Swearing in
11:45 - 12:45 pm	Brunch - to be served in the Standeasy Lounge and Corporals Mess.
12:50 - 1:30 pm	Sergeant Major's Parade - this will be held in the Drill Hall. Troop 19 will be performing their final noon parade and will be joined by other troops lined up according to seniority.

Grad program for Troop #19 – 2003/04

1:30 - 2:30 pm	Marching Display and Badge Presentation - this will be held at the Drill Hall immediately following the Sergeant Major's Parade. Troop 19 will be under the instruction of Cpl. Pullen of the Drill, Deportment and Tactical Unit. Following this will be the most anticipated moment at Depot: Badge Presentation.
6:30 - 7:00 pm	Cocktails at the Drill Hall - a bar will be open for cocktails preceding the graduation dinner.
7:00 pm	Graduation Dinner - in the Drill Hall
9:00 pm	Changing of the Numbers and Social - at this time the Graduating troop will be joined by the members of Troop 20 for the changing of the numbers, showing a new senior troop. Following this there is a social where friends and families meet and for the new Constables to say farewell to their fellow troopmates.

TROOP 19

Tim Whitehead	Fort St. John, BC	Kelly Hebert	Ritchibucto, NB
Amanda FitzPatrick	Vegreville, AB	Greg Morrow	Dease Lake, BC
Steve Larkin	Parksville, BC	Curtis Kuchta	Baddeck, NS
Mireille Sanchez	Maple Ridge, BC	Susan Aitchison	Surrey, BC
Naomi Kuban	Didsbury, AB	Shane Busch	Burnaby, BC
Mario Ouellette	Montreal, QC	Bruce McGilvray	Valleyview, AB
Maria Stoyles	Shamattawa, MB	Malcolm McAvoy	Langley, BC
Candace Pichach	Okotoks, AB	Chris Ivany	Williams Lake, BC
Amberia Sovdi	Surrey, BC	Carrie Cumming	Port Hawkesbury, NS
Luanne Gibb	Gimli, MB	Dean Webb	Kelowna, BC
David Chapieski	Coquitlam, BC	George Wootten	Shellbrook, SK
Chad Mehl	Onion Lake, SK	Yvonne Javorovic	Burnaby, BC
Jeremy Piper	Merritt, BC		
Andrea Neville	Pearson International Airport, ON		
Anita Gerwing	Rocky Mountain House, AB		

Prior to 1994, recruits were sworn into the RCMP as regular members just prior to the commencement of training at the Academy.

On April 1, 1999, the cadet training program was reduced from 26 to 22 weeks. The training program was increased to 24 weeks in 2001. From April 1, 1999, and as of 2006, cadets are not paid during basic training. They commence receiving a salary when they graduate.

Members of Troop #31, 1980/81

Members of Troop #19, 2003/04

Members of Troop #6, 2004/05, in the Chapel

CHAPTER 5 – TRAINING

Prior to the graduating troop's pass out, the troop marches past cadets still in training who applaud their success – 2005

Graduation

The changing of the graduating troop's number to that of the most senior troop, the next troop to graduate

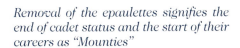

Removal of the epaulettes signifies the end of cadet status and the start of their careers as "Mounties"

Cpl. R.R. Bourget leading a graduating troop off Sleigh Square – spring 1997

Photo courtesy of Tourism Saskatchewan/Douglas E. Walker

To commemorate Inspector's Sheehan's last graduating troop inspection, the C.O. of "Depot," C/Supt. Tugnum, provided him with Sam Steele's sword to take on parade. This was just prior to his transfer to Ottawa – May 2004

C/Supt. Tugnum with Inspector Sheehan – May 2004

Cst. Danny O'Keefe at graduation – 2001

It's never too late –

The RCMP's oldest grad, Cst. Danny O'Keefe, was 53 on Graduation Day in 2001. A teacher in 1975, Danny joined the RCMP only to return to teaching in Newfoundland halfway through the program. However, his dream of becoming a "Mountie" stayed alive for 26 years and he signed up again as a cadet in 2000. After graduation in 2001, with his wife, Marie, and his three children, Danielle, Regan and André in attendance, he was posted to Bay Roberts, Newfoundland.

Oath of Allegiance

Swearing In

For over one hundred year, recruits of the North-West Mounted Police, the Royal Northwest Mounted Police and the Royal Canadian Mounted Police were usually sworn in as members of the Force in the province (division) in which they were recruited.

In 1994, a significant change occurred in which recruits, now called cadets, were sworn in upon the completion of the Cadet Training Program. Over the years, the wording has changed very little and the form utilized today is almost identical to that utilized in 1873.

Today, swearing in of a member of the RCMP is part of the graduation ceremonies. The Oath of Allegiance, Oath of Office and Oath of Secrecy are signed in front of family and loved ones and officially signify the start of the graduate's career as a member of the Force.

Photo 1990.106.70, Henry Keenan

The Oath of Allegiance required to be attested to by all recruits/cadets since the organization of the Force in 1873

Chapter 5 – Training

ENGAGEMENT DOCUMENT

PIB | CMP/P-PU-070

☐ Regular Member ☐ Civilian Member ☐ Special Constable Member

NOTE: To be taken before a Commissioned Officer of the Royal Canadian Mounted Police. All names are to be given in full.

I, _____ do hereby undertake to engage, enlist and serve in the Royal Canadian Mounted Police, subject to the exigencies of the Service, starting on _____ as a _____

I do acknowledge myself to be subject to all the provisions of the Royal Canadian Mounted Police Act, the Royal Canadian Mounted Police Superannuation Act and to any Acts amending the aforementioned Acts; and to all Regulations, Commissioner's Standing Orders and enactments made under the authority of the said Acts.

I understand that if I am found to be unsuitable for duties as a _____ of the Royal Canadian Mounted Police during the first two years of service in the Force, I may be subject to discharge from the Royal Canadian Mounted Police as a Probationary member under Part V of the Royal Canadian Mounted Police Act. I further understand that previous service with the Royal Canadian Mounted Police will be recognized and that the probationary period will be reduced by the amount of time previously served.

FOR SPECIAL CONSTABLE MEMBER ONLY

I further understand that I am engaged to fill the _____
(name of position)

position and that the Royal Canadian Mounted Police will only provide me with the training sufficient to allow me to perform satisfactorily in this position.

I further understand that this engagement offers me no opportunity for advancement in duty areas other than those for which I am being engaged.

Should I wish to promote to a rank or request a change of status outside the category of Special Constable Member, I understand that I will be obligated to satisfy all criteria for the rank / position which exist at the time the promotion / conversion is sought.

Signature _____ Date _____ Witness _____

TO BE COMPLETED FOR ALL CATEGORIES OF ENGAGEMENT

ENTERED INTO, this _____

at _____ in the Province/Territory of _____

I, _____, do hereby certify that I have not been charged with any criminal or other offence except as disclosed by me prior to this date. I do further understand that should the results of my medical examination in any way fail to meet the requirements of the Royal Canadian Mounted Police, I shall be liable to immediate discharge.

Signature _____ Date _____ Witness _____

OATHS / AFFIRMATIONS

NOTE: TO BE TAKEN BEFORE THE COMMISSIONER, OR ANY OFFICER OR ANY PERSON HAVING AUTHORITY TO ADMINISTER OATHS OR AFFIDAVITS

When affirmation taken in lieu of oath, amend form as follows:
1. In the title of each section change "OATH" TO "AFFIRMATION".   3. Change "swear" to "affirm".
2. Delete "So Help me God" from the end of each paragraph.   4. Change "sworn" to "taken".

I, _____, do _____ that I will be faithful and bear true allegiance to Her Majesty Queen Elizabeth the Second, Queen of Canada, Her Heirs and Successors.

before me at _____ in the Province/Territory of _____
This _____ day of _____ year _____
Signature _____ Witness _____

I, _____, solemnly _____ that I will faithfully diligently and impartially execute and perform the duties required of me as a member of the Royal Canadian Mounted Police, and will well and truly obey and perform all lawful orders and instructions that I receive as such, without fear, favour or affection of or toward any person.

before me at _____ in the Province/Territory of _____
This _____ day of _____ year _____
Signature _____ Witness _____

I, _____, solemnly _____ that I will not disclose or make known to any person not legally entitled thereto any knowledge or information obtained by me in the course of my employment with the Royal Canadian Mounted Police.

before me at _____ in the Province/Territory of _____
This _____ day of _____ year _____
Signature _____ Witness _____

RCMP GRC A114B (2002-11) FLO

Current Engagement Document

Prior to the commencement of the Cadet Training Program in 1994, recruits were sworn into the RCMP as members prior to training. Leanne Parsons affirms her allegiance at her swearing in on October 31, 1988 in St. John's, Newfoundland in front of Chief Superintendent R. Currie, the Commanding Officer of "B" Division

A cadet completes the Oath of Allegiance, Oath of Office and Oath of Secrecy in front of Commissioner G. Zaccardelli, his peers, family and friends on graduation day – December 12, 2005

Regimental Numbers

The RCMP has traditionally issued regimental numbers in sequential order since its inception in 1873. The original holder of regimental number one was Sergeant Major A.H. Griesbach, a late captain in the 15th Hussars and the Cape Mounted Rifles who was sworn into the Force in 1873. However, in 1875, due to an error in issuing regimental numbers, it was necessary to reissue numbers to all enlisted men. As Samuel Benfield Steele had been promoted to the unique rank of Chief Constable (today's equivalent of the Corps Sergeant Major), he was issued the new regimental number one. All regimental numbers today continue from his. (19)

On March 3, 2003, "Depot" Division reached a milestone as the badge bearing regimental number 50,000 was issued to Cadet Jason Pole by Inspector Dale Sheehan. A special ceremony was held as Cadet Pole was sworn in

Memories of "Depot"

Commissioner M.J. Nadon
Reg. #13863, (rtd.) 1975

Commissioner M.J. Nadon

When I joined the force in January of 1941, during WWII, training was reduced to six months in order to fill the many vacancies existing in the service at the time: i.e. three months Part I basic training in "N" Division Rockcliffe or "Depot" Division Regina, then on to field experience for 2 or 3 years, and back for Part II training. So after my initial training in Rockcliffe in 1941, I returned from Detachment to "Depot" Division for Part II training in November 1945.

Arriving in Regina with excess baggage I did not have sufficient funds to claim, I decided to wait till payday. Unfortunately some of the required uniforms were in the baggage held hostage so I appeared on parade improperly dressed. Any explanation offered did not satisfy the drill instructor. Thus followed parading before the Sergeant Major and then the Commanding Officer, who at the time was Assistant Commissioner R. Armitage, a policeman's policeman but not necessarily a disciplinarian. He listened to the explanation of my predicament, enquired as to excess baggage charges, reached into his pocket and gave me $10.00, refundable on payday.

Needless to say it was not what I or Sergeant Major expected, but I later found out that he had also helped out a number of other members in difficulty.

Although Assistant Commissioner Armitage did not make the grade as a training disciplinarian in some eyes, he certainly left a most favourable impression as a kindly, gentlemanly Officer worthy of emulation to most of us young serving members at the time.

A/Commissioner Robert J. (Bob) Mills
Reg. #15075, (rtd.)

A/Commr. Robert J. (Bob) Mills

Photo 19750714_MillRJ

Most have not likely given much thought to the title "Depot." The encyclopedia defines depot in a number of ways, one of which is appropriate. "A particular type of depot is one where recruits are received and undergo preliminary training before joining active troops."

Commissioner A.G. Irvine could never have envisioned a training depot that would grow and flourish for well over a hundred years when he made a recommendation in the 1880s, "that the training of recruits of the Force be trained at a depot similar to that of the Royal Irish Constabulary."

I arrived at "Depot" at the end of July 1947. I had been training in a number of army camps during 1945, and this place was different and somewhat intimidating. One incident stands out in my mind and had an impact on my service. It was as follows. S/Sgt. Arthur G. Cookson was our law instructor. Our first law exam, Cookson advised the class that some results were poor, mine was included with a 35%. Cookson, who later became Chief of the Regina Police Service, said, "You guys better hit the books, pull up your socks or you will be going out the north gate." I got the message, hit the books and kept my socks up thereafter.

I am currently amazed at the fellowship that is developed by passing through "Depot." Former members gather from across the country for squad/troop reunions. When members and ex-members meet for the first time the conversation quickly turns to the questions, "When were you at 'Depot'?" "What troop?"

Chapter 5 – Training

MEMORIES OF "DEPOT"

Constable Rene Cyr

Reg. #18907, "C" Troop 1955/56

In April 1955, our troop was the last to enjoy all the comforts of Old "F" Block. The walls were so cracked that snow accumulated between the beds during the nights.

A few weeks later we were "squaded" as "B" Troop and were one of the first troops to move into the brand new "C" Block. What luxury! Only six to a room. All this and all we could eat for a mere $1.50 a day deducted from our $203 per month basic pay.

Our troop leader was Stan Jaworski. Troop leaders were invaluable of course. They knew everything! He negotiated the purchase of hair clippers and steam irons from a previous troop at a moderate cost. I never suspected I had barbering talents until then.

Cpl. Stevens took us in charge as our Drill Instructor. Who could forget his colourful description of the intimate relationship between a monkey and a football! But Cst. Young was the martinet of the Parade Square. We swore he shaved in the mirror of his riding boots.

Cpl. Cave introduced us to the equine sciences, including the sanitation part. After a while some of us could ride while others, like me, were passengers. My horse, Whiskey, knew a lot more about riding than I ever did. He could perform all the manoeuvres, whether I was on board or not. Cpl. Cave's mount was a stallion and many a recruit bore the scars earned while cleaning its stall.

Cpl. Maguire undertook training our bodies with a vengeance and we all learned to climb up those ropes in the gym. Who could forget seeing Cpl. Pomfret doing one-handed push-ups from a handstand.

I believe our troop was the last one to be issued .455 Webleys as sidearms. We never fired them, however, much too dangerous! Brand new S & W .38 Specials reached us shortly thereafter.

There were lighter moments of course. Five-cent drafts at the Drake Hotel. Evenings at the Trianon Dance Hall under that spinning mirrored ball. And a brand-new television set in the mess; black and white of course.

And then came "N" Division.

Those were the days my friend, we thought they'd never end …

Cst. Rene Cyr

MEMORIES OF "DEPOT"

3rd Class Constable C.N. (Charlie) MacKinnon
Reg. #26295, Troop #23, 1967/68

Cst. C.N. (Charlie) MacKinnon

On November 17, 1967, I became the second of three brothers from Cape Breton Island who would join the Force. My older brother Mac joined in 1966 and my younger brother John in 1969. All three would serve 35-plus years. For me, the flight to Regina was my first time off the island. I arrived in the evening and was met at the airport by a uniformed member in brown serge. He was the recruit duty driver responsible for picking up all the new arrivals. At "Depot," I was taken to the guardroom in "C" Block and given bedding. Another recruit took me upstairs to temporary accommodation and showed me the proper way to make a bed with the aid of a coat hanger. The RCMP bed should bounce a quarter when made properly, I was told. I was then encouraged to practise until I had perfected the technique. I would stay in "C" Block until my troop formed up and then would be moved to a 32-man dorm in "B" Block.

The following morning all new arrivals were taken to the Division Clerk's office in "A" Block. On the way there I noted that large mirrors were everywhere and I thought, these mounties are a vain lot. Later, I learned they were for checking your appearance before going on parade, as a small piece of fluff on your uniform could mean extra duties and confined to barracks, a fate that befell me in short order. After the Division Clerk's office we were sent off for regimental haircuts and the issue of kit, this took most of the day. In the evening the more senior recruits came by and told us new arrivals what training was all about. These veterans had been in training for three or four weeks now and knew everything, or at least that is what they wanted us to believe.

The following day it was was back to the clerk's office to be assigned to one of the janitors for the blocks. I was assigned to the janitor in the museum. He was a nice chap who had me clean the public washrooms and change light bulbs. When I finished that he had me sweep and mop the floors. These special assignments by the Division Clerk continued until thirty-two (32) new arrivals had come to "Depot," enough to form a troop, my troop.

My older brother Mac had been in letter troop just one year prior, however, the Force had changed troop designation from letters to numbers. So when we formed up we became number 23 Troop. The instructors told us that the Force had indeed scraped the bottom of the barrel when they hired us. They all agreed we were the worst troop they had ever seen or would ever see again. They said we would have to work extremely hard if we were going to meet at least the minimum standard before pass out.

Early on I was introduced to fatigues, the horses may have been gone but other chores remained. There was an old adage in "Depot," "If it walks salute it, if it doesn't polish it." Fatigue parade was held every morning and recruits were assigned their polishing/cleaning jobs. It was, after all, winter in Regina so we got to sweep the snow from all the sidewalks on the base, including the private residences. It seemed that every morning after fatigues, when we had changed into our blues and were marching to the mess for breakfast, we would see the

CHAPTER 5 – TRAINING 275

little sidewalk tractor sweeping the same sidewalks that we had just swept. There was some sort of lesson there but I never figured out what it was. Training, of course, was from reveille to lights out and even at that there did not seem to be enough hours in the day to get everything done, from class assignments to polishing kit.

One day we were in a PT class doing isometrics when an instructor walked in looking for volunteers for the recruit choir. There were no volunteers. He turned to our instructor to confirm that this was a PT class and added that if he did not get any volunteers we could expect a very hard class. He again asked for volunteers and most of the troop volunteered. Our first choir practice was in mufti; we had no idea what mufti was so we all showed up in a shirt and tie. Our next practice we knew better.

Another day and another PT class, the fire alarm went off. Our PT gear consisted of white shorts and a white singlet. It was December in Regina; it was freezing and we had to go outside and form up in troop formation for roll call. As I shivered outside, I thought what bad luck to be caught in PT during a fire drill, until I saw another troop pour out of the building from a swimming class.

Another cherished memory from "Depot" was showering and lining up to go into the swimming pool. The PT staff's office was out behind the gym and pool in another building. The instructors would come in through a back door beside the pool door. They seemed to take a great deal of pleasure in holding the door open to the freezing Regina air as we stood wet and shivering. Their only comment was, "What's the matter girls, can't take a little cold air."

As with everything else, time passed and soon we were at the halfway point in our training. We learned that we would be going to "P" Division, Penhold, Alberta to finish training. We looked forward to Penhold as the intelligence reports we received indicated great food and no swimming. We piled into the bus that would take us to Alberta, thankful that we had survived the "Depot" experience.

MEMORIES OF "DEPOT" TRAINING

Inspector Jeff Dowling
Reg. #39886, Troop #20, 1988/89

Insp. Jeff Dowling

My strongest memories of "Depot" revolve around the weather. I was sworn in on February 12, 1988. The Force gave me 9 days to drive from my home in Prince Edward Island to "Depot," so I decided to take my time and make it a traveling vacation. I stayed with friends and family all the way across Canada, enjoying myself before what I knew would be 6 months of difficult training. On the way I drove through 4 different snow storms, the weather getting colder, windier and snowier the farther West I went. Staying in Winnipeg on the last night before arriving in Regina, it was -42°Celsius, with a wind out of the North at about 200 kilometers an hour. When I left the next day I stopped at the corner of Portage and Main, getting out of my car in -44 degree temperature to see what it was like (a cold day in P.E.I. is about -20°C). That was the coldest I've ever been, before or since.

Training in the cold was difficult. We ran outside if it wasn't colder than -25°C, often running on the golf course so we wouldn't slip on the ice on the roads. If Portage and Main was the coldest I'd been, a close second was the march from P.T. to the dorm while still wet from the shower and in a rush get ready for noon parade. Only recruits would go outside in weather that cold while wet. At night in the dorm many slept with their fur hats on for warmth, as the heating plant was losing the battle against the elements.

Things soon changed though. That summer Regina had the hottest heat wave in recorded history, and by the end of June it was +44°C. So in 4 months I experienced a change in temperature of 88°Celsius. For comparison, I believe the surface of the moon only has an 80 degree change. And it's not as windy.

Given the choice, my troopmates and I would rather trade the heat for the cold. We went weeks without seeing a cloud, and many suffered sunburn, rashes and nausea. It was a common sight to see a recruit collapse while marching to class or the mess hall. For 2 weeks in our non-air-conditioned dorm on the top floor of "D" Block it never got cooler than 35 degrees. We would leave a cold shower running all night, and recruits would stand under the water as long as they could to lower their body temperatures before going back to lie down wet on top of their beds. If you could fall asleep before the water evaporated, you had a chance to stay asleep.

We ran our 5-mile run at 13:30 hours in 40°C heat. I snuck into the instructors' office, while they were giving the troop instructions, and borrowed all the ice from their freezer. This I wrapped in a shirt, and wound it around my head, so as I ran it melted cold water over my face. I was quite proud I had finally gotten one over on the P.T. instructors, until I realized I was running 5 miles in 40 degree heat and they weren't. At least their Gatorade was warm.

Noon parade was the worst. The sun beat straight down on our heads, and the wind felt like someone had opened the oven to check on dinner. On parade, we would look down as the polish melted off our boots in minutes, leaving little puddles when we moved, and making the time spent polishing them the night before a waste. We averaged about 4 recruits passing out each day, and more when we had to wear our high browns. Noon parade, in mid-July, wearing high browns, a tight uniform and a new Stetson, in 42° Celsius weather, is the hottest I've ever been.

I returned to "Depot" in 2000 to instruct in APS. It was a great job which I enjoyed immensely, and I have many fond memories of my time there. In 3 years we had many cold days and many hot days, but nothing compared to 1988.

MEMORIES OF "DEPOT" TRAINING

Sergeant Raj Gill
Reg. #43063, Troop #22, 1990/91, Career Development and Resourcing Advisor NWR – "Depot" Division

Sgt. Raj Gill

Like most Regular Members of the Royal Canadian Mounted Police, my six months of Basic Recruit Training at "Depot" Division in 1991 brings back many fond memories. The best memories are those of the friendships made with my troop mates and of the "Depot" lifestyle. That term loosely translates to six months of hard work, a lack of sleep, full days of training, evenings of written assignments and practising newly learned skills, injuries, polishing kit, morning and noon hour parades, and, of course, that famous Mess food.

We all saw "Depot" as the biggest step to gaining our ultimate goal: to be Members of the RCMP, Canada's National Police Force with a reputation of excellence that is world renowned.

I rolled into Regina in the late afternoon of January 1, 1991. It was a typical Saskatchewan winter day, with a bright sky and brisk prairie wind. Unfortunately for me, dressed in a shirt and tie, that prairie wind blowing on a January day in Saskatchewan meant a freezing wind chill factor. That was a new term for me. Growing up in my hometown of Sparwood, British Columbia, in the heart of the Canadian Rockies, I'd never heard of a wind chill factor. Well, after my six months in Regina, and my subsequent postings in "F" Division (Saskatchewan), it's a term that I will never forget.

I came to "Depot" as a member of Troop #22, 1990/91. Unlike today's Cadet Training Program, the 32 recruits in my troop were already sworn-in Regular Members of the RCMP. I feel very fortunate to have been part of a group of individuals who took pride in their performance, worked hard in all aspects of the training program, and got along so well with each other.

Like all members who completed their time at "Depot" Division, I have a variety of good stories and amusing anecdotes. Of course, the most amusing and unusual events occurred in Drill class.

Our first Drill class, under the direction of Cpl. Bob Stewart, was an unforgettable experience. He was a man whose sharp voice and piercing stare could make you shake in your boots. If that was not intimidating enough, there were two other Drill Corporals strutting around behind our rank formation, also with their own intimidating voices. To say that I lost track of the number of "get down and give me ten" sets of push-ups that we did in that one hour session would be a gross understatement.

During this same drill class, after we had failed to follow Cpl. Stewart's specific direction, and as a result were required to "visit" several provinces and then return to our formation, an unusual incident occurred. As we returned to formation, one of my troop mates, with his shirt half soaked in perspiration, passed out and fell face first onto the shiny hardwood floor of the drill hall. I heard the thud and then saw my troop mate being helped to his feet by two other troop mates as he clutched his nose, which had started to bleed.

Naively, I expected Cpl. Stewart to be sympathetic and ask if my troop mate was all right. Instead, the words that bellowed out of Cpl. Stewart's mouth were to the effect of: "Get that man out of my drill hall. Don't you dare bleed on my drill floor. Do you hear me? Get out of my drill hall. GET OUT!!!" At that moment, I recall thinking to myself that this is going to be a tough six months!

Ironically, eleven years after that incident in the Drill Hall with Cpl. Bob Stewart, I was fortunate enough to be transferred to "Depot" Division as a Facilitator in the Applied Police Sciences Unit. During my move to Regina, my wife and I purchased a house in northwest Regina. Within days, I learned that Cpl. Bob Stewart, the man whose voice had made me and hundreds of other RCMP recruits quiver in our boots, lived directly across the street from me. He was now Sgt. Bob Steward, NCO i/c of the Drill Unit at "Depot."

It amused me greatly to see my then three-year-old daughter, Jenna, run up to him and say, "Hi, Bob." And then to see Bob reply to her in a gentle grandfatherly voice. Quite ironic, indeed.

Another effect that six months of training at "Depot" has is that you create some lifelong friendships with your troop mates. To this day, I still regularly keep in touch with some and converse via e-mails with others, but I remember them all. I know that if I were to sit down with one of them today, we could talk for hours about our time in "Depot," the memorable people we met and events that we experienced together.

Troop #22 of 1990/91 was an excellent collection of young men who left Regina with a little bit of "Depot" in them. Not only did we leave as newly trained Members of the Force but also as better people. That fact is in large part thanks to the men and women who were our instructors. Their knowledge, skills, experience and teaching abilities helped us not only to learn about police work but also about the proud history and traditions of the RCMP. They were role models for young fresh faces like ours, and they were who we wanted to be. Graduating from "Depot," I made it a personal goal to one day return as an instructor.

Today, I feel very fortunate to have had the opportunity to come back to "Depot" as an instructor. I taught the A.P.S. program for seven troops of Cadets during my 3.5 years in that position. I hope that, as my instructors did for me, I was able to leave a positive mark on these future leaders of our organization. I hope that I was able not only to teach them about basic police training, but also how to conduct themselves to maintain the integrity, history and traditions of the world-famous Royal Canadian Mounted Police.

MEMORIES OF "DEPOT" TRAINING

Constable M. Coulibaly
Reg. #50610, Troop #3, 2003/04

Cst. M. Coulibaly

It is often used lightly, overused and dismissed. It is the word HONOUR. I am honoured to have been invited to write about my RCMP training at "Depot." Some are journal entries from the 22-week journey and some are simply reflections of the journey to earning the Regimental number 50610.

Day 1, April 23, 2003 – Arrived at 14:00 today after a nervous afternoon in Regina with Susan. Shuttled in and signed some paperwork. ... It is all supposed to be a blur? Off to the guardroom to get bedding, etc. ... a rather humorous stroll trying to keep it all together literally and figuratively ... landed in "B" Block. Home. Bed 12. Sink 12.

Goodbye to the old me! ... or so I thought as I stood in my olive-coloured suit staring straight dead ahead. I was memorizing the 9th stair of the back of the bleachers and just then I began to dread the upcoming next 50 minutes. All this as the Drill Sergeant's high browns advanced across the drill hall floor. Welcome to DRILL class. I hadn't slept much in the last three nights, a massive room of single beds, 30-odd women living in a "glass jar." All visible, all present and yet all keeping to their little groups. It is funny how much one can try to maintain privacy in such an environment. I stood in the drill hall for the much-anticipated Drill Class. I had not wanted to laugh as I thought I would. I had not wanted to cry as I thought I would. Instead, as my mind was reeling and focusing on the Sergeant's voice, I found myself a stammering, bumbling seven year old. Barely able to answer the simplest of questions. Barely able to coordinate my right foot and left foot as we were so instructed. Less than an hour later, we were dismissed, but not before he had instilled in us that we were the worst he had seen.

It is with great ease that we can accomplish when we do believe. All we need is the hope, closely followed by action. I believed that there was nothing that could stop me from becoming a Mountie. The day I lived and breathed this truth was the day I passed my P.A.R.E. But that will come later.

Week one lasted forever. I couldn't fathom how 21 more weeks could possibly follow. Do not walk on the grass, stay away from the sidewalk, swing your arm with vigor, LIKE YOU MEAN IT, hold your head high, learn and respect the rank, never enter the drill hall without appropriate head dress, pretend you know what that means, eat fast, no giggling, do not fidget, certainly no crying, no hugging, don't ask why, do as you are told, be the Goddess of time management, polish, sleep, be patient, iron your bed, polish ... polish, and above all, whatever you do ... respect and understand that this is not the time to ask ... WHY?

Now for the PARE. ... I did learn early on that you do get out of life what you put into it. And so began what Erica, my troop mate, and I called the PARE challenge. I was certainly not the most apt, athletically speaking. I managed and pushed myself, watching the Olympians surpass me. Oh wait, those were my troop mates. I came to the realization early on that if I was going to graduate, I would have to OWN the PARE. Erica was on a similar page in this regard, or maybe she was just humouring me. We devised what we called the PARE CHALLENGE. One lap or two of PARE then to the stationary bike. One lap or two of PARE then to the stationary bike. One more lap or two of PARE and back to the stationary bike. So on and on until we collapsed or reached 45 minutes, whichever came first. This we did religiously. I had no fear in public speaking, no fear in class presentation, no fear in my law abilities, book work or intellectual abilities. I had great fear in my PARE ability. I feared that I would not succeed, that I would fall flat on my face, that I would go too slow, too fast at first and die out, trip, hit the mat each time, knock down sticks, that my legs would give out on me, that I would get confused and forget what I was doing and run in the wrong direction, that some greater power might take all the strength from my arms and render me weak and, of course, the fear that the string in my "Depot" issue shorts would give out – causing my shorts to fall off and expose my terribly sensible jockey-clad rear. THESE were my fears! The fears I refused to acknowledge and insisted on holding on to as though they were my comforts.

August 17, 2003 … I will own this. Empty the TANK.

With positive visualization and practiced physical ability, I ran. I ran with conviction this time, I ran BELIEVING that I could attain a goal previously unimaginable. I can recall with great detail all that I felt that day and on September 2, 2003 when I became a Mountie. The remaining tests and qualifications did not pose a great concern to me. This day I had in my mind and in my heart achieved what I set out to do. I was tense, there was no denying that. I brought it all to the table and right before, in the washroom, I began to cry. Stress and nervous tension. I completed the last cycle of weights and looked up at the timer. 3:48 … 3:48 … 3:48 was etched in my mind. Somewhere from my spent, empty tank I found it in myself to leap and cry out and forgo all appropriate behaviours and rules. I hugged each person who would allow me to hug them. I can't recall a greater feeling than that day. I passed! I believed and I had PRIDE in my accomplishment. What a thrill.

May 9, 2003 – My partner's mother died of breast cancer at the age of 61. I never met her and yet I've heard so much about her that in some small way I wanted my head shaving to make a difference. I had my head shaved.

While it can't bring my "mother-in-law" back, it may make a difference in someone else's life. Had this been an individual event, I would not have felt as touched and proud as I did today. Whether or not we were all personally affected by cancer, it was so very wonderful to see what a difference a small group of people can make. The lack of hair is a minor cosmetic issue, … Amazing what happens when a handful of people make time to make a positive difference.

A few weeks later, we were tasked to do a presentation on Child Abuse. I wondered if our facilitators expected something dry, boring, a simple regurgitation of the facts. Something they had seen before. Instead, we played a song, put some images up on the projector, and threw in a few props. This is what it was …

Sarah McLaughlin's haunting voice, single piano bars played and echoed. "In the arms … of the angel … far away from here. … In this dark cold hotel room … in the endlessness that you fear, you were born from the wreckage. …" The sweet voice, the chilling pitch … Images of children, like wreckage, illuminated the screen. A bruised eye, (something "tame" to whet the palate), then a broken nose, bruised limbs, burnt fingers … bludgeoned and tortured. A stretcher was wheeled in and on it lay a small lifeless body, covered in a sheet. The imagination filled in the blanks … hurt and broken … too young. We were now setting out to defend and speak for those who did not have a voice. Protect, maintain and, God willing, prevent.

As we presented, and completed our task, the lights went up in the darkened classroom. We watched our uniformed and stoic instructors dab tears from their eyes.

The PARE, a short presentation of child abuse, and shaving my head. Unlikely circumstances to be remembered. These were my memories of "Depot." Some troopmates to be forever remembered, unwavering support from my partner, family and friends, tears shed, blinding fatigue, pepper spray, battles of wits and strength, +30 Celsius in red serge on the parade square honouring those who came before us and knowing that all this was just the beginning.

It ended with a graduation. For me the journey ended with the song *Heart's Courageous* … "Give us ears to hear that still small voice, and give us lips forever willing to rejoice . . . our heart's courageous" The "Depot" choir sang and prayed that we may all be protected as we ventured into the real world. Our facilitator read from the Dr. Seuss book, *Oh, the Places You'll Go.*

So … be your name Buxbaum or Bixby or Bray or Modecai Ali Van Allen O'Shea, you're off to Great Places! Today is your day! Your mountain is waiting. So … get on your way!

And so … we began our journey.

RCMP Families

The MacRae Family

One of the many unique "family stories" at "Depot" started in July of 1960, when Regimental #15070, Officer #O.645, newly promoted Sergeant Major W.F. (Bill) MacRae arrived at "Depot." This arrival commenced a truly unique chapter in "Depot"s history. Over the next 20 years Bill MacRae became the most recognizable member associated with "Depot." During those 20 years he forged a reputation and image which is a blend of tradition and the progressive innovation that has contributed to the evolution of the RCMP and "Depot." It enabled Basic Recruit Training to keep pace with the requirements of providing a national police service which reflected the needs and expectations of Canadian Society.

Those who were recruits at "Depot" during Bill MacRae's tenure as Sergeant Major will remember two distinctive characteristics. First was his trademark full handlebar moustache, waxed at each end, which embodied the image of the traditional Sergeant Major and served notice to all that this was someone to be reckoned with. Secondly, there was "the voice." It is said that when Bill MacRae took command of the Parade Square that he could be heard all the way down 11th Avenue to the fairgrounds at Pasqua Street. It was a voice from which no one could hide. When he yelled, "On Parade," during the noontime Sergeant Major's parade, there was no question as to who owned that Parade Square.

Bill MacRae – circa 1963

Photo 0025

The Commissioner recognized Bill's presence and his contribution to the role of "Depot" S/M in 1960. Bill was promoted to the rank of Corps Sergeant Major in 1964, the senior NCO position in the Force. This rank had not been used since the retirement of Corps Sergeant Major Primrose in 1960. Bill's promotion to this rank was a significant achievement that contributed to the "legend" that was Bill MacRae in his role as Sergeant Major.

In October of 1966, C.S.M. MacRae and family were sent to assist in the opening of a new Basic Recruit Training base – "P" Division at CFB Penhold, Alberta. "P" Division was the Force's response to a need to increase capacity in turning out new members for the organization. It was recognized that the "Depot" experience was essential for new members so, to ensure that this experience continued, new recruits would spend the first three months of their training at "Depot" and then move to Penhold for their final three months.

The MacRaes spent only 10 months at Penhold because, in August of 1967, Bill MacRae received his commission – to the rank of Sub Inspector. Sub Insp. MacRae (O.645) returned to "Depot" to take on the role of Training Officer. This position was responsible for the operational rollout of the Basic Recruit Training program. Bill remained in the position of Training Officer until his retirement in December of 1979. While occupying this position he received two more promotions, to Inspector in 1969 and to Superintendent in 1972.

In 1964 S/M MacRae organized and participated in the parade that marked the lowering of the red ensign from the Parade Square Flagpole for the last time and then the raising of the new flag – the Maple Leaf.

The year 1966 saw the end of an era in the RCMP, when equitation was removed from the Basic Recruit Training program. The auction of the horses in September of 1966 was an emotional event and symbolically marked the start of a new era in the training of recruits, one that maintained tradition and discipline but also emphasized the need for police officers to be better prepared for the complexities of providing a police service to the Canadian public.

The year 1973 marked the Centennial of the RCMP. Throughout the year there were many initiatives and events that celebrated this historic anniversary. One of those events was the Centennial Parade at "Depot" in June. This parade was unique in the history of the Force. Participating in the parade were 300 members. The parade objective was to receive HRH Queen Elizabeth II and HRH Prince Philip, who were to oversee the retiring of the Force Guidon. During the parade Queen Elizabeth would also present the "new" Guidon to Commissioner Higgett and the Force. In response, the Force would be presenting Queen Elizabeth with one of the RCMP horses – named "Centenial," for the occasion.

"Three Cheers for Her Majesty the Queen." The parade commander, Supt. MacRae, leads the rousing cheer as the colour guard stands rigidly to attention with the Force's new Guidon – June 1973

This parade was one of Bill MacRae's proudest moments on the "Depot" Parade Square. As Parade Commander, the design and success of this parade was his responsibility. On June 25, the CBC was there to broadcast the parade live to the rest of Canada.

CHAPTER 5 – TRAINING

In 1973, Her Majesty Queen Elizabeth II presented a new Guidon to the Force during a drumhead service held at "Depot" Division. Her Majesty, escorted by Supt. MacRae, the parade commander, inspects the parade accompanied by Commr. W.L. Higgitt (rtd.)

September 16, 1974 was a day that forever changed the Royal Canadian Mounted Police. On this day Troop 17, the first female troop of recruits, was sworn in simultaneously across Canada. Given today's context it is difficult to describe the significance this day had for the Force and its members. For over 100 years the Force had been an exclusively male environment, in a profession where many thought only males were capable of operating. There were no uniforms or barrack quarters for females and there was no experience regarding female participation in Basic Recruit Training. As Training Officer, Bill MacRae played an integral part in the preparation for the arrival of Troop 17 and in ensuring that these women, and those who were to follow, were provided a fair opportunity to be successful in their basic recruit training.

During Bill MacRae's time as Training Officer at "Depot" Division, he was responsible for many innovations in the training syllabus that have survived to this day. It was through Bill MacRae's efforts that the inclusion of actors in scenario-based training was realized.

One story symbolizes the extent to which the family experience was interwoven into the "Depot" environment.

In 1961, there was a special ceremonial parade that included the Headquarters Ottawa marching band. It was a beautiful summer day at "Depot" and there was an even larger-than-usual crowd of spectators on hand. Sergeant Major MacRae, as usual, was putting the troops through their paces. He sensed that the troops were not responding in the style he had come to expect. He bellowed out a command. Instead of the usual response he observed something he had never seen before – many of the troops were smiling. He bellowed even louder and more emphatically. He was shocked to see that many of the troops were now outright laughing. He had never encountered anything like this. Out of the corner of his eye he spotted something that didn't seem quite part of the parade. He turned and discovered that his son Graham – four years of age and wearing a red Stetson and two toy six-gun cowboy pistols – had marched onto the Parade Square and taken aim at his dad with his pistols drawn. Without a second's hesitation the Sergeant Major bellowed at the young cowboy and sent Graham scurrying off the Parade Square with a well-aimed size-12 high brown boot in the direction of his backside for good measure. This action evoked a gasp from the crowd which quickly formed the opinion that this Sergeant Major was a cold-hearted scoundrel. The picture of young Graham, pistols now holstered, leaving the Parade Square, is a priceless memento of that day.

The MacRae tradition has continued with the transfer of Graham MacRae to "Depot" as a facilitator. Graham has spent the majority of his life living and working at "Depot."

Graham MacRae – 4 years old, marching – 1961

Supt. Bill MacRae saluting Queen Elizabeth II during her visit to "Depot" – 2005

Bill MacRae surrounded by his sons Graham, on the left, and Fraser, on the right

Chapter 5 – Training   285

Left to right – Steve Hadley, retired as a Sergeant; Gord Hadley, retired as a Staff/Sergeant; Gary Hadley, currently a Sergeant; Don Hadley Jr., ex-auxiliary member; Arnold Hadley, retired as a Staff/Sergeant; Jim Hadley, currently a Staff/Sergeant

The Hadley Clan

It is often said that the Royal Canadian Mounted Police is one large family. In one particular case, this is actually true. The Hadley family, parented by Donald Sr. and Adrienne, are particularly prominent in this respect.

Steve Hadley joined the Force in 1962, Reg. #22507. His brother Donald Jr. became an Auxiliary Constable and served for 13 years. Next were Arnold, who joined the Force in 1967, Reg. #25938, Gordon, 1970, Reg. #27689, and Gary, 1977, Reg. #34317. Finally, Jim, 1978, Reg. #34970, was engaged, totaling five brothers in the Force and one Auxiliary Constable. The only sister of the clan, Connie, is married to Denis Roy, also a member of the Force.

The Clare Brothers

Other examples of relatives in the Force are very common. At each graduation ceremony, it is not uncommon to see a relative present the badge to a graduating cadet. In 1918, three brothers (Constables Luther, Frank and Robert Clare) joined the Force on the same day and were assigned regimental numbers 7484, 7485 and 7486. Due in part to their excellent horse skills, the brothers were sent to Regina, quickly trained and dispatched as members of "B" Squadron to Vladivostok, Russia as part of an international expeditionary force to Eastern Siberia. (20)

Left to right – Inspector Craig Gibson, Constable Shawn Gibson, Constable Scott Gibson, A/Constable Sonny Gibson, Corporal Chad Gibson, MP/Corporal Curtis Gibson

The Gibson Family

In the heart of the Annopolis Valley in Nova Scotia there is a small, predominately Black community called Gibson Woods. The community families are closely related. Unique to this area is the connection to Law Enforcement and the Gibson extended family.

Cst. Ken Gibson, Reg. #33028, presently stationed in "O" Division, was the first member of the community to graduate from "Depot," in 1979. Ken's cousin Insp. Craig Gibson, Reg. #36587, O.2027 graduated next in 1981. He was followed by Craig's two nephews – Cst. Scott Gibson, Reg. #43784, graduated in 1990, and his brother Cst. Shawn Gibson, Reg. #46911, graduated in 1998.

Two of the Gibson family who did not attend "Depot," joined as RCMP Auxiliary constables. In the Annapolis Valley, Insp. Gibson's brother A/Cst. Charles (Sonny) Gibson, Reg, #A7915, is a member of Kings Detachment "H" Division and his sister Cheryl Byard (Gibson), Reg. #A6421, was a Special Supernumerary Cst. from May 1993 to August 1993 at "H" Division Halifax Detachment. She then became an auxiliary member from 1993 to 1996. On a side note, Insp. Gibson has another nephew who is a military police officer.

Left to right – Cst. Cheryl LaFosse, Louise LaFosse, Superintendent John LaFosse, Cst. Darrell LaFosse

The LaFosse Family

When Newfoundland joined Confederation on April 1, 1949, police officers with the Newfoundland Rangers were given the choice to join the Newfoundland Constabulary or the RCMP on April 1, 1950.

John Matthew LaFosse, Ranger Reg. #106 chose the RCMP and completed his lateral entry training in Newfoundland. He rose to the rank of Superintendent, Reg. #16187/O.734.

Supt. La Fosse (retired), had the distinct pleasure of swearing in his daughter, Cst. Cheryl Margaret LaFosse, Reg. #31812, and his son, A/Commr. Darrell LaFosse, Reg. #33759/O.1739.

Prior to joining the Rangers and the RCMP LaFosse was a school teacher in Bay-De-Lieu, a desolate settlement on the south coast of Newfoundland. One night he was called to a residence and requested to perform a baptismal ceremony on a critically ill newborn. He performed the baptism and also became the infant's godfather.

Although Supt. LaFosse never attended training at "Depot," he did present the badges to his two children. Also, twenty years after the event in Bay-De-Lieu, LaFosse was attending a course at "Depot" and met a recruit named Howard Kearly, undergoing basic training. Unbelievably, Kearly was the infant that Supt. LaFosse had baptized two decades earlier.

When all members of the first female troop were sworn in at the same time across the country to ensure no one could stake claim to being the first female constable in the RCMP, Cst. Cheryl LaFosse was sworn in in Newfoundland. Given the time change in the province, LaFosse was technically sworn in one-half hour prior to any other female recruit and thus can lay claim to being "the first female recruit" in the RCMP.

Life at "Depot"

Playing jokes on the newest tyros soon became a tradition at "Depot." In the 1880s, easterners still believed that the west was a wild and savage frontier inhabited by murderous Indians. Gullible new recruits could be sent out on their first night guard pale, scared out of their wits after being told that two or three members had been scalped recently. Another favourite ruse was to tell them that they had to go to the post carpenter to be measured for their own sentry box. The carpenter, who went along with these larks, took the necessary measurements, then reminded the recruit to be sure to pick up his box to take with him on his first guard duty. – S.W. Horrall – RCMP historian (20)

Life for a recruit was not easy. On the night he was detailed for guard duty, he mounted at 4:30 p.m. and was on duty until 6:30 a.m. the following day, without a break. If he took time for breakfast, he got to bed about 7:30 a.m. and was up again before noon, getting cleaned up for the afternoon parade. He was lucky to get about four hours sleep, after 24 hours on his feet. If he drew a Friday night guard, he was not permitted to go to bed at all, because of the Saturday morning inspection. The theory was, it seems, that the weekly "stand by your bed" inspection would be seriously disrupted by the horrid sight of one man in a 20-bed barrack room asleep in his iron cot. He was, of course, free to go to bed on Saturday afternoon. – ex-Cst. T. Jamieson Quirk, Reg. #11951, 1932 (21)

How to get in trouble in one easy lesson –

Early in February the Sergeant Major informed us, when we were on parade, that we would be going to Ottawa for 2nd part training. During the same parade, all of the squads were told that everyone was confined to barracks that evening. We had to clean the buildings to get them ready for an inspection by a Senior Commissioned Officer from Ottawa. It was a difficult task because almost all the buildings were old and rundown. When the Officer inspected, he was not satisfied with the cleanliness of the buildings. As a result, everyone was confined to barracks again that evening to clean everything again. We were told that, as an added punishment, there would be no midnight passes approved for a week.

There was a tradition in the training divisions that a squad held a celebration after its Pass Out Parade. Our Pass Out was going to take place during the week that no one would be given a midnight pass. Although we could go out after the parade, we had to be back in barracks by 9:00 p.m.

Finally, we had our Pass Out Parade and it went well. Everyone in the squad went downtown to celebrate afterward but we were back before 9:00 p.m. After the member in charge of the night guard called the roll, about half of us put our duffel bags on our beds and covered them with blankets. To anyone shining a flashlight in the room after the lights were turned out, it would appear that everyone was in bed asleep.

After arranging for a taxi to meet us off the Division grounds, we sneaked out and went back downtown to continue our celebration. I came back with two other members around 1:00 a.m.

The taxi driver dropped us off at the back gate of the division. We headed quietly to our barracks building and entered by a rear basement door. Just as we got inside, we heard someone coming down the stairs to the area where we were. The three of us took off outside as fast as thoroughbred horses out of a starting gate. I don't know what way the other two chaps went but I ran to the rear of the Chapel that was alongside our building. I hid there until my heart stopped pounding and then crept to the front of the Chapel. I lay in the snow for about twenty minutes. Finally, I slowly crawled on my hands and feet to the front steps of "C" Block. I went up the steps and after quietly opening the door, slipped inside. Just as I reached the second floor, the member in charge of the night guard stepped out of the library on the first floor. He turned his flashlight on me and quietly said that I was under Open Arrest. I gave a fleeting thought to darting into my room and jumping, fully dressed, into bed. When questioned, I would say that I was cold and had put my clothes on to keep warm. I decided against it because no one would be dumb enough to believe that story. It was the most intelligent decision I made that evening.

Of the thirteen of us caught that morning, the night guard only reported eleven to the Sergeant Major. After the Morning Parade, the Sergeant Major told us that we were going to be charged under the RCMP Act for being absent without leave.

The first evening after we were charged, the NCO in charge of the night guard, a Sergeant, told us that we were defaulters. His position on our status meant that we would have to turn out hourly during the evening dressed in our red serge tunics, Sam Browne equipment, breeches, long boots and Stetsons. I pointed out to the Sergeant that, according to the rules and regulations of the RCMP, a member was not a defaulter until after he had been convicted of an offence. Until we were convicted, we only had to attend the 6:00 p.m. and 10:00 p.m. parades and then only in our work uniforms.

Not letting the matter rest, two members of my squad went to see the Sergeant Major, but he wasn't home. They then visited the home of the Division Adjutant. He wouldn't do anything to help us – two strikes but we weren't out. Finally, two other members of my squad went to the home of the Officer Commanding and told one of his daughters, whom one of them had been dating, what had happened. She brought the matter to her father's attention and he ordered that we be taken off the defaulters' list.

Except for one or two instructors, the rest of the training staff felt that we had committed an unforgivable sin by going to the O.C. over the Sergeant's head. We felt good about winning the battle but we would soon find out that we have (sic) lost the war.

On February 8, 1954, I appeared before the O.C. charged with being absent without leave under the RCMP Act. After I pleaded guilty, he fined me two dollars and confined me to barracks for five days. Fortunately two of the days were spent on the train trip to Ottawa.
– Superintendent J. Regila (rtd.), Reg. #O.947, "H" Troop, 1953/54 (22)

Leave Pass

A weekend pass, which was rarely given, was from 1:30 p.m. Saturday, until lights out at 10:30 p.m. Sunday. Otherwise a Constable had to be in barracks and in bed every night at 10:30 p.m. except Saturday night, when he was allowed out until midnight. This made it rather difficult to take a lady to a dance. A constable either had to take his date home very early in the evening or hand her over to a friend before departing.

Annual leave didn't exist. Rules and Regulations, Section 528 in 1928 stated, "No leave is to be granted N.C. Officers or Constables without some apparent necessity for it." It was not completely impossible, however, and in the better part of eight years service, I had perhaps a total of 14 days leave. This monastic life accomplished one thing though. When the day finally came, months later, that we were assigned to a detachment, no matter how long the hours or arduous the task, it was no problem – and the freedom was wonderful! – ex-Cst. T. Jamieson Quirk, Reg. #11951, – 1932 (23)

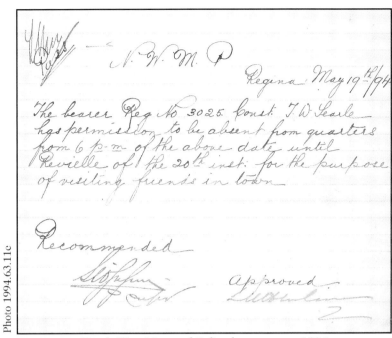

North-West Mounted Police leave pass – 1894

North-West Mounted Police leave pass – 1894

CHAPTER 5 – TRAINING   291

We were allowed two passes each week until midnight, otherwise, we had to be in our room by 9:00 p.m. We had to check into the Guard Room, whenever we left the grounds, and when we returned. We were off Saturday afternoon, Sundays and Statutory Holidays, unless detailed for duties on those days. Even when we were off on a Sunday or Statutory Holiday, we still had to turn out for the early morning Parade to do fatigues before breakfast. – Superintendent J. Regila (rtd.), Reg. #O.947, "H" Troop, 1953/54 (24)

Recruits in training are allowed time off as follows:
– Post orders No. 66

4. Recruit members with less than three complete months of training may be permitted:

    A. i) *to be absent from barracks after duties until 10:30 p.m. each evening, except Thursday.*
        ii) *to have three standing 1:30 a.m. passes during any given week, except Thursday evenings*
        iii) *to have weekend passes provided they are not scheduled for training or other duties.*

    B. *Members with over three months training may be permitted:*
        i) *to have standing 12:00 a.m. passes*
        ii) *to have standing 2:30 a.m. passes on Fridays and Saturdays plus one additional 2:30 a.m. pass on a night of their choice.*
        iii) *to have weekend passes provided they are not scheduled for training or other duties*
        iv) *to have a weekend pass from after duties Friday to 8:00 a.m. Sunday during Graduation weekend.* – Life at the RCMP Academy at "Depot" Division – 1977 (25)

During the early 1970s for a very brief period of time, staff members were ordered to tour the downtown bars to ensure that the recruits were behaving themselves. This stopped when the staff submitted expense claims for the drinks they felt obligated to buy when having to sit in the bars to observe the recruits.

Marriage

The RCMP initially only engaged single members into the Force. As the decades unfolded, the waiting period to marry declined from seven years, to five, to two, and currently married members are engaged. Initially, a written request to the Commissioner indicating that one was debt free and had completed the required service in a satisfactory manner was necessary prior to the marriage taking place.

Only single men were enlisted, but theoretically, after six and a half years, members of the Force could apply for permission to marry. This request was not granted automatically and by the time it was granted, the constable was usually crowding 29 years of age. The minimum joining age was 21. Of those who remained in the service, those in my group were probably 35 by the time they married. – ex-Cst. T. Jamieson Quirk, Reg. #11951 – 1932 (26)

Marriage Regulations

Those desiring to marry must make application in writing to the Commissioner through regular channels. The application will not be considered unless the member is 21 years of age or over, debt free and has served in a satisfactory manner for at least two years. – A Career in Scarlet, 1969 (27)

Rumour had it that a friend of the Force used to lend $500.00 interest-free to members for the brief time it took the Force to check the members' bank accounts.

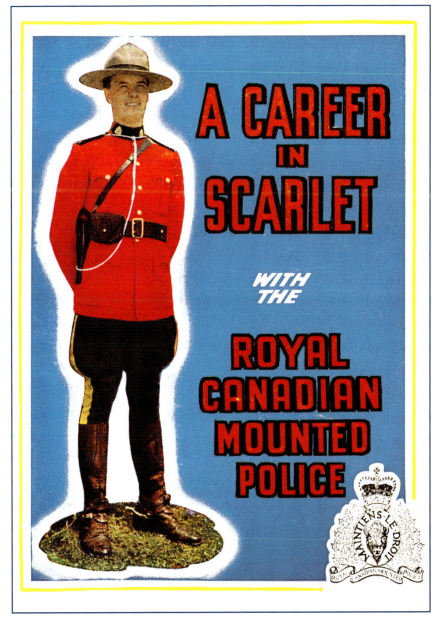

RCMP recruiting booklet with Cst. Bob Camm on the cover

To the Wives

The wedding of Cst. and Mrs. G. Muir in the Chapel – December 10, 1975

The year 1974 produced major changes to the RCMP recruiting policies, which included the acceptance of married personnel. Contained within the recruit handbook was the following passage.

Upon engagement, in the RCM Police, your husband will be posted to the RCMP Academy at "Depot" Division, Regina, Saskatchewan, for an intensive six month Recruit Training Programme. This, as well as a subsequent six-month field training period, is very demanding. As the first year of service (probationary) can set the momentum of a very successful or not so successful career, we suggest that for the benefit of your family as a whole his first priority should be to his training. Hopefully you will be able to take a back seat for this short one year time span, in a thirty five year career.
– Life at the RCMP Academy at "Depot" Division – 1977 (28)

"Depot" Chapel Marriage Certificate

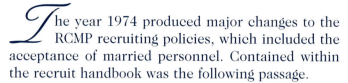

Wedding party in front of the Chapel – circa 1945. The steeple was added in 1939

294   BEHIND THE BADGE

Native Special Constable Training

Native Special Constable Training – 1986

In 1972, the Minister of Indian Affairs and Northern Development authorized a task force to study policing on reserves. In 1973, the task force recommended an increased emphasis on the recruitment of Native Special Constables to police the Canadian native community. The program allowed flexibility for differences in culture and ethnic backgrounds but attempted to conform as closely as possible to the qualifications required for a regular member.

At the completion of the nine-week program at "Depot," the special constables became members of the Force, wore uniforms and would normally work out of a detachment nearest their home reserve. The Constables possessed the powers of a regular member but would concentrate their efforts on community policing and prevention.

Some Native Special Constables, after acquiring experience, have chosen to become regular members of the Force, subsequently opening new career opportunities. (29)

The first native special constable troop completed its training on March 14, 1975.

Display commemorating the first Native Special Troop

Training Syllabus for the Native Special Constable Program – 9 weeks in duration

Academic Subjects	Hours		Physical Subjects	Hours
Criminal Law	54		Self-Defence	30
Federal Statutes	8		Physical Training	20
Operational Techniques	43		**Total**	**50**
Human Relations	51			
Technical Services	4			
Total	**160**			

Skill Subjects	Hours			
Small Arms	44		Miscellaneous	26
Drill	20			
Driver Training	38			
Total	**102**		**Total Hours**	**339** (30)

This program was later discontinued to encourage aboriginal members to become regular members of the Force.

Pay/Salary

At the start of the NWMP, few members of Canada's national police force saw it as a career opportunity. Men joined the force for adventure, a means of traveling west and establishing a homestead, or pursuing a military career. Starting salary was little better than a labouring wage. The pay for a recruit in 1873 was 75 cents a day. This was lowered to 40 cents in 1880, increased to 60 cents in 1905, and to 75 cents a day in 1912.

Pay as of May 26th, 1874:

Commissioner	$2600 per annum
Assistant Commissioner	$1600
Inspectors	$1400
Sub Inspectors	$1000
Surgeon	$1400
Veterinary Surgeon	$ 700 (31)

Regulations and Orders for the Government North-West Mounted Police 1889:   **2005 annual salary:**

Staff Sergeants	$1.00 to 1.50 per day	$81,090
Sergeants	$1.00 per day	$74,237
Corporal	.85 c per day	$67,581
Constables* according to length of service	.50 to .75 c per day	$39,535 (32)

* Constables received .50 c per day in first year plus .05 c per day annual increment up to the maximum of .75 c per day. (33)

Out of a recruit's pay of $2 per day in 1923, a $2 mess fee and 50 cents per month library fee were deducted. In addition of course were laundry, dry cleaning, shoe polish, silvo, brasso, blanco and saddle soap if one were to escape the wrath of the inspecting officer. Should one frequent the Division Canteen and afford the luxury of a girlfriend, he might well find his pay cheque exhausted before the end of the month and still owe a canteen bill.
– ex-Cst. Glenn Victor Wellman, Reg. #9948 – 1923 (34)

In 1987, recruits in training received the following salary and allotments:

APPENDIX "A" FINANCES

Without Dependants		With Dependants (based on wife and one child)	
Monthly gross income	$1062.00	Monthly gross income	$1062.00
		Daily incidental allowance ($2.15 x 30)	64.50
		One telephone call* home per week approx.	20.00
			$1146.50

DEDUCTIONS			
Meals	$72.00	No deductions for meals or quarters	
Quarters	28.00		
Income tax, pension, insurance etc.	312.00	Income tax, pension, insurance etc.	$260.00
	$412.00		$260.00
Average monthly pay after deductions	$663.00	Average monthly pay after deductions	$874.00
Pay every two weeks	$330.00	Pay every two weeks	$437.00

* limited to five minutes, station to station, operator placed at weekend rates (35)

Recruits in training received a salary. In an effort to reduce costs, since 1994 cadets in training have not received a salary.

Pay Parades

The RCMP paid us once a month. After lunch on paydays, the squads lined up in the gym in order of seniority. After everyone in a squad had been paid, the squad was dismissed and given the rest of the afternoon off to take care of personal business. Being paid first was one of the privileges that the senior squad was given. The pay parade was time consuming, because only one member was paid at a time. When your name was finally called, you came to attention, marched to the front of the gym and halted in front of a table that had been set up. Even though we were paid by cheque, we still had to sign for the cheque. After being paid, you marched back to your squad. When we were the junior squad, I found it was plain agony waiting to be given my cheque, so that I could get away from the Division for the rest of the afternoon. Time away from the Division was worth its weight in gold.
– Supt. J. Religa (rtd.), Reg. #O9.47, "H" Troop, 1953/54 (36)

Cadets in training are placed on the payroll once they have successfully completed the Cadet Training Program and are sworn in as regular members of the RCMP on grad day.

Physical Training

A number of display boards can be found in the hallway of the gym. These boards list the names of recruits, cadets and staff who have achieved personal goals on their own time in the form of the various categories that are displayed. The display boards include:

The PARE (Physical Abilities Requirement Evaluation) board lists –

- the "all-time" record times for males and females completing the PARE
- the best time for males and females currently in training completing the PARE
- the "all-time" record times for males and females completing the Cooper's Run (1.5 miles)
- the best times for males and females currently in training completing the Cooper's Run (1.5 miles)
- the "all-time" record time for males and females completing the 3-mile run
- the best times for males and females currently in training completing the 3-mile run

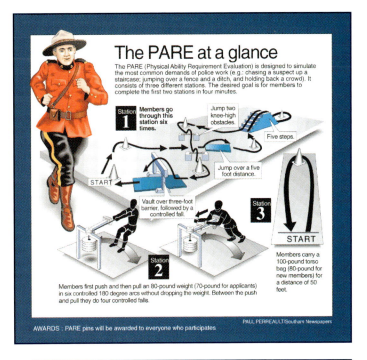

Volleyball in the old Gym – circa 1950s

"E" Squad in the old Gym – 1935/36

CHAPTER 5 – TRAINING

Gymnastics in the old Gym – circa 1950s

Warming up for PT class – circa 1990

Recruits, cadets and staff have a number of opportunities to challenge themselves physically.

"200 Mile Club" (322 km Club), (cadets only) – cadets who achieve this mileage receive a certificate of achievement signed by the C.O.

"500 Mile Club" (800 km Club) cadets who achieve this mileage receive a certificate and name plate on the board in the gym hallway.

"1,000 Mile Club" (1600 km Club) Cpl. Pat Baker Club – cadets/members/staff who achieve this mileage receive a certificate, keeper plaque and a name plate on the board in the gym. Cpl. Pat Baker was an avid runner who worked out of "Depot."

"English Channel Swim" 1,290 lengths of the "Depot" pool (length of English Channel) – cadets receive a certificate of achievement and a name plate on the board in the pool.

"Diefenbaker Swim" the length of Diefenbaker Lake (100 miles/160 kms) – cadets receive a certificate, a keeper plaque and name plate in the pool lobby.

Roll up and tuck – circa 1990

C.O. C/Supt. Harper Boucher completing the P.A.R.E. in 1998

Cst. Marion Craig, at the time of her graduation in February 1986, was the **first female** to complete the "1,000 mile club" running requirements and the first recruit to complete both the "1,000 Mile Club," and the "Diefenbaker Swim."

Bench Press Board – Cadets and staff have an opportunity to place their name on this board if they can bench press:

150% body weight (males)
100% body weight (females)

The fitness component of the Cadet Training Program is designed to develop cadets' commitment to a lifelong healthy lifestyle to ensure their physical and mental readiness for police duties. The program addresses issues of nutrition and stress management. Cadets are taught safe and effective techniques to develop their resistance through weight training, anaerobic, aerobic and cardio-vascular capabilities through a variety of methods. The program is designed in two phases progressively from instructor centred to learner centred. Once cadets have learned appropriate physical training techniques, they establish in consultation with their instructors, fitness and lifestyle objectives and select those techniques best suited to them to maintain standards set. Cadets participate in a series of challenge exercises to understand their limits and use this knowledge in risk assessments when involved in policing situations.

Cadets must complete the P.A.R.E. (Physical Ability Requirements Examination) standard of 4 minutes to successfully complete the program.– Overview of the Cadet Training Program – 2004 (37)

Cst. Marion Craig, won 8 gold medals at the Can Am Police Fire games held at "Depot" in 1998. This included the "Toughest Cop Alive" competition. This event consisted of a 3-mile run, 100 metre sprint, shot put, 100 metre swim, rope climb, bench press, pull-ups and obstacle course which were all completed in one day.

TEST / L'EPREUVE		MEMBER / MEMBRE	TROOP / TROUPE	DATE	SCORE / RESULTAT
3 MILE TIMED RUN	MALE / HOMME	LEEF	4	98-08-07	15:13
COURSE DE 3 MILLES CHRONOMÉTRÉ	FEMALE / FEMME	ZUBYCK	1	97-07-14	18:37
PRESENT RECORD FOR CADET IN TRAINING	MALE / HOMME	JESSOME	34	05-05-17	17:49
RECORD DE CADET PRÉSENTEMENT EN FORMATION	FEMALE / FEMME	GRAND-CLEMENT	26	05-03-14	20:14
P.A.R.E.	MALE / HOMME	WHITE, BRIAN	18	00-12-18	2:25
T.A.P.E.	FEMALE / FEMME	JACKSON	6	96-11-05	2:45
PRESENT RECORD FOR CADET IN TRAINING	MALE / HOMME	GREEN	26	05-05-18	2:46
RECORD DE CADET PRÉSENTEMENT EN FORMATION	FEMALE / FEMME	GRAND-CLEMENT	26	05-05-18	3:13
COOPER'S 1.5 MILE RUN	MALE / HOMME	LEEF	4	98-10-27	7:09
L'ÉPREUVE COOPER DE 1.5 MILLES	FEMALE / FEMME	DICKMAN	20	96-06-04	8:29
PRESENT RECORD FOR CADET IN TRAINING	MALE / HOMME	JESSOME	34	05-05-02	8:15
RECORD DE CADET PRÉSENTEMENT EN FORMATION	FEMALE / FEMME	GRAND-CLEMENT	26	05-02-28	9:38

P.A.R.E. Board – June 2005

CHAPTER 5 – TRAINING

Weight training is an integral part of the Fitness and Lifestyle program

Physical training in the Force calls for a great deal of self control, and a high standard of discipline is necessary. The recruit is taught that he must carry out instructions to the exact detail, which in turn will develop leadership qualities, assuring that when he is on his own he will set a good example as a member of the Force. – Cpl. E.C. Curtain – 1956 (38)

Quick-Change Artists

We were always changing our clothes – fatigues to uniform to gym clothes to uniform to swimming trunks. The problem was that we did not have much time to do it in, and it was a never-ending routine. It was pure luck to have physical training and swimming class one after the other. There was usually a classroom subject or lunch, to which we had to wear our uniform, between the two.

We were changing into our white gym clothes so often that it was difficult to keep them clean. The instructors always could find some dirt on someone's shorts, T-shirt, or running shoes. It usually meant push-ups or if an instructor was in a bad mood, extra duties. – Supt. J. Religa (rtd.), Reg. #O.947, "H" Troop, 1953/54 (39)

Today's cadets experience this reality with the same time restrictions as their predecessors.

Weight Room – 2005

Let's make a Deal!

As a rule, the only time you could be injured physically during training was in the police holds and boxing classes. Almost everyone in my Squad had an understanding when it came to boxing classes. If either of the members who were to box together had a date on the weekend or had something special coming up, it was understood that both members would pull their punches during their match. The way we looked at it there was no use sporting a black eye or a bruised face when taking out a young woman. – Supt. J. Religa (rtd.), Reg. #O.947, "H" Troop, 1953/54 (40)

Circuit Training – 2005

Prior to the introduction of the PARE in the cadet training program in 1994, recruits were required to meet the following minimum standards prior to graduation.

Benchmarks – In 1988, these were the minimum standards that had to be met to successfully complete the physical training portion of training at "Depot."

Exercise	Minimum Standard			
	Male		Female	
Cooper's Test (1.5 mile timed run)	10:45	Age 20-29	13:30	Age 20-29
	11:00	Age 30-39	14:30	Age 30-39
Push-ups	30	Age 20-29	23	Age 20-29
	24	Age 30-39	22	Age 30-39
Sit-ups	40	Age 20-29	31	Age 20-29
	33	Age 30-39	24	Age 30-39
POPAT*	4 minutes 15 seconds for both genders			

* "POPAT (Police Officer Physical Abilities Test) was designed to test a person's physical capabilities in direct relation to what a peace officer is required to preform at various times in the field." (38) It simulates a brief but intense encounter situation similar to what one could anticipate as a police officer in a stressful situation. The test includes stairs, jumping over low obstacles, pushing, pulling, lifting and carrying weight.

GYMNASIUM

Kit – issue – running shoes, white jersey, white shorts, socks
 – non-issue – athletic support necessary – available at canteen in "C" Block

How to wear – Shoes laced to top, socks in a fold approximately two inches wide down over the top of the shoe, shirt inside shorts. No items of jewellry or metal, such as rings, watches, pendants, etc., may be worn.

Laces – Preferably the wide issue laces. Starting at the bottom of the shoe, the lace is placed through the opposing eyelets from the top or outside, with an equal length of lace on each side. Continue the lacing by placing the loose ends of the lace into the next eyelet on the opposite side, always working into the eyelet from the outside. This results in a criss-cross lacing. The loose ends of the lace, after a suitable knot is tied, are placed upright along the sock which is then folded down over the top of the shoe.

Cst. Doug Doige, Troop #26, whitening his runners for PT in F-2 barracks – January 1956

CLEANING KIT

Shoes – white shoe cream is essential and is available at the canteen. Wet an issue button brush, squeeze a small amount of the cream onto the shoe, and brush it into the shoe with a damp brush. The shoe laces must also be kept white and this is done by washing after each use and whitening with shoe cream.

Socks – wash in lukewarm water and soap. Rinse thoroughly, dry on sock stretchers.

Shorts – wash in water which is not too hot for hand, otherwise the elastic band will be ruined. Use soap and a small amount of bleach. Press and crease as ordinary trousers.

Shirt – clean as you do the shorts. Press with no creases.

INSPECTIONS

You will be inspected at the beginning of every physical training period. The following items receive the strictest attention:

1. Personal body cleanliness
2. Cleanliness and condition of kit
3. Condition of skin (pimples, boils, etc.)
4. Haircuts
5. Posture
6. Occasional inspections of towels, underwear, etc., will also be made.

Police Defensive Tactics

Members of Troop #6 in judo attire changing in the basement of the old Gym – 1989/90

The Police Defensive Tactics component of the Cadet Training Program is designed to provide cadets with safe and effective techniques to manage policing-related incidents within the context of the RCMP Incident Management Intervention Model (IMIM). The Model was designed based on the following principles:

- the primary objective of any intervention is public safety
- police officer safety is essential to public safety
- the intervention model must always be applied in the context of a careful risk assessment
- risk assessment must take into account the likelihood and extent of life loss, injury and damage to property
- risk assessment is a continuous process and risk management must evolve as situations change
- the best strategy is the least intrusive intervention necessary to manage risk
- the best intervention causes the least harm or damage

Ground fighting – 1990

Warming up for the class by performing the wheelbarrow – 1990

Reinforcing techniques taught in class through detachment scenarios – 1990

Preparing for a boxing stint – 2002

Cadets learn and practice different techniques under a variety of simulated circumstances. The techniques taught include joint locks, take downs, use of Oleoresin Capsicum (OC), suspects through doorways, stances, blocks, strikes, use of batons, carotid control hold, grappling, ground defence, body hold releases, handcuffing and searching suspects and use of weapon defences. – Overview of The Cadet Training Program – 2004 (41)

Cpl. Tammy Patterson providing direction to two cadets – 2002

Today's recruit will have 4½ weeks of physical conditioning behind him before ever setting foot in the self-defence gymnasium. His training commences with instruction in the basics of collegiate-style wrestling. This beginning has proven a satisfactory introduction into heavy body contact while restricting the recruit to a system of rules. The recruit progresses from wrestling into what is termed "ground fighting." During this phase each man is placed in a variety of extreme situations involving considerable stress, always with the policeman at a distinct disadvantage – straddled by a heavier and stronger opponent applying a choke. He is taught simple effective methods to not only escape from this predicament, but in many cases he will have established control over his assailant.– Cpl. W.D. Pitcher – 1973 (42)

Police Driving Unit
– The Moving Classroom

The driver training curriculum is designed to provide cadets with police driving skills and related knowledge to ensure public and police safety while on patrol and when responding to incidents. Cadets learn to gather appropriate evidence to ensure the fair outcomes of investigations of traffic related incidents, and to identify opportunities for crime prevention while on patrol. They learn about the laws and policies pertaining to the use of police vehicles, appropriate use of police vehicle equipment; observational skills and use of the radio while driving are emphasized.

Opportunities are provided to apply knowledge and skills in situations calling for officer/violator contact, making sketches, taking measurements and photographs at scenes of motor vehicle accidents, identification and handling of traffic collision-related evidence and identification of preventive opportunities through good observational skills. – Overview of The Cadet Training Program – 2005 (43)

The decision maker – driving technique taught to avoid unanticipated obstacles on the roadway – circa early 1980s

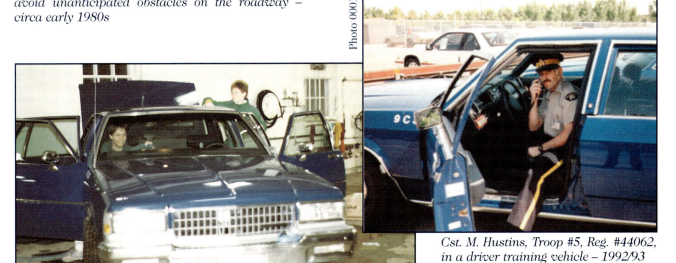

Troop duties include the maintenance of their driving car – members of Troop #13 ensure that their efforts will be approved by their driving instructor – 1988/89

Cst. M. Hustins, Troop #5, Reg. #44062, in a driver training vehicle – 1992/93

CHAPTER 5 – TRAINING

In October 1982 a Driver Training Range was opened at "Depot" for recruits and in-service training. This new facility was designed specifically for the recruit-training program, but has also served the needs of advanced-driver-training courses as well. It consists of a paved serpentine track measuring one-half mile in length and a large rectangular skill course.

Learning the mechanics of vehicle dynamics on the Shwaykowski track

The unique feature of the serpentine track is that high-speed vehicle movement is duplicated at low speeds. This permits the student driver to become aware of a vehicle's capabilities while discovering the limits of his own ability to skilfully handle a motor vehicle during-high speed operation. Equally important is the degree of safety inherent in the low-speed training exercise; driver training accident is virtually terminated. – Sgt. James Scott – 1983 (44)

In October of 2004, an advanced second track was completed which features curves, apexes, curved elevations spread on a 2.7 kilometer two-lane highway surface. The new track provides greater flexibility and represents road conditions that are closer to "real life," allowing the cadets to experience advanced driving in a controlled environment. The basic principles of advanced driving remain the same, however the cadets are now able to apply the techniques in two different environments. – Depot Digest – 2004 (45)

An aerial of the new advanced-driver-training track – 2005

Recruits and cadets have been taught various acronyms or short bundles as a means of reinforcing the physical skills taught while in their moving classroom.

Recruit Training Program	Cadet Training Program
Smith system of driving	**SIPDE**
– Aim high in steering	S Search
– Get the big picture	I Identify
– Keep your eyes moving	P Predict
– Make sure they see you	D Decide
– Leave yourself an out	E Execute
– Get the big picture	

Driver Training Classroom Syllabus – Lesson Plan No. 4 – circa 1965

Subject	• Rules of the Road • **Time 3 minutes**
Lesson Objective	• To show two short films covering rules of the road and proper driving habits.
Training Aids	• Blackboard and chalk • Film – *Driving in the City* • Film – *Practice Makes Perfect Drivers*
References	• Regina City Traffic bylaw • Saskatchewan Auto Insurance and Safety Guide • American Automobile Association **Time 37 minutes**

1. ***Driving in the City***
   (black & white, 20 minutes)
   (a) Outline main points of film on blackboard
   (b) Film showing
   (c) Questions and discussion

2. ***Practice Makes Perfect Drivers*** (black & white 10 minutes)
   (a) Outline main points of film on blackboard
   (b) Film showing
   (c) Questions and discussion

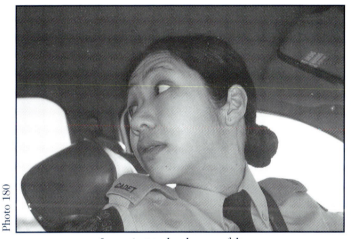

Learning to back up safely

Prepatrol inspection – "Depot" – 1990

Recruit Training

Recruit Training Manual – 1932

Every recruit is to be trained for the first four months of his service in –
1. *Foot and Arm drill*
2. *Equitation and Cavalry drill*
3. *Rules and Regulations of the Force*
4. *First Aid to the injured, as called for by the Canadian branch of the St. John Ambulance Association, for the candidate to obtain the first certificate.*
5. *The history of the Force and its present organization.*
6. *The Constable's Manual*

At the conclusion of the period of four months' training, the Officer Commanding of "Depot" will appoint a board of two officers to conduct an examination in all six subjects.

Each recruit will be required to obtain 60% of the total marks and will be put back for further instruction if he fails.

Those who obtain the necessary 60% will be passed out and will then be instructed in –
- *(a) Musketry and revolver shooting*
- *(b) The Criminal Code*
- *(c) Federal Act*
- *(d) Detachment returns and the use of a typewriter*
- *(e) The operation and care of mechanical transport.*

At the conclusion of this period of two months' training, a report is to be rendered on each man, showing the opinion of the Officer Commanding as to his fitness for appointment to the rank of second class Constable, and setting forth his knowledge of the subjects referred to immediately above. – Office of the Commissioner – 1932 (46)

Sleigh Square – circa 1930

Regular Basic Recruit Training (25 weeks) – April 1977

Tactical Training practice at "Depot" – early 70s

	Hours
Criminal Law	65
Federal Statutes	28
Administrative Manual	15
Human Relations	62
History of the Force	13
Effective Speaking	21
Practical Training	42
Typing	28
Report Writing	19
First Aid	11
Telecommunications (CPIC)	20
Technical Services Unit	36
Miscellaneous	90
Cross-Cultural Education	18
Hours	**468**

	Hours
Physical Training (aerobic exercises, cross country running, weight training, calisthenics)	85
Swimming (back, breast, side strokes and water safety)	40
Self-Defence (judo, karate, ground fighting, wrestling and police holds)	68
Hours	**193**

	Hours
Drill (including crowd control, gas training)	70
Driver Training (classroom lectures, defensive driving, police techniques)	68
Firearms (safety and handling and cleaning of weapons, along with range practice of revolvers, rifles and shotguns)	56
Hours	**194**
TOTAL HOURS	**855**

Collision investigation at "Depot" – early 70s

Basic Recruit Training (26 weeks) 1988

Canadian Police Information Centre (CPIC) and Police Information Retrieval System (PIRS) are taught in the APS portion of the program

Scenario training – 1990

Troop enroute to Self-Defence Class – 1990

The Academic Section is comprised of four instructional units as follows:

Human Relations, Identification, Law, Operational Training

Academic Subjects	Periods
Human Relations	121
Crime Prevention	8
Effective Presentation	17
Applied Human Behaviour	29
Cross-Culture	20
Victimology	41
Ethical Conduct	6
Identification	38
Law Unit	113
Federal Statutes	27
Operational Training	149
Telecommunications	4
First Aid	18
Notebooks	3
Typing	8
Report Writing	18
Prisoners	10
CPIC & PIRS	40
Practical Training	46

Driving	
Lectures	23
Practical Drives	35
Circuit Driving	11

Physical Training	80
Self-Defence	68
Swimming, survival & rescue	39
Cardio Pulmonary Resuscitation	12

Firearms	58
Drill	59
Study Periods	19
Miscellaneous (debriefings, photos, kit, language testing, Division Staff Relations Rep)	58
Total Hours	1178

Reserves

In 1937, the Royal Canadian Mounted Police Act was amended by Parliament, authorizing the formation of a Reserve. Previously, the provisions were that the Reserve membership could only be held by previously serving members of the Force. With the amendments, men without previous service could apply, and the Force now had the ability to appoint Non-Commissioned Officers and prescribe training.

Several hundred men applied, qualified and went onto a waiting list. Five hundred men were contacted and 278 reserves were enlisted for training. Training camps were set up in Fredericton, Gaspe Peninsula, "Depot" and Vancouver. The training period was held simultaneously across Canada from July 2nd to August 31st.

The Reservists were trained in physical training, drill, police work, the Constables Manual, Revolver Drill and the History of the Force. The training was deemed a success and it was noted that no member of the Reserve had been convicted in the Orderly Room for any breach of discipline. – Supt. V.A.M. Kemp, 1937 (47)

RCMP Reserve – 1937

The Reserves were ready for any resulting duties that required additional police assistance. The training continued for several years and many of the Reservists eventually signed on to full-time duties in the Force.

Chapter 5 – Training

Reveille

When reveille sounded, our feet hit the floor. I should have said that nearly everyone's feet hit the floor, because there were always some people who hated to get up. It was a quick wash and then into our fatigue clothes. Some late risers went straight from their bed to their clothes. Now and again, a member went to bed with his clothes on. We did not have much time to do anything, because we had to be on the Parade Square before 6:30 a.m. If you were late, it usually meant extra duties or some other punishment. – Supt. J. Religa (rtd.), Reg. #O.947, "H" Troop, 1953/54 (48)

"Depot" Division Trump Calls

Reveille	6:00 a.m.
Quarter Dress	6:15 a.m.
Markers	6:25 a.m.
Fall-in	6:30 a.m.
Quarter Dress	12:50 p.m.
Markers	1:00 p.m.
Fall-in	1:05 p.m.
Quarter Dress	5:45 p.m.
Markers	5:55 p.m.
Guard Mount	6:00 p.m.
Retreat	Time as per sunset
First Post	10:00 p.m.
Last Post	10:30 p.m.
Lights Out	10:45 p.m.

Trumpeters at "Depot"

The last boy trumpeter at "Depot" was Bill Perry who later became head of the Physical Education section at "Depot." After leaving the Force, Perry headed up the Regina Exhibition facility.

Reveille – in front of the A.B. Perry Building – May 1936

Boy Buglers in front of the Guardroom – 1905

Rites of Passage

Throughout the years at "Depot" Division, there were, and are, many formal and informal "Rites of Passage" that recruits and cadets pass through.

Seniority plays a large part in the majority of these advancements, and although they have to be earned, they can also be taken away.

Recruits and cadets enter "Depot" as the junior troop and, after each graduation, move up towards senior troop designation. Along the way, over six months, however, there are several stepping stones for both personal and troop achievements.

Junior cadets commence training in a modified uniform called fatigues. They are not issued Force black boots as the troops have to earn the right to wear them.

"Doubling" as it is known at "Depot," involves troops running or jogging together in troop formation between classes. This commences the concept of working in a team, promotes physical fitness and teaches the cadets some basic drill movements. Only after a practical test in front of the Drill Instructor, combined with verbal questioning about historical and academic issues, will a troop receive "their blues" (navy blue pants with yellow stripes). Called the "Blues Challenge," this permits the troop to march, as opposed to doubling everywhere. It is one of the most anticipated rites through the training program. Once a level of competence has been

Cst. L.M. Tuchscherer, Reg. #44212, Troop #10, 1992/93, wearing the senior troop designated uniform of the day

achieved, this does not mean that a troop can rest on its laurels. For the action of several, or only one cadet, troops can be stripped of their blues, while enjoying senior status, and suffer the consequences and wrath of troops junior to them.

Once a troop is deemed proficient in drill manoeuvres, it receives its "Marching Orders." They commence the rite of Noon Parade, with the newest (junior) troop at the back of the parade. As troops move up in seniority, they move up to the front of the Parade Square, ultimately becoming the senior troop, in Red Serge, on graduation day.

Along with moving up on the Parade Square, senior troops used to move up in the Mess by eating at the most preferred, designated dining tables, which had tablecloths.

The Halfway party is another milestone at "Depot." Held at the halfway point through training, the troop hosts a party in the Stand Easy Lounge to mark the occasion. This tradition has been adopted by several other RCMP training courses.

Senior troops at "Depot" have also been granted the privilege of walking on sidewalks. The origin of this tradition is unknown. However, in the late 1990s when senior management ruled it permissible for all cadets to use the sidewalks, an informal adherence to the tradition continued, with junior troops circumventing the utilization of the sidewalks.

Recruits on parade – they have yet to earn their "blues" – circa 1990

Upon arriving at "Depot," depending on the era, one had to obtain permission to leave the base. Leave Passes were granted, usually one weekend per month, and could be revoked at any time. Being CB'd (confined to barracks), for anything deemed worthy by the Sergeant Major, was very difficult to take given the limited amount of free time off the base.

Senior troops also have the responsibility of lowering and raising the Canadian flag each day, assisting in identifying inappropriate actions of junior cadets, and setting an example for junior troops.

Another rite of passage is for junior troops to serve senior troops at their graduation banquet. This duty is passed down to junior troops so that all graduates are provided the service from the undergraduates.

About graduation there were many truths and myths: from throwing the fedoras into Wascana Creek, burning the PT running shoes or other troop rituals, many of which were seen as rites of passage from a junior troop to senior graduates ready to begin their policing careers.

These rites of passage are held in high regard by all cadets and several have become traditions of their own.

No doubt, every member who passed through "Depot," could offer amusing stories of their training days. For example, at one time, prior to 1974, a Commanding Officer declared that all recruits must wear a "proper" hat when in mufti. The fedora-style hat was not popular among young men in those days, with the result that there was some difficulty in finding these hats at a reasonable price. Nevertheless, the Army & Navy store came to the rescue and stocked a line of "cheap hats" which served the needs of the recruits. This form of dress also became a symbol of a "rite of passage" as troops graduated from training. It became a custom among recruits to hurl these hats into Wascana Creek as they departed "Depot." To see a cluster of hats floating in the creek must have intrigued the many residents living in that area. – Inspector Dale Sheehan

Malcolm Wake, former Director of the "Depot" Museum, shares a great story told by S/M Bill Pomfret:
During the time of the mandatory fedoras, recruits were "supposed" to have a $100 bill in the top pocket of their uniform pocket. This was the result of a Friday morning inspection when the C.O. asked a recruit what was in that particular pocket. When the recruit said, "Nothing Sir," the C.O. turned to the S/M and asked him to tell the recruit what should be there. The S/M hadn't a clue what the C.O. was getting at and blurted out, "a $100 bill." "Quite right," said the C.O. and they carried on. This was repeated for a couple of weeks until the C.O. asked the S/M why the $100 bill. The S/M told him that at the time he had no idea what the C.O. had wanted him to say, so he just said the first thing that popped into his head.

Saturday Inspection

I never looked forward to Saturday mornings, because that was when a commissioned officer and his entourage came around to inspect your room, your equipment, your bed, your pit and, finally, you. If you were ever going to get in trouble for something, this was the time. You always knew a commissioned officer from a non-commissioned officer. The former had a lot of brass on his shoulders. One Saturday, at the morning parade, the instructor sent our squad to do fatigues in "B" Block. Although we finished our work in good time, the Sergeant in Charge of our detail kept us hanging around until just before the inspection was due to start. We rushed back to our room because we had only minutes to get ready. The only thing that we had going for us was that we were not the first squad to be inspected. Still, we had to get into our dress uniforms, and put everything in order. We were still getting into our uniforms and had fatigue clothes, towels and other things to put away, when we heard the inspection party on the first floor. There was only one solution. It was to finish dressing as quickly as possible and then throw everything that we had not put away down the fire escape. We did this and just made it to our pits in time to stand at ease before the inspection party entered room. Thank God, no one opened the door to the fire escape. – Supt. J. Religa (rtd.), Reg. #O.947, "H" Troop, 1953/54 (49)

Malcolm Wake, former director of the "Depot" Museum, recalls an incident when Commissioner Higgitt was visiting "Depot" with his father and they had gone on what was now the Friday inspection. He asked if he could take his father back into the dorm on Saturday morning. Despite pleas by the Commanding Officer and Corps Sergeant Major not to do this, the Commissioner explained that he wanted to show his father what a mess the dorm was following the weekly inspection. Sure enough, the dorm was not in its previous day's neatness and the recruits were suitably embarrassed, except for the one member sleeping

Members of Troop #26 preparing for inspection – 1991

buck naked on top of his bed, who later refused to believe that the Commissioner had revisited the dorm and thought his troop mates were playing a joke on him.

Sports

NWMP Rugby Football team – Commissioner Herchmer is standing in the rear row wearing a white summer tunic – Regina, May 26, 1891

As physical fitness played such a large part of grooming and training future Mounties, all sports were strongly encouraged and implemented in the Physical Fitness program and extracurricular activities. In the late 1800s, playing sports was a means of passing idle time. Years later, sports were integrated into the basic training program. Inter-troop rivalries and competitions were essential in developing recruits, emphasizing esprit de corps, fitness and sportsmanship.

Commissioner L.W. Herchmer put in an extensive effort promoting sports. Given the geography of outposts in the west, early settlers tended to gather near the barracks for protection and the NWMP assumed the role of community leaders as well as law enforcement officers. "In 1890, $1600 was spent on outfitting a bowling alley." (50)

Winners of Manitoba and North-West Territory Rugby Union Cup – Commissioner Herchmer is standing in the centre of the back row – 1894

The NWMP have been credited with introducing and growing such sports as rugby in the west. By 1890 numerous sports teams has been formed: baseball, cricket, football, lacrosse. On holidays like Victoria Day and Dominion Day, contests between teams from the barracks and town became regular fixtures. The wives of the officers and NCOs often played a big part in promoting recreation for the recruits. Mrs. Herchmer was the founder and president of the baseball team which was familiarly referred to as "Herchmer's Pets." (51)

In 1891, the Regina NWMP Roughriders represented the NWMP in the Hamilton Cup, championship of the North-West. (52)

Building #29 Curling Rink rear view of the north and west sides – July 1956

The RCMP was competitive in city and provincial sports and often reported that it was difficult to develop any first-class teams because they could not overcome the continual rotations of the staff. That did not, however, stop recruits from excelling in sports. In the fall of 1937, "Depot" converted one of the old stables into a one-sheet curling rink. A RCMP Police Curling Club was formed and had a membership of sixty members. (53)

In 1939, a "Depot" basketball team entered the Regina City League and was defeated in the finals by the Regina "Dales." (54) In 1938, Constable Primrose won the Provincial Heavyweight Boxing title for Saskatchewan. (55). In 1915, two instructors, Csts. Shank and Olinkin, held the Saskatchewan Amateur Heavy and Middleweight Championship Trophies for the year. (56)

"Depot" hosted numerous sporting events both internally and for the City of Regina and the Province of Saskatchewan. In 1934, His Honour the Lieutenant Governor, Brig.-Gen. Gordon, and Officers of M.D. 12 attended a wrestling exhibition and 9 bouts of boxing with medals being presented to the winners. (57)

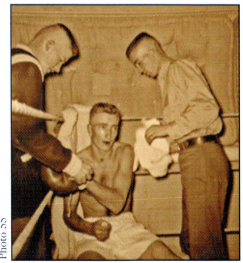

Cst. Merv Dickie boxing at "Depot" – 1955

CHAPTER 5 – TRAINING

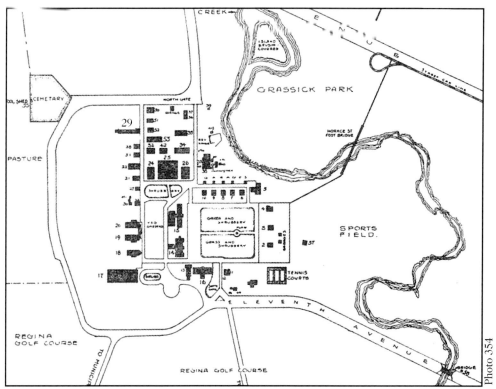

"Depot" Division – Curling Rink – Building #29 – 1950

Members of the RCMP who excelled in sports were often encouraged to participate in professional sports as well. In 1934 two members of "Depot" Division, Constables J.H.A.P. Miller and G.L. Sprague were chosen to play for the Regina Roughriders football team in the Western Championship finals at Vancouver, winning a two-game match 22-2 and 7-2. Both players also participated in the Dominion Finals and, although it was a losing effort, their efforts were reported as one of a good impression of their sportsmanship. (58)

This was not the only occasion that a member of the RCMP was selected to play for the Roughriders. In 1931, Stirling "Lighthouse" McNeil, as he was known to Rider fans, played with the team with the provision that the Roughriders signed a waiver in the event that he was injured, as they would have to bear all of the expenses. (59)

Regina Roughriders, Dominion Finalists 1931

Why was the "Depot" golf course sold?

During the Mulroney era, the federal government was short of funds and ordered that all unused government land must be sold. As part of the sales agreement, it was stated that if for any reason the Royal Regina Golf Club closed, they must offer it back to the Force to maintain a buffer between "Depot" and the City of Regina. Previous to this sale, a 99-year lease existed on the golf course, ensuring that the Force would eventually have the option to receive it back.

Original golf clubhouse on the left and the old "Depot" hospital on the right

"Depot" golf course

Tennis courts – east side of the Crime Lab

In 1936, three new tennis courts at the Barracks were completed and attracted a large group of recruits and staff. The tennis courts no longer exist on the base.

Track and field event on the Schrader Anson Sports Field

CHAPTER 5 – TRAINING

RNWMP hockey team – 1912

The old custom of holding organized sports on Wednesday afternoons was revived in 1941. The break in the week's work and studies was greatly appreciated by all. Participation included baseball, softball, tennis, soccer, field and mounted sports. Interest in water polo is being stimulated and two games have been played. (60)

Perhaps one of the most significant shifts towards sports was in 1967, which was the end of an era for "Depot" Division. Equitation was eliminated from training and the horses and equipment were shipped to Ottawa. The result was empty buildings, one of which was transformed into a hockey rink. The City of Regina and surrounding communities immediately benefited from the new facility with hockey tournaments and figure skating enthusiasts utilizing the ice to its full capacity.

"Depot" hockey team – 1937

Ice rink on the Parade Square

Recruits playing hockey – winter of 1955/56

The Arena

Centre ice at "Depot" Arena

"Depot" hockey team – 1979

In 2000, the Arena was closed down and redeveloped into a Training Scenario Complex. Many recruits and Saskatchewan residents have fond memories of the games played in the "Depot" ice rink, and it was with a heavy heart that facility was transformed.

Today, inter-troop competitions in sporting events do not occur as frequently as the Cadet Training Program is geared to a fitness and lifestyle program. When scheduled, however, sporting events and troop tournaments bring out the best in cadets and the competitiveness quickly accelerates, bringing back memories of training days gone by.

Members of "Depot" and "F" Divisions – Western Finals – 2003

Chapter 5 – Training   325

Swimming

Excavation of the base of the Swimming Pool – the deep end of the pool is in the foreground – 1940

Recognizing the importance of life-saving knowledge to a peace officer, the Force has provided the facilities to include swimming in the recruit training curriculum. "Depot" Division has one of the finest pools in Canada. – Special Cst. Canning – 1951 (61)

View of the south end of the pool – 1942

Relay races, inter-troop competitions such as murder ball and leisure activities were all a part of a lifestyle the pool provided. In 1971, as part of a fitness program, recruits were also encouraged to complete enough laps in their own time to swim the English Channel. The swim totaled 21.5 miles or 34.6 kilometers (1290 lengths of the pool). Those that did so were presented with a certificate of achievement.

The City of Regina also benefited from the pool, providing Red Cross classes and lessons to citizens. "In 1978 a Canadian record in professional long-distance swimming was established in the 'Depot' pool. Cpl. R. Cusson, an instructor at 'Depot,' and Mr. D. Pellitier, a swimming instructor with the Centre de Development Physique, Montreal, relayed for every two hours from 2 a.m. until 6 p.m. to achieve the new record, at the time, of 30 miles." (62)

In 2001, the swimming time allocated to training was one hour, concentrating on basic life saving skills. The pool was subsequently closed in the spring of 2002 due to a high level of mold infestation and structural issues. The pool is scheduled to reopen in the summer of 2006.

The main entrance to the Gymnasium/Pool Complex – 2006

Training

The meaning of the word "training," insofar as the Royal Canadian Mounted Police is concerned, is to educate in all the duties and knowledge required of a policeman and to teach him discipline. – Office of the Commissioner, Ottawa, Ontario, September 30, 1927

Lecture in "C" Block – 1936

Lectures in APS Building – circa 1975

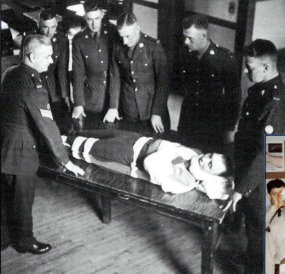

First Aid training – 1936

First Aid training – circa 1965

BEHIND THE BADGE

Cst. M.M.L. Malette, Troop #9, 1982/83, fingerprinting

Fingerprinting Techniques – 1936

Recruit Typing Class – circa 1965

Cst. M.M.L. Malette – Troop #9, 1982/83 – developing CPIC skills

Cst. R. Cook, Reg. #28122, joined the Force in 1970 and has served the last 20 years at "Depot," currently as a S/Sgt. with Executive Management Services

CHAPTER 5 – TRAINING 329

Lecture on basic engine dynamics – 1936

Care and Operation of Mechanical Transport – In the early years, a full series of lectures and practical demonstrations were given to all members, including tests in driving a car. Through the kindness of the Ford Motor Company, each squad of recruits was given a whole day's instruction and demonstration, by a Ford Motor expert, on the care and upkeep of cars, with a stripped car before them. This was done at one of the automotive sales offices in Regina and was of benefit to the recruits during their lectures and afterwards, when they were in charge of cars on detachment.

Learning the fundamentals of traffic control – circa 1990

Traffic Collision Investigation – circa early 1970s

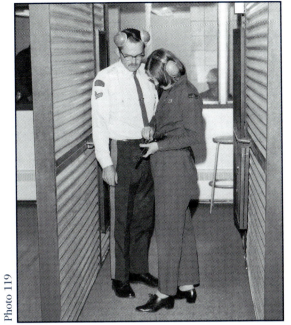
Firearms – revolver training – circa 1975

"Depot" Firearms Range – 1936

C&D Squad performing gymnastic displays – 1940

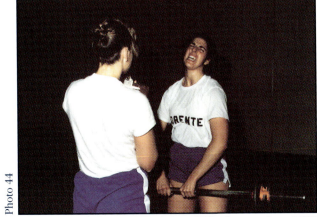
The agony of Physical Training (PT) class – circa 1990

An expectation, push ups! – circa 1995

*Death mask class
– July 1941
– Cst. G.R. Ruggles*

(Death masks of victims were used to make it easier on families when identifying a victim.)

Cpl. John Pullen conducting a drill class – April 2006

Daily lectures for the No 1 and 2 squads were given by the officers of the "Depot" in connection with the NWMP Police Constables Manual, Rules and Regulations, the Criminal Code, local ordinances and statutes, prairie and camp duties, veterinary matters, care of the horse, shoeing and subjects generally, which experience has shown to be necessary in the training of the recruit. – RNWMP Annual Report 1909 – Superintendent Routledge

RNWMP recruiting class on raising a sick horse – "Getting Up" instruction class – Cst. Ernie Feyer – 1917

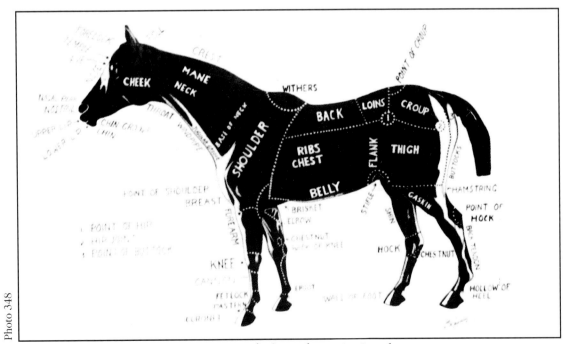

Cross-section of a horse for equitation class

CHAPTER 5 – TRAINING

Training Day – Tuesday, 26 January 1954

Reveille	6:00 a.m. Stables
Got done in good time	5 minutes lae (sic)
RCMP Act	review
PT	pass out drill and police holds
Portrait Parle	looked over types of questions
	Noon time and room still cold
Swimming	21 lengths – no clothes – 7/7/7
	High & low diving, treading water in fatigues (about 10)
Foot drill	pass out drill in gym
Studied first aid	for about an hour
	Put ground sheets over windows to keep wind out
	Got to sleep about 10.00

– Supt. J. Religa (rtd.), Reg. 0.947, "H" Troop, 1953/54 (63)

Training Day 1977

Daily Routine:

Following is the outline of a typical working day for recruits in training:

6:00 a.m.	Reveille
6:30 a.m.	Roll Call
6:45 a.m. – 7:45 a.m.	Breakfast
8:00 a.m. – 12:05 a.m.	Training (e.g., drill, lectures, swimming, P.T., etc.)
12:05 p.m. – 1:00 p.m.	Lunch
1:00 p.m.	Corps Sergeant Major's Parade
1:30 p.m. – 4:30 p.m.	Training
4:30 p.m. – 5:30 p.m.	Dinner

Evening spent studying, polishing kit, extra swimming, visit to Constables' Lounge, etc.

10:45 p.m.	Lights out

– Life at the RCMP Academy at "Depot" Division 1977 (64)

Courtroom – lower level of Applied Police Sciences building – 1977

Training Day 1987

Our training day starts early in the morning at "Depot" and frequently continues on into the late hours. Besides the normal training activities, you will be assigned extra duties to help maintain and run the Division, which also serves to provide you with a valuable training exercise in itself. A typical training day is as follows:

0600 hrs	Reveille – recruits rise, prepare dorms, make beds
0630 hrs	D.O. Parade – Roll Call taken by Senior Troop
0630 hrs – 0800 hrs	Breakfast at Division Mess
0800 hrs – 1205 hrs	Four training classes (50 minutes with 15 minute break)
1205 hrs – 1300 hrs	Lunch at Division Mess
1300 hrs – 1330 hrs	Sgt./Major's Parade
1330 hrs – 1630 hrs	Three training classes (50 minutes each with 15 minute break)
1630 hrs – 1730 hrs	Dinner at Division Mess
1800 hrs – 2230 hrs	Perform assignments as per duty roster, or free time if no duties
2245 hrs	Lights out (64)

– RCMP Academy at "Depot" Division – 1987 (65)

Training Day 2005

A typical day as a cadet at the RCMP Training Academy is as follows:

0600 hrs	Reveille
0630 hrs – 0700 hrs	Morning Parade
0700 hrs – 0800 hrs	Breakfast
0800 hrs – 1205 hrs	Classes
1205 hrs – 1300 hrs	Lunch
1250 hrs – 1320 hrs	Sgt./Major's Parade (on designated days)
1330 hrs – 1630 hrs	Classes
1630 hrs – 1830 hrs	Dinner
1800 hrs – 2300 hrs	Assignments and skill practice
2300 hrs	Lights out (66)

Cpl. Redd Oosten with members of Troop #20 discussing traffic collision investigation – 2002/03

Flip Charting – 2005

Chapter 6

Badges and Insignia

Royal Canadian Mounted Police Regimental Badge

The first regimental badges appeared on RCMP uniforms circa 1876.

The principle elements on the early badges can still be seen today: these include a bison head facing forward; the motto – *Maintiens Le Droit*; maple leaves; a scroll containing the title of the Force; a crown at the top of the badge over the word "Canada."

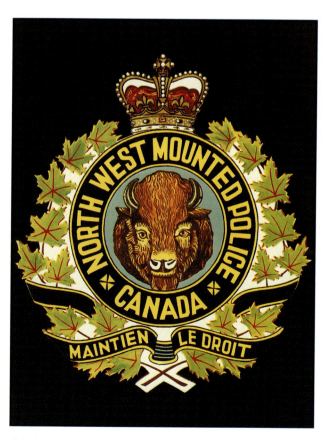

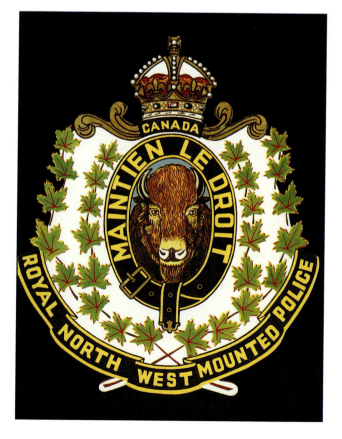

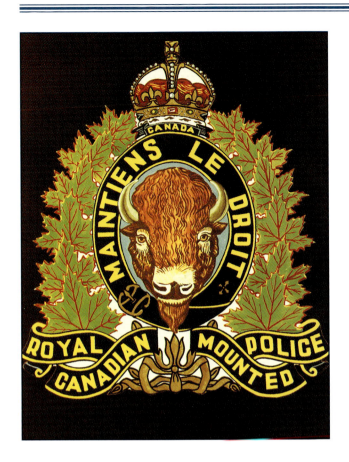

The "North-West Mounted Police" experienced two further name changes. In 1904 it became the "Royal Northwest Mounted Police," in 1920 the "Royal Canadian Mounted Police." The crown at the top of the badge has also changed to conform with the reigning Monarch – St. Edward's crown was adopted for Her Majesty Queen Elizabeth II.

The precise circumstances under which the bison head was chosen is unknown, however it seems appropriate of the close association of the RCMP with the prairie grasslands where early members depended on the buffalo for food, fuel and clothing. The adoption of the French motto gave the badge a bilingual character from the very beginning. At first the word "Maintiens" was spelled without the "s." In 1953 the badge was submitted to the College of Arms in England for redesign according to heraldic procedures. The newly designed badge, authorized by Order-in Council in 1954, used the motto Maintiens Le Droit. (1)

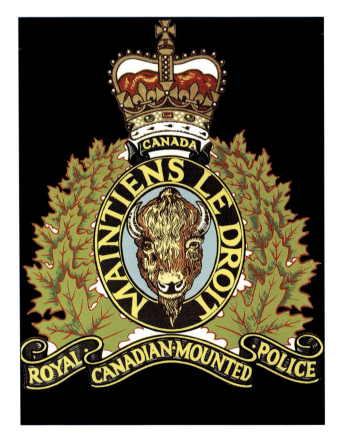

CHAPTER 6 – BADGES AND INSIGNIA

Force's Name Changes to RCMP – 1920

H. R. H. THE PRINCE OF WALES
NOW HONORARY COMMANDANT
Of Royal Canadian Mounted Police (formerly the Royal Northwest Mounted Police)--Reasons for the Change of Title

THE FACT that His Royal Highness the Prince of Wales has accepted the position of honorary commandant of the Royal Canadian Mounted Police came as an agreeable surprise to the Mounted Police as well as to the people of Canada, who esteem the honor thus conferred by His Royal Highness upon that historic force. It was also equally surprising but less gratifying when it was announced that the title of Canada's famous mounted corps had been changed. The following reprint is taken from Hansard, March 12th last, and is self-explanatory. It was during the debate on pensions for retired Mounted Policemen when this occurred:

Hon. N. W. Rowell (president of the council): The matter which I desire to mention to the committee arises out of the visit of His Royal Highness the Prince of Wales to Canada. While His Royal Highness was in western Canada, the Mounted Police provided him with an escort in the various cities which he visited; and, like other distinguished visitors, he evinced a very great interest in and appreciation of the work of the Mounted Police. I am glad to say that I have received a cable from Sir George Perley, Canadian High Commissioner, to the following effect:

> With His Majesty's approval, the Prince of Wales has graciously consented to accept the position of Honorary Commandant of the Royal Canadian Mounted Police, and His Royal Highness asks me to tell you how pleased he is to be associated with the force in this way.

Needless to say the Mounted Police greatly appreciate this conspicuous evidence of His Royal Highness' favor.

Hon. Mackenzie King: The force, as well as the people of the Dominion, will, I am sure, appreciate the honor which has been conferred upon that distinguished body by His Royal Highness. Most of the honorable members on the other side have spoken of the force as the "Royal Northwest Mounted Police." That title has a great deal of historic significance and naturally brings to one's mind past associations to which considerable importance is attached, particularly to those who reside in the west. There is a section of opinion in the country which seems to indicate that it might be advisable to retain the old title. I wonder if the government have further considered that suggestion.

Hon. N. W. Rowell: The bill of last session simply changed the word "Northwest" in the title to the word "Canadian," the title now being "The Royal Canadian Mounted Police." As the work of the force has been extended into eastern Canada, I am sure that members of the force in the west, who are good and true Canadians, will be quite

prepared to accept the change. The matter was carefully considered, and the approval of the executive officers of the force was secured before the change was made. Generally speaking, I have found that it has met with a great deal of public approval, although I am ready to admit that a few representations have been made to retain the old title.

Reasons for the Change of Title

Last summer quite a lot of controversial talk was indulged in, both inside and outside of parliament, regarding the change of name of the "Royal Northwest Mounted Police" to that of the "Royal Canadian Mounted Police." A sentimental attachment to the old name is held by the members of this world-famous force, especially by those who, in the days when Indians had to be conquered, went out into the wild west country, endured great hardships, and practically saved the western plains for Canada. All old-timers of western Canada have a fellow-feeling for the initials R. N. W. M. P. and for what they stand for, and it will take a lot of practice to say R. C. M. P. and to realize that the changed times have warranted the dropping the word Northwest and substituting the term Canadian therefor. The reason for this alteration is that the Federal government has established a new system in the organization of its police force.

Formerly there was a small police force for Canada in all the provinces, but now there shall be only one such force for all the Dominion. Now, instead of the Dominion Police and the Royal Northwest Mounted Police, there will be but one force whose ramifications and operations will now extend from the Atlantic to the Pacific and from the international boundary to the Arctic ocean. The government holds that this is a reasonable arrangement, because if Canada must maintain an army of federal police, there is no reason why it should be restricted to the prairies and the far distant North.

The Western provinces are just as peaceable as those of Eastern Canada, and the provincial authorities can keep order as well as those of Ontario, Quebec and the Maritime Provinces, and it does not follow that police will be stationed where they are not necessary.

It will be readily understood that police services may be municipal, provincial or national in character, and these should each be under appropriate jurisdiction. The question is not whether there should be a national police, as that matter was settled many years ago, but what should be its strength and cost, and how it should be distributed. This is a matter in which the federal government might take control conjointly with the provinces.

It will probably be found that most provinces will be agreeable to this plan or even ask for an inconsiderable body of men for serious and unusual emergencies, and for action in matters under national jurisdiction.

Photo courtesy of Regina Leader Post

HRH The Prince of Wales becomes first Honourary RCMP Commissioner; Her Majesty Queen Elizabeth II now holds this position

Guidon

The Guidon of the Royal Canadian Mounted Police was presented to the Force on April 13, 1935 at Regina, Saskatchewan by His Excellency the Earl of Bessborough, then Governor-General of Canada. The inclement weather resulted in the cancellation of an outdoor ceremony and it was subsequently held in the Riding School. One hundred and fifty members participated in the parade, which also included His Honour, the Lieutenant Governor of Saskatchewan and Mrs Munroe and Commissioner J.H. MacBrien.

Original Guidon

The Guidon "bears the crest of the Force in the centre in blue and gold on a scarlet background, the Guidon itself being fringed with an edging of gold. In addition to the Royal Cypher of His Majesty King George V in the top left and lower right corners, the letters RCMP are inscribed on the Guidon in the top right and lower left corners opposite to His Majesty's Cypher. Battle honours of the Force descriptive of the part taken in North-West Canada 1885; the South African War 1900-02: France and Flanders 1918 and Siberia 1918-19 appear to the right and left of crest." (2) At the bottom centre is the insignia of the Canadian Army Provost Corps, honouring the part members played in WWII by forming No. 1 Provost Company.

Interior of the Riding School during the presentation of the original Guidon – 1935

CHAPTER 6 – BADGES AND INSIGNIA

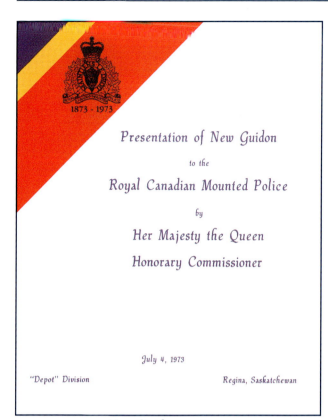

New Guidon program

The original Guidon performed its last official function July 4, 1973, when Her Majesty Queen Elizabeth II and Prince Philip participated in the parading of the new Guidon. The old Guidon was retired and is on display in the Force Chapel. At this ceremonial occasion, Her Majesty was presented with a new parade horse, "Centenial." The new Guidon performed its first official function at the Calgary Stampede on July 5, 1973 as part of a mounted escort for Her Majesty and is on display at the RCMP Headquarters in Ottawa.

New Guidon presented to the Force by Her Majesty Queen Elizabeth II in 1973

The Guidon on parade during the Memorial Parade – circa 1990

The Guidon of the RCMP serves as a unique standard for the Force and follows the regimental tradition of cavalry regiments deriving from the British Army.

The Guidon party is a small unit which carries the Guidon on parade and consists of a Guidon bearer Sergeant Major, armed Guidon escorts, Sergeant and a Guidon Orderly Corporal.

The Guidon is always paraded by itself or with other military colours only. It may not be paraded with other flags or ensigns.

The Guidon may be paraded:
- on the Sovereign's birthday
- at the funeral of a dignitary entitled to a 100-member guard of honour
- at a change of command ceremony for a new commissioner
- at a ceremonial commissioner's inspection parade
- at an RCMP Memorial church service and parade honouring members who have died in the line of duty
- at other mounted/dismounted ceremonial parades as approved by the Commissioner. (3)

CHAPTER 6 – BADGES AND INSIGNIA

How the Divisions Came to Have Their Letters

Ever wonder why "M" Division is called "M" Division? Or why the division letters from west to east don't flow in alphabetical order? Or which three divisions never got their letter designations? Did you know that the RCMP once had a "P" Division?

Force historian Bill Beahen provided the following explanation. "The first six troops of the NWMP were named using the first six letters of the alphabet from A to F. When they set up forts in the new territory, the letters designated their divisions. That's the simple answer. As the Force changed its organization, they just kept going down the alphabet, but they kept moving the divisions around. That's when it got complicated." Commissioners and their successors would reassign division designations. The RCMP had divisions named "Marine," "Air" and "Security Service" for which letters were never used.

The original divisions –
- "A" Division   1874, Fort Edmonton – 1920 provided to the National Capital Region
- "B" Division   1874, Fort MacLeod – 1949 provided to St. John's, Newfoundland
- "C" Division   1874, Fort MacLeod – 1932 provided to Montreal, Quebec
- "D" Division   1874, Fort Dufferin – 1919 provided to Winnipeg, Manitoba
- "E" Division   1874, Swan River – 1919 provided to Vancouver, British Columbia
- "F" Division   1874, Fort MacLeod – 1932 provided to Regina, Saskatchewan

Still curious about "P" Division? It was the training academy in Penhold, Alberta in 1966. (4)

The Royal Canadian Mounted Police Headquarters is located in Ottawa. There are four Regions, Pacific, North West, Central and Atlantic. Each region consists of Divisions which are identified by a letter of the alphabet.

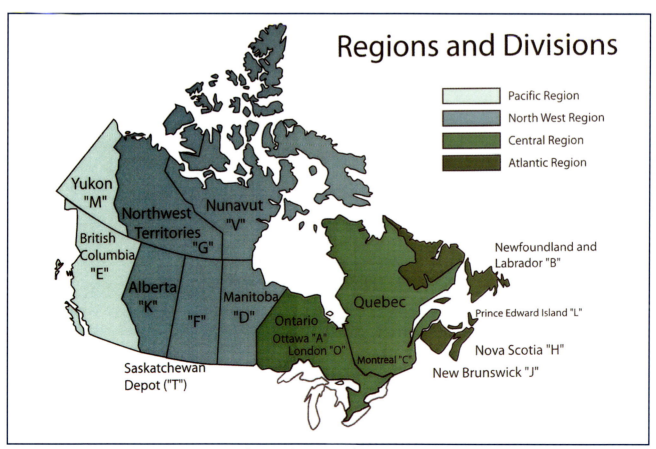

Current Regions and Divisions

342   BEHIND THE BADGE

Insignia of the Royal Canadian Mounted Police

Commissioned by Ranks

The three badges of the RCMP that indicate the commissioned ranks are: A crown, a star and a crossed sword and baton. Depending on the dress, the badges are worn on slip-ons, shoulder boards, or directly on the epaulettes.

The commissioned ranks of the RCMP are as follows:

Non-commissioned officers

Since 1990, the non-commissioned officers' rank insignia has been embroidered on the epaulette slip-ons and continue to be based on British army patterns. Non-commissioned rank badges are worn on the right sleeve of the scarlet/blue tunic and blue jacket.

The non-commissioned ranks of the RCMP are as follows:

Commissioner

Chief Superintendent

Corps Sergeant Major

Staff Sergeant

Deputy Commissioner

Superintendent

Sergeant Major

Sergeant

Assistant Commissioner

Inspector

Staff Sergeant Major

Corporal

Chapter 6 – Badges and Insignia

RCMP Corps Ensign

"Depot" Division RCMP Corps Ensign

… to be borne and used for ever hereafter by the Royal Canadian Mounted Police according to the law of arms of Canada.

In 1991, the Governor General, the Right Honourable Ramon J. Hnatyshyn, presented Commissioner N.D. Inkster the new RCMP Corps Ensign. During this ceremony, the Commissioner presented divisional ensigns to the provincial Lieutenant Governors and Commissioners of the two territories. Ensigns were also unveiled for the Commissioner, Headquarters, the Equitation Section and "Depot" Division.

The RCMP Academy at "Depot" Division is described as follows; Sabres crossed in saltire ensigned by an antique lamp all Argent – this badge combines crossed cavalry sabres representative of the Force's cavalry lineage and the hard police skills such as drill, self-defence, weaponry and in general the physical qualities of speed, strength and agility. This is surmounted by a lamp of learning which is the symbol of knowledge and wisdom. (5)

Mounties "Always get their Man"

A Hollywood theme reinforces that the Mounties "always get their man"

The saying that the Mounties "always get their man," is considered to be the creation of Hollywood. But, surprisingly, the phrase can be traced to 1877, many years before the film industry. In April of 1877, the Fort Benton (Montana) Report published the following story from Fort MacLeod.

Thanks to the vigilance of Major Irvine and the energy of Captain Winder, of the N.W. Mounted Police, another attempt to smuggle whiskey has been frustrated by the arrest of three men, who were tried, found guilty and sentenced to pay a fine of five hundred dollars each or be imprisoned for the minor period of six months. They preferred the former. Horses were sacrificed for the arrest, but the M.P.s are worse than bloodhounds when they scent the track of a smuggler, and they fetch their men every time.

This is the earliest record of the phrase that was later made famous by Hollywood. Interestingly, people often confuse this saying with the official motto of the Force, "Maintiens Le Droit." (6)

Wyatt Earp, marveling at the relative tranquility of Dawson while his own town exploded with violence and death, is reported to have said. "If I'd had a couple of those red-coated fellas behind me we'd have kept Tombstone clean for sure." (7)

Chapter 7

ACTIVITIES
Horses

A.J. Barker breaking a RNWMP remount in October 1919

S/M "Tim" Griffin, Reg. #10571, at "Depot" – circa 1920

When the Dominion Parliament passed an Act in 1873 to provide for the establishment of a "Mounted Police Force for the North-West Territories," the horses were vital to the work of the Force. The riders and horses faced formidable challenges with weather, lack of water, lack of experienced riders, unbroken horses and insufficient supplies on their westward march to the prairies. The horses proved very valuable for the thousands of miles of patrols that were required to maintain order through the decades, as settlements were established and the need for policing increased.

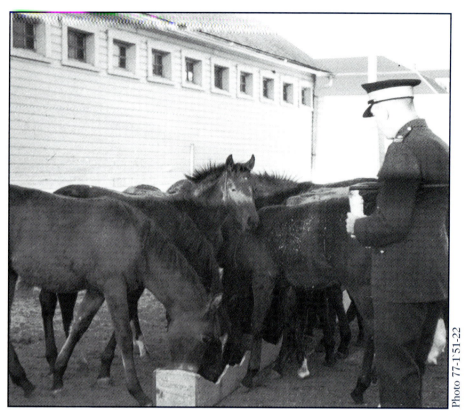

The procedure on the morning ride was for the men who had regular horses to saddle up and be ready to get on parade. Those not lucky enough to have a horse were to go to No. 4 Stable, an ancient structure dating, I am sure, from the last century. There, we took our pick of the unassigned horses. In wintertime, we had to grab an axe handle to break ice on the surcingle buckle to get at the saddles which, being stored in an unheated room, were covered with frost. The next job was to hammer the caulks into the horseshoes. This job was often impeded by the fact that all shoes did not always take the same size caulk, hence by the time the luckless trooper got going, he was dead certain to be late on parade and subject to the sulfurous recriminations of Griffin. At times, the corps sergeant major used more than his tongue to instill discipline. In the jumping lane, known as "suicide alley," the usual procedure of jumping with crossed stirrups and reins tied was often carried out with Griffin watching from the sidelines. Any man so cowardly as to "pull leather," i.e., grab the pommel, risked having large clumps of turf hurled at him as he attempted to stay mounted. This technique ensured that the guilty party's name was literally mud. – ex-Cst. T. Jamieson Quirk, Reg. #11951 – 1932 (2)

"Take care of your horse and gun and they will take care of you, were words of advice given to recruits in veterinary and musketry lectures." – ex-Cst. G.V. Wellman, Reg. #9948 – 1923 (1)

"Don't give your son money; give him horses'. No one ever came to grief–except honorable grief–through riding. No hour of life is lost that is spent in the saddle. Young men have often been ruined through owning horses, or through backing them, but never through riding them; unless of course they break their necks, which, taken at a gallop, is a very good death to die." Churchill.

This quote by Sir Winston Churchill hung in the Senior NCOs' Mess until its closure in March 2006

Cst. Milt Tyreman and Cst. Pete Whittemore – "Depot" Division Pasture – October 1955

By 1940, the practicality of horse patrols became obsolete with the advent of the motorized vehicle. However, the equitation training program at "Depot" remained sporadic due to the outbreak of the Second World War. By 1947, the equitation program was fully reinstated. In 1954, general recruit training was extended to two, three-month sessions and then to two, four-and-a-half month sessions. With the extension of the program, equitation was integrated, allowing for 100 hours of riding and 50 hours of stable duty. The recruit training syllabus in 1962 notes

Cst. Dennis Murphy, Troop #26, 1955/56, with "Pepper"

140 hours of equitation and 70 hours of stable management. During this time, the Treasury Board constantly questioned the value of recruit equitation training in relation to the costs involved. In the summer of 1966, with the need to economize, the federal government announced that the equitation program at "Depot" would cease. The Musical Ride was moved to "N" Division at Rockcliffe barracks on the outskirts of Ottawa and the breeding program moved from Saskatchewan to Packenham, in the Ottawa Valley.

Last Horse Parade just prior to final horse auction – September 16, 1966, "A" Troop on Parade – left to right, Cpl. Tex Shearer, S/Sgt. Harry Armstrong, Supt. K.B.M. Fraser, C.O. Supt. Vic Currie, C.S.M. Bill MacRae

CHAPTER 7 – ACTIVITIES

Cst. Matt Smith of "F" Division and Cpl. Raj Gill of "Depot" Division

Did you know that the brand of the RCMP – "MP" fused together was registered in 1887? The saddle cloth or horse blanket is called a shabrack – the "MP" can be found on the rear corner of the shabrack. (3)

The thought was appropriate –

The Force has been the recipient of many kind deeds and expressions of gratitude relating to its centennial. "Depot" Division has received its fair share of congratulatory messages – in varying forms.

The strangest was received on May 23 as a birthday gift for the Force on its 100th birthday from Bob Ruby, a disc-jockey for radio station WWL, New Orleans, Louisiana, which was attached to a carton containing 50 pounds of fresh carrots.

Much speculation surrounded the receipt of this parcel, until it was finally decided the contents were probably meant for our four-legged performers that are so well known to US admirers.

Surprisingly enough, no problems were experienced in dispensing the goodies. – RCMP Quarterly – 1973 (4)

"Depot" Horses

On June 6, 1999 two retired Musical Ride horses were donated to the Friends of the Mounted Museum through the kindness of C/Supt. Andre Thouin, Director, Public Affairs and Information Directorate.

The original horses donated, "Pedro" (a gelding, age 23, regimental #691) and "Wings" (a mare, age 18, regimental # 764), had both previously performed in the 100th Anniversary of the Musical Ride at "Depot" Division in July of 1987.

Currently, horses Falcon, Pepper and Pulsar continue to be crowd pleasers and are stabled at "Depot."

The role of the horses with their riders is to promote the Force through their appearance in Sunset Ceremonies, Noon Parade and local community parades during the tourist season.

The Friends of the Museum provided, at their cost, construction of the paddock and a permanent stable facility located in the northwest corner of the "Depot" arena. (5)

A new truck and horse trailer were loaned to transport the riders and horses to community events during the Saskatchewan Centennial in 2005.

Paddock at "Depot" – 2005

Fun at "Depot" Division

When "Depot" was a horse Division in the 1920s, we recruits looked forward to Wednesday afternoon when we took our mounts to the sports fields near the barracks for "fun and games." Wednesday afternoons could include familiar games such as tent pegging with lance and sword, tilt the bucket, jumping, boots and saddles, push ball and balaclava melee.

Boots and Saddles

Any number of men could participate in this game. All players went to one end of the sports field, removed all outside uniform, except britches, and all equipment from horses, except head gear, put all this in a pile and rode back to the other end of the field. When the players were assembled, a signal was given and everyone made a mad dash for his pile of clothing and equipment. The first one properly dressed and saddled would return to the starting point. This sounds simple, but to hang onto a horse that is plunging and fooling around and at the same time lace up a pair of riding boots is something else again.

Wrestling on horseback – 1917

RNWMP Sports Day Regina – "Tilting the Bucket" – 1917

Sports Day – 1936

Chapter 7 – Activities 349

Push Ball – 1936

Push Ball

The horses in this game had more fun than the riders. A push ball was identical to a soccer ball except that it was six feet in diameter and held 50 lbs. of air. The ball was placed at centre field and six mounted men on opposing teams lined up on each side of it. Each team endeavored to push the ball with the horses' chest and score goals. The horses would inevitably enter into the spirit of the games and would rear up in their excitement and put their front feet on top of the ball. Of course, they would roll off it. In a few minutes there were men and horses lying all over the field.

Balaclava Melee

Balaclava Melee

This game always ended up with many well-bruised bodies.

Each player wore a vest of white material, padded and quilted on the back, and a wicker helmet with a face piece (which offered absolutely no protection) and a four-inch red or blue plume on top of it. The players then lined up, red plumes on one side, blue on the other. Each man was given a wooden broomstick about three feet long and a wicker hand guard.

On the signal to start hostilities, the object was to knock the opposing team's plumes off their helmets with the broomsticks. It was a real melee with mounted men clubbing men and horses all over the field. The last man with his plume still in place won the game.
– ex-Cst. Dave Mason – 1980 (6)

Horse Troughing

Members of Troop #26, 1955/56 – A troop mate being escorted to the trough

The routine was hard, but high spirits prevailed, although at times it may have been somewhat unregimental. There was an old, but rarely exercised custom at "Depot" called "horse troughing." It consisted of seizing a man from his bed in the middle of the night and conveying him bodily to an outdoor horse trough, where he was dumped into icy water, after which the conspirators beat a hasty retreat to their barrack rooms. This punishment exercise was reserved for any individual considered a "real stinker." I recall only one such incident, where the victim was a decidedly unpopular lance corporal, whom I considered had earned the treatment. – ex-Cst. T. Jamieson Quirk, Reg. #9948, 1923 (7)

Horse troughing was an accepted practice then, but it has been banned since. It was one method that a squad had of punishing one of its members who was not giving one hundred percent to the squad's training activities.

Two methods of horse troughing evolved. The first was to take the person out back of the stables, where there was a ditch filled with a mixture of urine and manure that had run out of the stables. The member then was held down in the mixture and made to swim. The second method was a lot cleaner. The member was rolled up in his blanket when he was asleep. He then was taken to a trough in a nearby field. The member would be dumped unceremoniously into the water and left to fend for himself. – Supt. J. Religa (rtd.), Reg. #O.947, "H" Troop, 1953/54 (8)

Moustache parade was also practiced. This was where a member would be tied to his bed and then, as he slept, quietly hoisted, with his bed, to the ceiling rafters in "F" Block barracks.

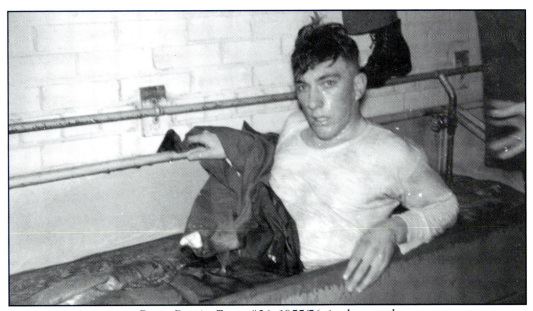

Roger Barrie, Troop #26, 1955/56, in the trough

CHAPTER 7 – ACTIVITIES

Horse Auction

During the 1950s and the early 60s, the Treasury Board of the federal government constantly questioned the value of recruit equitation training in relation to the expense involved. They pointed to the fact that the efficiency of the Force had not suffered during the war and suggested that perhaps mounted training should be abolished.

Many RCMP officers disagreed. They believed that young recruits matured through the discipline acquired by learning to care for horses and to ride in cavalry style. The riding master at Regina agreed with those officers stating, "The Mounted Police horse … is the equine detector of courage, or lack of it, in police candidates. Skilled tuition in equitation will replace timidity with boldness and develop a disregard for the inevitable bodily bruises which even the most proficient must experience. Handling of horses promotes mental alertness and rapid acceleration of muscular reflexes." (9)

Other senior members of the RCMP, although acknowledging the value of recruit equitation training, agreed with Treasury Board and pointed out that thousands of efficient members of other police forces had never taken equitation.

In the summer of 1966, the need to economize drove the federal government to announce that mounted training of RCMP recruits would be discontinued.

On September 17, 1966, the horses were auctioned.

Horse auction poster

Horses being auctioned off at "Depot," after the RCMP discontinued equitation training in 1966

Cars

Commissioner A.B. Perry, a man of vision and innovation, lobbied to ensure the Force progressed in their ability to police efficiently. Since 1914, the Commissioner had requested, and ultimately received permission to purchase a seven-passenger Model 55 McLaughlin in 1917, becoming the first car to Regina Headquarters. The vehicle had approximately 40-45 horsepower and was made in Winnipeg.

The first vehicle was utilized to transport prisoners from the "Depot" Division guardroom to the jail in Regina and other duties that assisted in effective policing. Horses were still, however, the main method of patrol and monitoring the Canada United States border into the late 1930s. (10)

Seven-passenger Model 55 McLaughlin – Regina – 1917

One interesting vehicle in the Museum's collection is a 1964 armored Cadillac, which was purchased by the Force in the U.S. The acquisition was from the United States Secret Services in 1968 and was one of four utilized for transporting and protecting President L.B. Johnson and other high profile dignitaries.

The RCMP utilized the armored Cadillac from 1968 to 1970 for Prime Minister P.E. Trudeau. In the early 1970s, the Prime Minister requested, and received, a new vehicle and the 1964 Cadillac was retired. (11)

Bill MacKay, RCMP Museum Director, with the 1964 Cadillac used to transport the President of the United States and the Prime Minister of Canada. It was later purchased for a visit by the late Queen Mother

Marked Police Car – 1999

Chapter 7 – Activities

Sergeant G.W. Brinkworth

Sgt. G.W. Brinkworth at "Depot" – circa 1912

A combined shot showing the original riding school on fire in 1887 and the school built to replace it

The interior of the Chapel used as an illustration in Haydon's Riders of the Plains *– 1910*

George Walton Brinkworth joined the North-West Mounted Police as a special constable in 1898. He served in Saskatchewan before going to South Africa during the Boer War. On his return, Brinkworth took up photography as a part-time hobby. Documents do not indicate that Brinkworth was an official Force photographer, but he was assigned the task with the implementation of the fingerprinting program, which required a photograph attached to the set of prints.

Brinkworth was one of several who was trained as a fingerprint photographer, and he was paid a dollar a photograph. Recruits also often paid Brinkworth to take pictures of themselves on horseback. Some recall that Brinkworth actually ran a studio right out of a building at "Depot." It is not known how Brinkworth was permitted to enjoy employment outside of the Force which, at the time, was contrary to the Rules and Regulations of the North-West Mounted Police.

Brinkworth was at times criticized for dereliction of duty due to being absent taking photos when he should have been working. However, due to the large number of officer photos that he took, he was able to avoid reprimands.

Brinkworth was promoted to Corporal and started publishing postcards. He was promoted to Sergeant and retired in 1912, leaving behind an incredible display of photographs documenting the history of the Force. He then began a career as a chauffeur for the Lieutenant Governor of Saskatchewan, maintaining his passion for photography in a small shack behind Government House.

"Depot" Guardroom – circa 1910

Old and new Officers' Residences at "Depot" Division on the north side of the Parade Square – it is believed that the toppled chimneys are as a result of the devastating tornado which hit Regina on June 30, 1912

Over the years, Brinkworth photographed many historical scenes and events for the Force, including the Prince of Wales' visit in 1919. Brinkworth's work has been credited with preserving the heritage of the wooden seats in the Chapel. When renovations were to occur, and the wooden benches to be replaced, a Brinkworth photograph circa 1909 showed the original pews in place and, subsequently, the renovators decided to preserve history and leave them intact, where they still stand today.

"A" Block and "B" Block – 1913

Sadly, the majority of Brinkworth's glass plate negatives were stripped of their exposed emulsion to provide glass for a greenhouse. However, the RCMP Centennial Museum received, through a donation, three dozen Brinkworth plate glass negatives which are safely secured today.

Sgt. Brinkworth's visual portrayal of the Force's history gives us a glimpse of a remarkable time in the NWMP and the RNWMP.

RNWMP muster parade – 1919

CHAPTER 7 – ACTIVITIES

Horses of RNWMP drafted for Siberia – 1918

The caption that this photo is the Prince of Wales arriving at "Depot" in 1919 is disputed by Force members due to the inappropriate deportment of the members lined up against "B" Block. Others feel a wedding party is departing from the Chapel – "C" Block is under construction on the left

Prince of Wales, centre, with Commissioner Perry on his left – 1919

Cst. A.A. Lunkie's Album

Cst. Antti Alfreet Lunkie, Reg. #12730, joined the RCMP in July of 1935. He died at the age of 29 during a flying accident on active service near Delacour, Alberta on April 14, 1943.

He left behind a treasury of photographs documenting RCMP activities.

Cst. Lunkie – 1936

Decoration Day, Regina, a day to remember fallen comrades – 1935

Barracks at night – February 1936

#4 Troop on the west side of the Riding Stable – 1936

#4 Troop on parade – 1936

Rifle Drill – Sleigh Square – 1936

RCMP Bands

The RCMP, from its inception as the NWMP, had musicians amongst the membership. Similar to the Musical Ride, boredom and camaraderie were instrumental to the formalization of the RCMP Band. The first band was formed in 1873 and there were occasional bands from that time on.

The mounted band was organized in Regina in 1887 by Sergeant J.F. Farmer, mounted left foreground. This band was very popular with the citizens of Regina. On occasion the mounted band would ride through the streets of town entertaining the residents. These bandsmen provided the musical accompaniment for the first musical rides.

Boredom has been the cause of most of the misconduct among the men, they had to seek any little amusement they enjoyed in the company of the usual inhabitants of frontier towns in billiard salons. The entire absence of theatres, concerts and other sources of amusement being extremely hard on young men, generally of good education, but with the advent of good recreation rooms and the establishment of bands in many of the divisions most of these drawbacks will be forgotten. – NWMP Annual Report 1886

In 1878, Sgt. Harry Walker, Reg. #308, joined the NWMP. As a bugle player in Fort Walsh, he was transferred and promoted to Regina when it became Headquarters. Undertaking to form a band, he had many talented men to chose from. Commissioner Herchmer was an ardent supporter of the band and did everything possible to gather instruments.

"The contributions of the Regina Band are credited with laying a foundation for the musical history in Western Canada." (12) Many pieces, still played to this day, are a heritage from the first band.

The monthly social balls were the high point for the community and countryside. With walls adorned with flags and trophies, red-serge-clad Mounties and a musical spectacle, the events were very popular.

The "Depot" band and recruits on foot parade. The Sergeants' Mess is located in the far left corner – NWMP, Regina, NWT – 1890

NWMP Regina – front centre is Sergeant Harry Walker, Bandmaster – 1892

True to the Force's background, there was even a concept and an attempt to have a mounted Band. Cliff Walker, Reg. #3760, stationed at "Depot" Division for several years, recalled that the Officer Commanding decided to organize a mounted band. They got the horses fairly "gentled" to carrying the instruments but the nervous animals never became docile enough to allow music to be produced upon their backs. Mr. Walker recalled that on a mounted parade in 1905, the horses snorted with fright as soon as the music struck up. Several of the riders were thrown and, with tails and manes streaming, their horses started westward. The O.C. came running out shouting to the young rough rider: "Walker! Get on a fast horse, gallop down to Regina Station and wire to our detachment in Moose Jaw to intercept the horses before they get any further into the "wilderness." (13)

In 1939, a RCMP Band was formed. Thirty-nine musicians, 7 cornets, 1 oboe, 9 clarinets, 1 alto saxophone, 1 tenor saxophone, 4 french horns, 1 baritone, 1 euphonium, 6 trombones, 3 basses and 3 drums. Recruiting of fully trained musicians took place in all parts of the Dominion. All members of the band had to meet the physical and educational standards of the Force, and were deployed to the Band. (14)

"The first official appearance of the Band was on May 25, 1939, to celebrate the Royal visit of the King and Queen to the barracks." (15) Concerts continued to be played for the community in and around Regina. Concerts at Wascana Park were a frequent occurrence and very well attended.

NWMP band on Parade Square – 1895

The force had two part-time bands, one in Ottawa and one in Regina "Depot." The members were made up of regular RCMP officers who had administration duties in the morning and band duties in the afternoon. The band in Ottawa was under the direction of Insp. Brown.

In 1958 the two bands amalgamated into one full-time band in Ottawa under the direction of Insp. E.J. (Ted) Lydall. The fulltime band had 28 members. In 1966 they recruited enough members to have a 36-piece band in preparation for Centennial Year and a six-month tour across Canada as part of the Centennial review. – Kenneth Iles – former RCMP band member.

During the early 1960s, Assistant Commissioner Perlson often lamented the loss of the "Depot" Band and, in his frequent meetings with Sergeant Major Bill MacRae, he would discuss some of the possible remedies. One of the early attempts to fill this void and provide martial music for the parade was to pipe recorded band music from the Guardroom with Sgt. Bill Perry standing in the window of "C" Block watching the parade with a record player arm in his hand. As the quick march command was given to commence the parade, Sgt. Perry attempted to match the cadence with marching music played over the PA system. The scratching and skipping music was more than S/M MacRae could take and he evaluated this initiative as an unblemished failure. Nevertheless, the Commanding Officer was determined to find a way. The idea of trying to create a band from among recruit "volunteers" emerged as an urgent project.

Bill Perry, a member of the Physical Training staff, had been a member of the "Depot" Band and had displayed his talent on the trumpet from time to time, playing at Remembrance Day services and funerals at "Depot." Perry was a trained drill instructor, a fact which was not lost on the S/M. The A/Commissioner was aware of this, and in his discussions with the S/M he indicated that perhaps Perry would try to form a band. To the

Cadet Tammy Um, Troop #1, 2002/03, preparing for Sunset Ceremonies

reader this might seem a casual observation. To the S/M (who understood the C.O.) it was clear that Sgt. Perry should start immediately.

With a long weekend coming up, it was agreed that Perry would gather some volunteers, with previous band experience, and shape them into the new "Depot" band – by Tuesday. Perry didn't let the C.O. down. As the 1 p.m. parade was forming that Tuesday, Bill Perry led the new band to the Square. There were 4 trumpeters, 3 drummers and Sgt. Perry directing the band with the aid of a shortened pool cue. The band clearly had some work to do. Nevertheless, as time went on and other recruits joined the band, it became a tradition which has endured for more than 45 years. The "Depot" recruit band functioned as a volunteer activity by replacing graduating members with new volunteers. New members were taught by those remaining and thus was formed a "Depot" Band which remains active to this day. Over the years the band has played in a variety of parades, including the Royal Parades in 1973 and 2005 when Her Majesty the Queen visited the Division.

As the original band grew and began to achieve some success, the A/Commissioner, began talking about developing a formal parade to which the public would be invited. His plan was to form a Tattoo display reminiscent of earlier times when bugles and drums were employed in signaling the troops to return. Today, Sunset Ceremonies can be viewed throughout the summer.

Cadet Dan Block leading the RCMP Cadet Band at Sunset Ceremony – 2001

As each troop starts training, a request for 3 volunteer cadets is made, musical talent or not, to join the band. The band members are coached and mentored by senior troop band members, and are quickly placed on parade. Within a very short time, these cadets are on parade with their instruments and, within weeks, can play several tunes and begin the process all over again, teaching newer cadets. Tourists and guests attending graduations and noon parades marvel at the accomplishments achieved by the cadet band in such a short time.

Over the years, the bands have come and gone in the RCMP. Today, the cadet band is utilized at every Sergeant Major's Parade and Sunset Ceremony and, with the RCMP Pipe and Drum Band, embodies the pride and glory of the Force bands of earlier days.

RCMP band at Sunset Ceremony – 2005

The Nine-Pounder Field Guns

Members standing behind the nine-pounder field gun and limber on the Parade Square – the NCOs' Residences are in the background – circa 1915

Two nine-pounder field guns came from the Imperial Ordinance Store in 1874 and were pulled from Fort Dufferin, Manitoba to Fort Whoop Up in Southern Alberta. The nine pounders, weighing 4,400 lbs., were known as "horse killers." The artillery were pulled by a four-horse team, and over the dirt hills of southern Saskatchewan six horses were required. The nine-pounders played significant roles in the Northwest Rebellion in 1885 and the fall of Almighty Voice in 1897.

The guns have been ceremoniously fired on a number of occasions. This included the formation of the provinces of Saskatchewan and Alberta, the Coronation of King George V in 1911, and during the Force's centennial year.

On May 28, 2000, the RCMP museum's 9-pounder gun and limber had the honour of carrying the remains of Canada's Unknown Soldier for interment from Capital Hill to the National Cenotaph in Ottawa. (16)

The nine-pounder is still used today during the Sunset Ceremonies. "Mounted on the cannon is **Honi Soit Qui Mal Y Pense** (Shame on him who thinks ill of it) stated by King Edward the III when a lady dropped her garter and he picked it up and put it on." This is the motto of the Order of the Garter.

Removing the cannon from Sleigh Square during Sunset Ceremonies

The Seven-Pound Bronze Mark II Field Guns

Cst. Pelletier standing beside the seven-pound bronze Mark II field guns – Regina 1935

Photo 3 courtesy of Cst. Lunkie

The acquisition of the 7-pound bronze guns by the NWMP in 1876 was in response to the threatened influx of Sioux Indians and their allies from the United States. Flushed with victory after annihilating General Custer's command, but fearful of US military reprisal, the Sioux fled to Canada to seek refuge. In the fall of 1876 and spring of 1877, approximately 4,000 Sioux crossed the border and camped at Wood Mountain, close to Fort Walsh. The anxiety of the NWMP command, concerning the precariousness of Fort Walsh, prompted the purchase of the four bronze guns for $4,464,40.

The guns proved useless on the prairie with their small narrow "mountain" carriages and limbers suited to pack horse hauling. The relations with the Sioux were for the most part friendly and the guns fired only during battery drills.

With the establishment of a new permanent headquarters in Regina in 1882, two bronze guns were transferred there. The bronze guns that currently flank the cenotaph were used at the Battle of Cutknife Hill in 1885 and the siege of Almighty Voice in 1897. (17)

CHAPTER 8

UNIFORMS

Evolution of the Uniform

One of the most recognizable Canadian and international symbols is the scarlet tunic of the Royal Canadian Mounted Police, often called the Red Serge by members of the Force. It is, without a doubt, one of new members' proudest days when they don their red serge one final time for the Sergeant Major's Parade and graduation pass out prior to leaving "Depot."

The Mountie uniform has been on Canadian currency, postage stamps, postcards, used to promote Canadian tourism, and is proudly on display at practically every significant national event.

The official dress uniform of the RCMP has undergone several changes since 1873. On the March West in 1873, the original members wore the Scarlet Tunic and the Indians regarded it as a symbol of honesty and fairness of the British soldiers in the West. Thus, the Mounties adopted it as their own uniform. The basis of choosing this uniform was to ensure that the North-West Mounted Police would be quickly identifiable with their British predecessors, as opposed to the Americans who were dressed in blue.

"It was once said that fifty men in red would be better than one hundred in any other colour." (1)

Superintendent R.B. Deane noted in his 1885 Annual Report that "the suitability of the present dress had long been a moot point. On the one hand, the red coat, from long association has the confidence of the Indians,

The earliest photo of members wearing official uniform – 1874 – in Fort Dufferin – scarlet Norfolk jacket, steel grey or beige-coloured beeches, blue trousers with white stripe, black or brown boots, pillbox or white helmet. The uniform became more ornate in 1876. Sub/Inspector John French (brother of the commissioner) is seated and Sub/Inspector F.J. Dickens (son of Charles Dickens) is second from right

Various orders of dress – circa 1900

Members standing in front of "A" Block – circa 1930

and conduced to the smartness and soldierly appears of the men. On the other hand, a red coat loses its colour amid the dust and dirt of the prairie travel."

In the early nineteen hundreds, after years of documented complaints, the uniform was revamped. The current-day broad-brimmed, felt hat, called the Stetson, replaced the original blue pill-box hat. The riding breeches are blue with a yellow cavalry stripe; they were originally a greyish beige.

When the Mounties were granted the prefix "Royal" in 1904, dark blue was added to the collar, shoulder straps and on officers' cuffs of the red tunic. Over the years, various badges depicting rank and service were also added. Members on the Musical Ride, Band, or other units have special insignia on their Red Serge.

The traditional dress uniform is still worn for parades, special events and formal duties, and is a staple on the RCMP Musical Ride. This uniform is called the "Review Order" and is the one most likely to be seen in Hollywood movies or television shows. Given the media exposure, it is not uncommon for tourists to be disappointed or surprised to discover that the Mounties do not wear the dress uniform for daily duties.

As the day-to-day duties of the Mountie changed, so too did the uniform requirements. Todays' Review Order uniform is a direct descendant of the original, which was replaced for practicality.

Members standing in front of the Riding School – circa 1905 (left to right) Sgt. Geo. W. Brinkworth, Sgt. Ike Phillips, S/Sgt. Littleholes, S/Sgt. Cunning, Sgt. Jacko Robinson

The day-to-day working uniform has also changed on several occasions. The Mountie on duty now wears a black Sam Browne, black shoes or boots, blue trousers with a yellow stripe and a peaked cloth cap.

Issued items such as Buffalo coats, moccasins, leather chaps, headgear, gloves, mitts, cold weather wear, have all evolved over the years to parkas, rain gear, storm coats and other protective clothing.

The original issued sidearm equipment was a leather belt with a bullet pouch and holster, which was carried on the left side. Later, the famous Sam Browne belt and shoulder strap was instituted with the bullet pouch and holster on the right side.

The Kit – 1901

UNIFORM

The changes which have been approved by Order in Council came into force on January 1, 1901.

The object is to make the uniform more serviceable, suitable for the work we have to do, and adapted to the service in both territories.

Pipeclay and blacking are discarded. Gloves and boots are of brown leather and can be readily cleaned. The proposed changes are as follows :—

Discarded—
- Helmet.
- Forge cap.
- White gloves and gauntlets.
- Tunic.
- Black boots.
- Cloak and cape.
- Black fur cap.
- Black lambskin coat.
- Mocassins.

Adopted—
- Felt hat.
- Service cap.
- Brown gloves and gauntlets.
- Brown boots (Strathcona pattern).
- Brown ankle boots.
- Field service jacket.
- Field service pantaloons.
- Fur cap, (Klondyke pattern).
- Elk mitts, with woolen mitts worn inside.
- Felt boots and black stockings.
- Pea jackets.
- Slicker and Sou-Wester

Proposed regulations for officers uniform, similar to that approved for the men' have been drawn up and will be submitted for your approval.

Articles adopted and discarded – January 1901

RCMP Tartan

In 1998, the 125th Anniversary of the Force, a tartan specific to the RCMP was approved and was presented to the Force by HRH The Princess Royal, Princess Anne, in Ottawa. The colours are derived from the colours of the Force's uniform and badge. Blue is for the traditional breeches; scarlet red for the tunic; yellow represents the cavalry stripe on the trousers of the ceremonial uniform, the band on the hat and the crown and gilt letters on the badge; the sienna brown represents the buffalo which is the centrepiece of the badge; forest green represents the Canadian maple leaf; white represents the lanyard; the sky blue colour is associated with the hat worn by the RCMP peacekeepers.

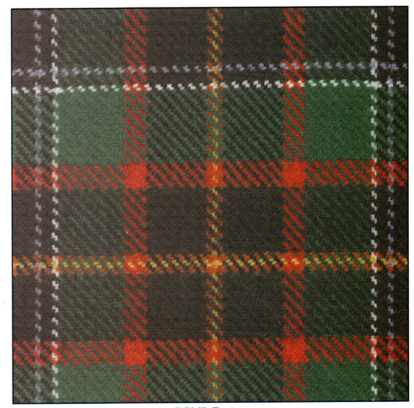

RCMP Tartan

Uniform modifications throughout the years

Sgt. Bob Stewart overseeing a troop during Sunset Ceremony – 2005

Cadets in Review order #1 – 2003

BEHIND THE BADGE

The Stetson

Members standing in front of the Stables – circa 1900

The same remark applies to the helmet, future issues of which should be of buff and brown leather. It would be better, also, if they were not so tall as the present pattern, which presents an unnecessary surface to the wind on the prairie, and is thereby rendered very uncomfortable to the wearer. – NWMP Annual Report 1885 – Superintendent R.B. Deane (2)

The pith helmets and pillbox hats quickly proved to be impractical headgear for patrol work and conditions in the West. The members began to buy their own items in what came to be known as, "prairie dress." The headpiece found to be the most practical was the wide-brimmed cowboy hat. The hats were initially pleated in a variety of shapes and styles – resulting in a lack of uniformity, and they were also made by several different manufacturers. The hats made by I.B. Stetson of Philadelphia were thought to be of superior quality, so the term "Stetson" became the description of the hat.

The Force's attendance at Queen Victoria's Diamond Jubilee in London in 1897 required the Force to make a decision to formalize the "prairie dress" of the Force. The headgear became a brown broad-brimmed felt hat with a brown leather hatband, with four pleats or indentations in the crown.

The Stetson hat, along with the red tunic, has become an integral part of the image of the Force.

The Buffalo Coat

Constable wearing a buffalo coat

The schedule of free kit in 1882 entitled every recruit to a buffalo coat, with an expected life of five years. Although heavy, the buffalo coats were very popular as they were capable of keeping the body warm in the coldest of prairie temperatures. The buffalo coat had large, rolled collars which could be pulled up to protect the neck and ears. They were made in several lengths, short for mounted duty and long for teamsters or dismounted guard duty.

The impossibility of furnishing the men who have joined this year with Buffalo overcoats has afforded me the greatest uneasiness, as the force in winter is quite useless without such protection and as yet no efficient substitute has been found. For this winter we are, however, well supplied by the arrival of seventy-five guard coats, with which we can manage this season. – NWMP Annual Report 1885 – Superintendent R.B. Deane (3)

Due to the rapid decline of buffalo herds, in 1887 the coats were removed from the list of free kit. Thus all new supplies of buffalo coats were retained in Division Stores and only loaned when duty necessitated it.

In 1887, a board of officers examined samples of kangaroo, sheepskin and calfskin as possible substitutes. Kangaroo was too expensive and the black dye on the sheep and calfskins bled on the faces, hands and tunics when wet. In 1898 it was reported that the last of the usable coats were supplied to men transferred to the Yukon that year.

The kits of the men are now generally very complete and the articles of clothing issued satisfactory, with the exception of the great coats which neither possess the strength nor are sufficiently waterproof for the use of a Force exposed to so much hard work and weather. The disappearance of the buffalo and the difficulty in replacing the coat of that fur hitherto in use with a suitable substitute, has rendered us short of fur coats. At present we are trying an article called "Montana Calf," and if natural black skins of this quality could be used instead of dyed ones, I think this want would be met. The coats supplied this year are long and split-tailed, affording good protection to the men's legs either riding or driving. – NWMP Annual Report 1887 – Commissioner L.W. Herchmer (4)

In 1930, the Force was able to obtain seven hundred buffalo skins through the National Parks Branch and the buffalo coat was once again issued.

In 1951, the Commanding Officers were polled concerning the winter outerwear of the Force. The consensus was that the buffalo coat was too heavy and cumbersome. Malcolm Wake recounted that when on foot patrol some members would find a dark spot on a wall with a spike sticking out on which they could hang the coat collar while they relaxed inside once the weight was removed.

By 1954, the short buffalo coat was replaced with the regimental parka. The full-length buffalo coats used on Parliament Hill were replaced by a blue coat in 1961.

Kit – Stores

Currently, cadets are issued kit three times during their stay at "Depot." This occurs during their first week of training, between the 9th to 12th week of training and the 15th to 17th week of training.

The cost to kit a male cadet to become field ready is $3,142.97; for a female cadet it is, $3,056.27.

Stores Services has a 'first day' to 'last day' relationship with cadets. Upon arrival at the Academy Guard room, cadets are issued with bedding that has also been prepared in advance by Store's staff. Bedding, issued on loan, includes 2 blankets, 2 fitted sheets, 2 flat sheets, 2 pillow cases, 1 pillow with 1 zippered cover and 3 towels. At 7:00 a.m. on the first Monday or Tuesday of training, a troop receives a one hour welcome and introduction, which tells cadets about the kit issue process. They are loaned judo gis, issued with numbered red plastic guns which have to be returned at the end of training and gym bags with contents that don't have to be sized. These bags are prepacked by Store's staff.

An interior view of Stores – in the basement of "C" Block – 2005

On the last day at the Academy, Stores sees cadets again as they ship personal effects to their detachments. At this time they may use some of the 6,000 cardboard boxes that staff assemble and tape, and may purchase one of the 900 wardrobe boxes used each year. Stores staff see each troop a minimum of three times during the 22 weeks of training.

A basic cadet kit issue costs approximately $3,200.00 and consists of more than fifty individual items, the majority of which need to be fitted or altered in some way. RCMP stetsons, for example, come in 48 sizes. It takes a great deal of understanding to get the fit just right. About 2,000 line items are stocked, with a total average inventory value, including ammunition, of nearly three million dollars. This fiscal year they will issue in excess of $3.2 million worth of uniforms. (5)

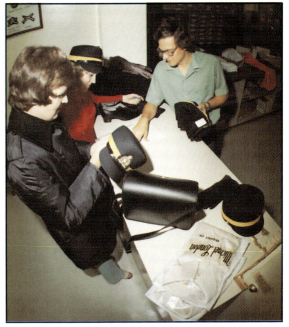
Female recruits issued kit – circa 1975

SCHEDULE of Free Kit issued to Constables.

Articles issued on joining, to be kept in serviceable condition at the Constable's expense during his whole term of service:—

Buffalo Robe	1
Blankets	2 pair.
Waterproof Sheet	1
Buffalo Coat	1
Cloth Overcoat	1
Helmet	1
Fur Cap	1
Gauntlets, Buckskin	1 pair.
Drawers, Woollen	2 "
Undershirts, Woollen	2
Overshirts, Flannel	2
Socks, Woollen	4 pair.
Stockings, Woollen	2 "
Mitts, Woollen	1 "
Spurs	1 "
Towels	2
Kit Bag	1
Haversack	1
Mocassins	1 pair.
Holdall	1
Knife	1
Fork	1
Spoon	1
Razor and Case	1
Comb	1
Shaving Brush	1
Blacking "	1
Polishing "	1
Cloth "	1
Button "	1
" Brass	1
Sponge	1
Burnisher	1
Cup	1
Saucer	1
Plate	1

Articles issued annually, to be kept in serviceable condition at the Constable's expense:—

Forage Cap	1
Tunic, Serge	1
Jacket, Stable	1
Breeches, Cloth	2 pair.
Trousers, Stable	1 "
Boots, Long	1 "
" Short	1 "

One Scarlet Cloth Tunic will be issued to each Constable on joining, and another during his third year of service.

Kit issued to Constables – circa 1900

Troop forming up in front of Applied Police Sciences – carrying issue gym bags – circa 1990

Cadet Gym Bag Issue:

- spurs, per set (2 for males, 1 for females)
- suspenders
- flashlights
- batteries
- film
- VCR tape
- ASP baton and holder
- DNA kit
- ball cap
- cap covers
- scarves
- collar and shoulder badges
- ceremonial buckle
- lanyard
- mouth guard
- handcuffs
- purse for females

Winter issue Gortex boots – 2002

Issuing kit – 1975

CHAPTER 8 – UNIFORMS 373

Preston Haynee assisting a cadet with gloves – 2002

Your kit will be issued to you in the Q.M. stores. Get your kit together as soon as possible. It is against regulations to buy and sell kit. Certain articles of kit may be purchased on repayment from the Q.M. stores, the price of which will be deducted from your monthly cheque. Make sure you really want the article before you buy it in this way. You will need some money for that leave period that is coming. – A Guide To Success – 1960 (6)

In 1990, the RCMP canteen at "Depot" Division exhausted their supply of Kiwi Shoe Polish "Mahogany" brand. This brand gave the Mounties the distinctive "spit and polish" shine on their high brown boots and Sam Browne leather kit. The problem was, that given the insignificant sale the brand generated, that Kiwi discontinued producing same. As a result of negotiations, Kiwi agreed to produce another 10,000 cans exclusively for the RCMP. (7)

Rick McIlvenna ensuring a good-fitting storm coat – 2002

Cost of placing a Member in Red Serge – 1 February 2006

	Male	Female	Cost in 1973 (8)
Stetson	$ 145.93	$ 145.93	$ 16.30
Leather Hatband – Stetson	10.07	10.07	1.10
Strathcona Boots	386.83	372.21	29.50
Breeches	102.82	112.07	21.00
Brown Gloves	28.48	36.72	4.15
Lanyard	2.79	2.79	0.90
Scarlet Tunic	181.05	182.76	48.10
Collar Badges	2.16 x 2	2.16 x 2	0.90
Shoulder Badges	2.59 x 2	2.59 x 2	0.90
Straps/Tabs	25.50	25.50	
Spurs, Jack	27.19	27.19	3.90
Brown Holster	29.44	29.44	19.95
Sharpshooter Badges	.39	.39	(for brown holster & Sam Browne Assembly)
Sam Browne Assembly	90.38	90.38	
Hat Strap	1.90	1.90	
Total	**$ 1,042.27**	**$1,046.85**	**$146.70**

Stetson $145.93
Hat Band $10.07
Badge Collar $2.16
Badge Shoulder $2.59
Lanyard $2.79
Scarlet Tunic $181.05
Sam Browne Holster $29.44
Sam Browne Assembly $90.38
Sharp Shooter Badges $0.39
Brown Gloves Unlined $28.48
Breeches $102.82
Boots $386.83
Straps & Tabs $25.50
Jack Spurs $27.19

Chapter 8 – Uniforms

Clothing Stores

The following clothing items known as Scale "A" will be issued to you in your first week at the training division. This clothing is free but should it wear out or become lost then you will be required to purchase replacements on repayment (Form S 201). You will receive a Kit Upkeep Allowance of $6.00 per month. This amount is included on your pay cheque each month. Purchases of kit and clothing are paid for by "pay stoppage" and it is deducted from month end pay cheque.

Kit descriptions and price lists are posted in the typing rooms. Sample copy of S 201 the repayment requisition is found in the typing room and clothing stores. Scale "A" purchases may be picked up at the clothing stores between 8:30 a.m. and 12:00 noon and from 1:00 p.m. to 5:00 p.m. each day Monday through Friday.

Scale "A":

1 Grey Blanket and 1 Brown Rug will be loaned to you while in Training at Regina. Both items will be returned to Stores before you leave this Division.

Badges, cap – 2	Clips, tie – 1	Shirts, under – 2
Badges, collar – 4	Drawer, pr – 2	Shirts, gym – 3
Badges, shoulder – 4	Gloves, lined, pr – 1	Shorts, gym – 3
Bags, dunnage – 1	Gloves, unlined, pr – 1	Slips, pillow – 2
Bands, hat – 1	Haversacks – 1	Socks, pr – 6
Batons – 1	Lanyards – 2	Spurs, box pr – 1
Belts – waist – 1	Mitts, leather, pr – 1	Spurs, jack pr – 1
Boots, ankle – 2	Mitts, woolen, pr – 1	Straps, hat – 1
Boots, congress – 1	Over boots, pr – 1	Sweater, pullover – 1
Boots, gym – 1	Pillows – 1	Ties, blue – 3
Braces – 2	Sheets, cotton – 4	Towels, bath – 3
Caps, cloth – 2	Shirts, over – 4	Towels, hand – 3

The following items of clothing are also a free issue, but the Force is responsible for the upkeep of these articles which are classified as Scale "B." This means that they may be exchanged after being condemned by an Officer and approved by the Commanding Officer. Copies of the way the forms should be submitted are hanging in the clothing stores, and may be perused at any time the Stores are open. Kit which is to be condemned should first be brought to the attention of the Drill Staff before a requisition is made for new kit.

Immediately after the clothing has been issued to you, all items that require alteration or adjustment should be taken to the Tailor Shop or the Saddler's shop.

Should kit issue be the wrong size, then return it immediately unused to the clothing stores, and a form S 2222 J will be completed for the exchange to the right size.

Every time kit is obtained from Clothing Stores, ENSURE YOU HAVE SIGNED FOR IT AND THAT THE ITEM(S) ARE IN GOOD CONDITION.

Scale "B":

Blouses, field – 2	Caps, fur – 1	Peajacket – 1
Books, Constables Manual – 1	Equipment – Sam Browne – 1	Slickers, black – 1
Books, First Aid – 1	Hats, felt – 1	Trousers, blue pr – 1
Boots, long pr – 1	Jackets, brown – 1	Trousers, field pr – 1
Breeches, pr – 1	Overalls, blue pr – 1	Tunic, scarlet – 1

Scale "B" kit may be exchanged at any time on all days from Monday to Friday inclusive. Extra issues of brass buttons and fittings for Sam Browne equipment are not available.

Tailor Shop and Leather Craft Shop

The image of the Royal Canadian Mounted Police is world renowned. The red serge is used in Canadian tourism promotions, Hollywood movies, television shows, postcards and souvenirs. One need not look far in Canada or abroad to recognize the uniform of the RCMP.

All this begins at "Depot" Division, where the pride and significance of the uniform is passed on to cadets. Behind the scenes at "Depot" are hard-working employees who first issue kit to cadets and then specifically alter, tailor and prepare kit for each cadet.

NWMP Annual Report 1886:

The physique of the force is very fine and improving all the time, the trouble being to get clothing large enough; but now that our clothing is generally made in Canada, with proper size rolls there should be no difficulty in guarding against this mistake.

NWMP Annual Report 1887
– Superintendent R.B. Deane

The clothing and kit supplied are generally satisfactory, but the want of competent tailors is much felt. I would very strongly recommend the establishment of a master tailor and staff at headquarters, by whom the several articles of uniform are, at all times, made strictly according to the measurements of the various sizes and, required or not, a certain amount of alteration is invariably necessary, entailing inconsistent and undue expense.

To keep this Force dressed as it should be, a year's supply of clothing should always be on hand at Regina, under the present system since I have taken command, we have always been short.

The Leather Shop customizes the RCMP kit, including all leather and footwear. Although the uniforms are manufactured in Ottawa and Montreal, and the high brown boots in Alberta, this is just the preliminary step in ensuring the uniform is custom-made for each cadet.

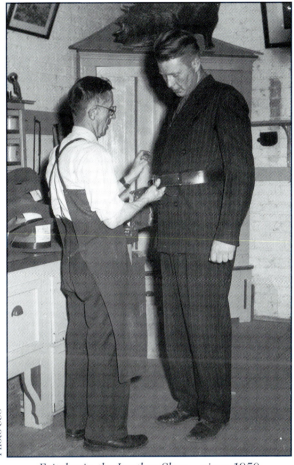

Fritzler in the Leather Shop – circa 1950

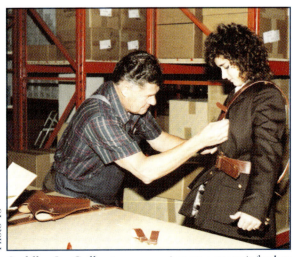

Saddler Joe Gallenger measuring up a recruit for her Sam Browne – 1990

Chapter 8 – Uniforms

Trying on the "Strathcona boots" – 1990

Aside from the regular uniform which is worn on a day-to-day basis by the members of the Force, altering Stetsons, red serges, boots and breeches is a complex operation. Over the years, special and unorthodox methods have been tried and true in the Leather Shop, including soaking the leather high browns in water to give them special shapes.

As for the tailors, there are few places that can actually tailor breeches in the proficient manner in which it is done at "Depot." Faced with so many measurements, the RCMP breeches are a unique challenge for even the highest caliber of tailor.

Over the years, the tailor and leather shops have experienced a wide variety of challenges. With cadets that range from 4'9" to 7'4" and from 95 lbs. to 340 lbs., from size 5 boots to size 15, they are prepared for every challenge.

There are three leather-crafts persons and thirteen tailors, all having state-of-the-art abilities and qualifications.

The employees behind the scenes still get satisfaction on a daily basis when they measure up cadets for the famous red serge or high brown boots. Watching the cadets marching on graduation day means a "finished product for these employees – they share in the pride."

Name Tags

In the 1970s the saddler made black leather name tags for recruits to wear. The recruits had their names written in black tape until they were senior troop, at which time they switched to red to signify their new responsibilities.

Tailor Shop – circa 1950

Making adjustments – Dan Heiberg in the leather shop

Theresa Tran working on a red serge – 2002

Chapter 9

HISTORICAL CALENDAR

1869   Sir John A Macdonald proposed the formation of a mounted police force to establish law and order in the North-West Territories.

1873   Order in Council approved the creation of the North-West Mounted Police.

1875   Headquarters based at Swan River barracks near Pelly, Saskatchewan.

1876   Headquarters moved to Fort McLeod.

1878   Headquarters moved to Fort Walsh.

1882   Headquarters transferred to Regina from Fort Walsh – Prefabricated buildings arrived from eastern Canada and reassembled over the winter of 1882/83.

1883   Mess Hall erected by local artisan (currently the RCMP Chapel). Senior NCOs' Mess built on the south side of the Parade Square.

1884   Cst. W. Armstrong first member to be buried at the "Depot" Cemetery.

1885   Commissioner A.G.Irvine urged the government to establish a permanent training centre. On November 1, "Depot" Division was created. Louis Riel executed at the Guardroom. The erection and repair of Force buildings turned over to the Department of Public Works.

1886   Prime Minister Sir John A. Macdonald visits "Depot." Officers' Mess sanctioned by Sir John A. Macdonald. Original Riding School built – 68 meters by 37 – largest structure in Regina.

Original Riding School built in 1886

"A" & "B" Block constructed in 1887

1887 Original "A" Block and "B" Block completed. Mounted Band organized by Sergeant J.F. Farmer. First officially recorded Musical Ride performed in Regina. Commissioner's House built on the northeast corner of the Parade Square. Post Hospital constructed. Original Riding School burns to the ground.

1889 Riding School rebuilt – almost identical to the original. Mess Hall converted to a reading room and Post Canteen. Boardwalk was extended to connect the Academy with Regina.

1890 First trees, obtained from Dominion Experimental Farms, planted; most did not survive and were replanted in 1891. Twenty-meter water tower erected on the Square.

Near Water Tower, erected in 1890, Squads #1 and #2 preparing for transfer to the Yukon

1893   Commissioner's annual report indicated prefab buildings were not standing up well, very costly to heat and recommended their replacement.

Church Parade – NWMP – Regina, on Parade Square – 1895

1895   Kitchen fire in Mess Hall resulted in Mrs Herchmer suggesting structure become a chapel.

1896   First electric lights installed throughout "Depot."

1900   Division Mess built and attached to the rear of "B" Block.

Two cement light pillars were installed on either side of the south entrance to "Depot" in 1896 – this photo circa 1915

1904   King Edward VII bestowed the prefix "Royal" on the NWMP in recognition of the Force's service to Canada.

1907   "Depot" hooked up to the Regina water system.

CHAPTER 9 – HISTORICAL CALENDAR

Preparation for King George V's coronation – 1911

1910 Water tower demolished and lumber used to build a new bridge over Wascana Creek.

1911 82 members and 80 horses attend King George V's coronation in London.

1912 "A" Block destroyed by fire and rebuilt – currently the A.B. Perry Building. Officers' Mess demolished and moved to former Commissioner's residence. Library and 2,300 volumes contained in "A" Block destroyed by fire.

"A" Block destroyed by fire and rebuilt in 1912

1913 Senior NCOs' Mess relocated to "A" Block.

1914 Heating Plant opened.

1917 First car arrived at "Depot" – seven-passenger Model 55 McLaughlin.

Prince of Wales visits "Depot" in 1919

1919   The Prince of Wales visited "Depot." "C" Block was hastily erected due to several hundred men who had returned from Siberia and were housed in tents in November.

1920   RNWMP changed to RCMP and assumed responsibility of the Dominion Police which resulted in a broader mandate and a jurisdiction that extended from sea to sea. Headquarters moved to Ottawa. Second Riding School destroyed by fire.

Members returned from Siberia in 1919 and were housed in tents near Riding School #2 which was destroyed by fire in 1920

CHAPTER 9 – HISTORICAL CALENDAR

1925	His Royal Highness The Duke of Connaught inspected "Depot" Division.
1929	Riding School rebuilt – presently the Drill Hall.
1930/31	Post Garage built, later extended to the north in 1953.
1931/32	Duplex on the south side of the Parade Square built.
1932/34	Training divided into two parts – academic and physical.
1933	Museum established.
1934/35	Central Heating plant is built.
1935	Cenotaph was unveiled. Guidon presented to the Force by His Excellency the Earl of Bessborough. Mid-30s, Memorial Service became an annual event to honour fallen comrades.
1936	Crime Lab created in the Officers' Mess. Original "D" Block constructed, also known as the Artisan's Workshop (currently the Resource Centre).
1937	Parliament authorized the formation of Police Reserves, resulting in subsequent training at "Depot."
1937/38	Two-storey brick addition to "A" Block to house extra offices – Self-Defence Building erected (old PDT Gym).
1938	"A" Block renovated. Crime lab moved to "C" Block. Rifle Range built in the basement of the Gym (currently PDT Gym).
1939	Their Majesties King George VI and Queen Elizabeth honoured "Depot" by their visit. Lecture Hall built. Steeple added to the Chapel.

King George V and Queen Elizabeth depart from the Chapel during their visit in 1939

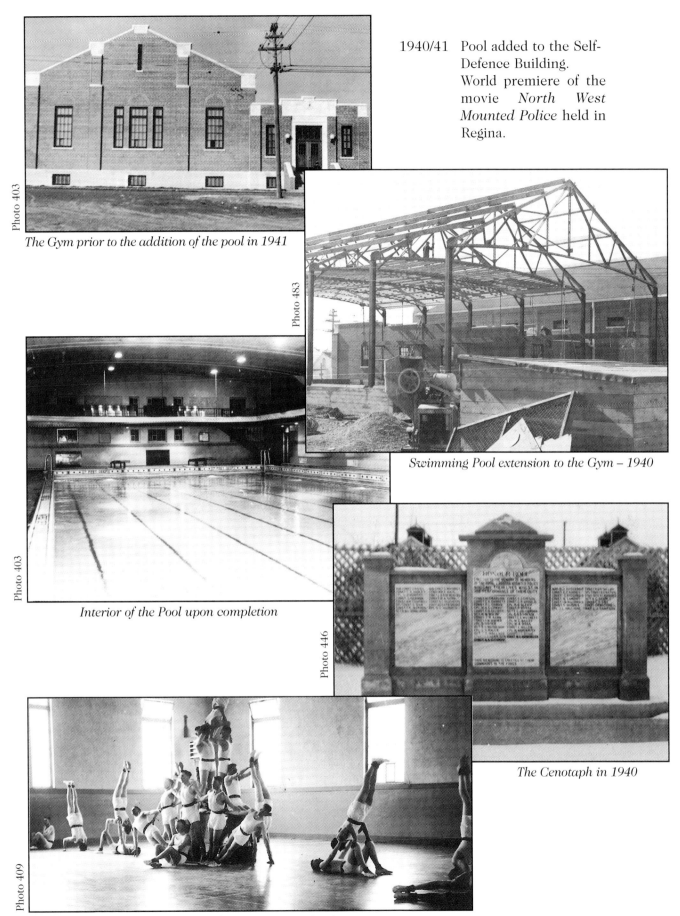

The Gym prior to the addition of the pool in 1941

1940/41 Pool added to the Self-Defence Building. World premiere of the movie *North West Mounted Police* held in Regina.

Swimming Pool extension to the Gym – 1940

Interior of the Pool upon completion

The Cenotaph in 1940

C and D Squads perform gymnastic displays in 1940

CHAPTER 9 – HISTORICAL CALENDAR

1942   30,000 caragana seedlings, 800 young trees and 25,000 plants were set at "Depot."

1943   MTC erected (formerly known as the Post Hospital – renamed 1974/75). Flagpole erected at the east side of Sleigh Square by "P" Squad in September 1943.

A view of "Depot" from the Commanding Officer's Residence – circa 1945

1949   Walk-through tunnels for heating piping commenced.

1950   Unveiling of the St Roch monument on Sleigh Square.

1952   1,000 trees planted at the Schrader Anson Sports field.

1953   Crime Detection Laboratory was built.

1953/54 New Riding School built (currently the Arena). Old Riding School converted to the Drill Hall. New "C" Block built – Corporals' Mess located in the basement of the east wing. Post garage extended.

1956   The last of the old barrack buildings disappeared when "B" Block was dismantled.

1957   Current Mess was constructed.

1958   New Officers' Mess built on the site of the old Officers' Mess and staff residence, "B" Block, was completed.

1959   Visit to "Depot" by Her Majesty Queen Elizabeth II and Prince Philip. New Officers' Mess completed and opened.

Old Officers' Mess was demolished in 1958

Queen Elizabeth II and Prince Philip visit the Museum in 1959

early 60s   Initiation of the Sunset Ceremonies.

1966   Equitation discontinued and horses sold at public auction. Riding School converted into an arena.

1971   Pistol Range and Armourers' Shop completed. Old "C" Block demolished. Artificial ice plant installed in the Arena. CF-MPH, a Beechcraft D18S aircraft, retired to the Museum Collection.

Old "C" Block is demolished in 1971

1972   Academic Building constructed and opened by Commissioner W.L. Higgitt.

1973 Gas training area and compound erected. Original Guidon was retired and displayed in the Chapel. New Centennial Museum opened. Queen Elizabeth II and Prince Philip visit "Depot" during the Force's Centennial.

1974 Rifle range completed. 32 women began training as the first females in the Force in Troop #17. South Saskatchewan Lily Society started a plot at the Dewdney entrance to "Depot."

Queen Elizabeth II is escorted by Supt. W.F. MacRae during her visit in 1973

Females join the RCMP in 1974

First Native Special Constable Troop graduated in 1975

1975 First female troop graduated March 3rd. First Native Special Constable troop graduated on March 14. "Depot" was renamed RCMP Academy at "Depot" Division. Old outdoor revolver range disassembled and relocated at the new range complex. Stand Easy Lounge officially opened.

1976 Carden Estate campground officially opened May 24. "D" Block opened November 29 by Commissioner Nadon. Corporals' Mess moved to the basement of "Depot" Division Mess from "C" Block.

1977 First Inuit Special Constable Troop graduated on March 4.

1982 Shwaykowski Driving Track opened at "Depot."

1991 RCMP Corps Ensign unveiled at "Depot."

1994 Recruit training evolved to cadet training program. Buffalo Detachment and Scenario residences opened.

1998 Centralized Training Complex opened. Firearms Training Complex opened. "A" Block renamed A.B. Perry Building to commemorate the 125th Anniversary of the Force.

First Inuit troop graduates in 1977

"Depot" celebrates the Force's 125th Anniversary – 1998

2000 Due to an increase in the cadet load, additional classrooms and offices were added to the north end of the Applied Police Sciences building. Norwalk virus outbreak.

2002 "Depot" provided tactical troop to G8 summit in Kananaskis, Alberta. RCMP Heritage Centre site plan unveiled. Sweat Lodge opened.

"Depot" Tactical troop members prepare for G8 in Kananaskis, Alberta – 2002

CHAPTER 9 – HISTORICAL CALENDAR   389

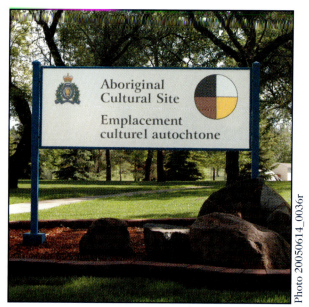

Sweat Lodge opens at "Depot" – 2002

2003   50,000th regimental number issued.

2004   Cadet training program increased from 22 weeks to 24 weeks. Second driving track opened at "Depot."

Queen Elizabeth II visits "Depot" – 2005

2005   Queen Elizabeth II and Prince Philip visited "Depot" on May 19, 2005 to lay a wreath honouring the deaths of Cst. Brock Myrol, Cst. Lionide Johnston, Cst. Peter Schiemann and Cst. Anthony Gordon in Mayerthorpe, Alberta on March 3, 2005. Her Majesty met with the families of the fallen members in the Chapel.

Parade Square made larger to accommodate bleachers for Sunset Ceremonies. Connaught Cup is updated with additional tiers for mounting plates. Cenotaph was upgraded with lattice and divisional ensigns.

Construction of Heritage Centre – April 2006

2006   Construction of Heritage Centre begins. Bunk beds placed in centralized training to accommodate "ramp up" at "Depot." Employee access to "Depot" available through McCarthy Boulevard.

Cenotaph – 2005

Through the Decades

1880s

The original Riding School

The Bagley Pony – owned by Trumpeter Fred Bagley, the youngest recruit to join the March West at age 15. He retired from the Force at age 40

"Depot" – circa 1889

1890s

Church Parade – circa 1890

Commanding Officer's team and sleigh – circa 1890

CHAPTER 10 – PHOTOS BY DECADES

1900s

Keeping warm in buffalo coats – circa 1909

Cst. J.C. Stedman, Reg. #4827, on "Dandy" – July 1909

1910s

On the west side of the Stables – circa 1910

"Depot" Division – in front of "B" Block decorated with black crepe paper in mourning for the death of King Edward VII on May 6, 1910

Horse tricks on the Parade Square, S/M Tim Griffen standing behind his horse – circa 1920

1920s

Rifle drill in front of the old "C" Block – circa 1925

BEHIND THE BADGE

1930s

Division Mess – 1934

King George VI and Queen Elizabeth visit "Depot" – 1939

Tent living – 1935

1940s

Looking westward across Sleigh Square – circa 1940

Looking southeast across Sleigh Square – 1940

1950s

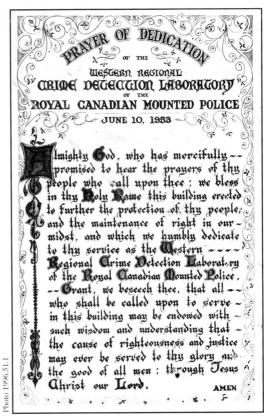
Formal social – circa 1958

Opening of the Crime Lab – June 10, 1953

CHAPTER 10 – PHOTOS BY DECADES

1960s

Lowering the Red Ensign in preparation for the raising of the "Canadian" Flag on February 15, 1965

1970s

Female graduating troop in the Gym – circa 1978

Queen Elizabeth II, Honourary Commissioner of the Force, was presented with a token horse by Commissioner W.L. Higgitt to commemorate the Forces' 100th birthday in 1973. On August 2, she visited Rockcliffe barracks and selected "Jerry," whose name was changed to "Centennial," the spelling of which was modified to "Centenial"

1980s

Applied Police Sciences – PIRS Classroom – 1986

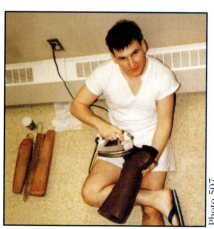

Cst. D.H.J. Dupasquier Reg. #38978, Troop 9, 1986/87, ironing his boots

1990s

Members of a troop form up and await instruction from their right marker prior to attending their next class – 1990

Members of the band enter Sleigh Square for Noon Parade – circa 1990

2000s

Cadet Dan Block at Sunset Ceremony – 2001

Prime Minister Chrétien inspecting a troop in front of the Chapel in October of 2000. He is escorted by S/M Tardif and C.O. Twardosky

Remembering fallen comrades – September 9, 2001

HRM Queen Elizabeth II and Commissioner G. Zaccardelli at "Depot" – May 2005

Chapter 10 – Photos by Decades

Historical Centre of "Depot"

The history of "Depot" comes alive as you sit in front of the Chapel and scan the horizon.

①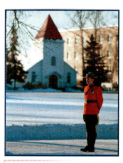

As you enter "Depot" from the north gate, you see the Chapel, the enduring symbol of the spiritual history of the RCMP. This is the oldest building in Regina.

②

"C" BLOCK – the "new" C Block was constructed in 1953/54, replacing the old "C" Block which was on the east side of the Chapel.

③

DRILL HALL – Built in 1929, as the third Riding School, it is currently the Drill Hall.

④

DIVISION MESS – The new Division Mess, built in 1957, is in the left foreground. The former Mess, with the prominent roof, is in the centre.

⑤

A.B. PERRY BUILDING – Formerly known as "A" Block, this building was named after Commissioner Aylesworth Bowes Perry during the 125th Anniversary of the Force. It is the administrative centre of "Depot."

⑥

CENOTAPH – Built in 1935 to honour the memory of our fallen comrades.

⑦

"B" BLOCK – The last of the old barrack buildings disappeared when "B" Block was dismantled in 1956, vastly altering the appearance of Sleigh Square.

⑧

POST GARAGE – Built in 1931/32, this building stores Force vehicles, houses chauffeur service and the gun-cleaning area for the cadets.

⑨

FIREHALL – The former Firehall is now used as a mock courthouse as part of the Cadet Training Program.

⑩

MONUMENT TO THE ST ROCH – Commemorates the voyage of the RCMP arctic patrol vessel St Roch through the Northwest Passage, from the Pacific to the Atlantic – June 23, 1940 to October 8, 1942.

⑪

SLEIGH SQUARE – The Parade Square was named in honour of Cpl. R.B. Sleigh, Reg. #565, killed at age 27 at Cutknife Hill, North-West Territories on May 2, 1885.

⑫

OFFICERS' MESS – The current building was designed by Sgt. J.C. Coughlin of "Depot" Division and built in 1959.

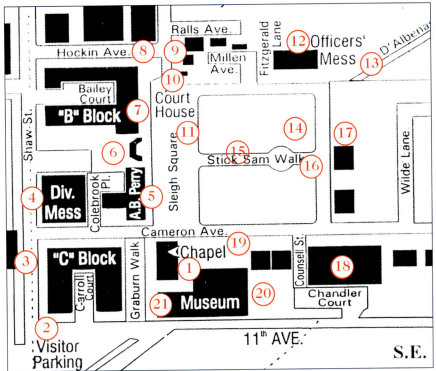

Police Driving Unit – Also Informatics, this was built in 1953, and was the site of the Crime Lab.

RCMP Beechcraft D18S – On display in front of the RCMP Centennial Museum, this was the first new plane purchased by the Force after WWII. It was used by RCMP Air Services for 24 years.

Sweat lodge – On January 18, 2002, "Depot" opened a Sweat Lodge to foster better understanding of aboriginal culture by sharing customs and spiritual practices.

Street sign – S/Cst. Stick Sam, age unknown, was one of the first Special Constables serving in the north. He drowned crossing Kaskawulsh River, YT on horseback while on patrol on July 19, 1903.

Guard house – Louis Riel was hung at the rear of the Guardroom in November of 1885 after being found guilty of treason. Photo circa 1890.

Sundial – This "Depot" artifact has remained relatively unnoticed given its location just north of the Flagpole base. The Sundial was donated to "Depot" by a Regina resident in 1947.

Flagpole – Erected by members of "P" Squad on Sleigh Square at "Depot" on September 14, 1943.

Museum – Built in 1973 to commemorate the RCMP 100th Anniversary, the Museum recounts over 125 years of RCMP service in Canada. It attracts visitors from around the world.

Commanding Officer's Residence – On the east side of Sleigh Square, it has a spectacular view of "Depot." The identical residence to the south was the former residence of the Commanding Officer of "F" Division.

Historical Centre of "Depot"

"DEPOT" – An Overview

circa 1927

circa 1945

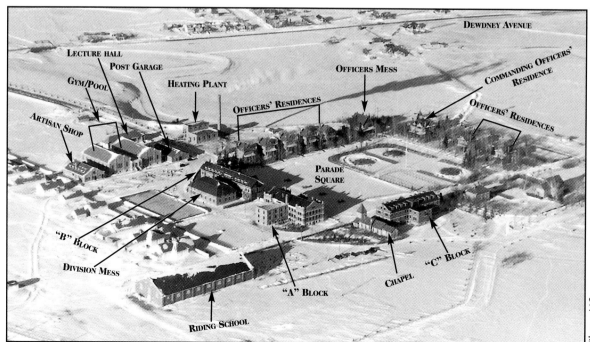

circa 1953

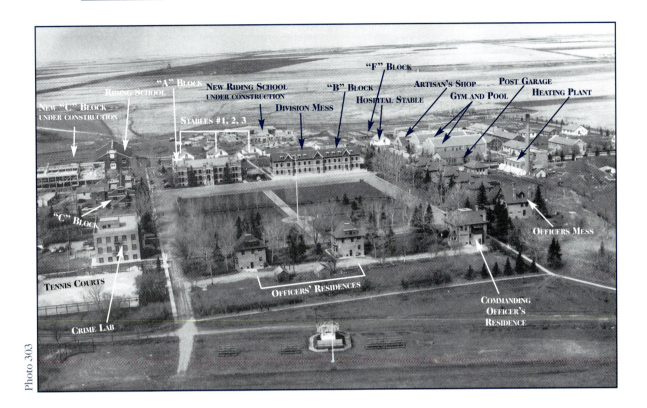

circa 1980

Chapter 11 – Aerial Shots

HONOUR ROLL

*T*he Royal Canadian Mounted Police Honour Roll lists the men and women of the North-West Mounted Police, Royal Northwest Mounted Police and Royal Canadian Mounted Police who sacrificed their lives in the line of duty.

Sub. Cst. John Nash
Sub. Cst. George Mahoney
Cst. Marmaduke Graburn
Cst. Claudius S. Hooley
Cst. Adam Wahl
Cst. Thomas James Gibson
Cst. George Knox Garrett
Cst. George Pearce Arnold
Cst. David Latimer Cowan
Cpl. Ralph Bateman Sleigh
Cst. Patrick Burke
Cpl. William Hay Talbot Lowry
Cst. Frank Orlando Elliott
Sgt. Albert Ernest Garland Montgomery
Cst. George Quiqueran Rene Saveuse DeBeaujeu
Cpl. Harry Oliver Morphy
Cst. William Tyrrell Reading
Cst. James Herron
Sgt. Colin Campbell Colebrook
Cst. Oscar Alexander Kern
Sgt. William Brock Wilde
Cst. John Randolph Kerr
Cpl. Charles Horne Sterling Hockin
Cst. Norman Malcolm Campbell
Cst. Spencer Gilbert Heathcote
S/Cst. Stick Sam
S/Sgt. Arthur F.M. Brooke
Cst. Joseph Russell
Cst. Thomas Robert Jackson
Cpl. Alexander Gardner Haddock
Assistant Surgeon Walter Stafford Flood
Cst. George Ernest Willmett
Sgt. Ralph Morton L. Donaldson
S/Cst. Samuel Carter
Insp. Francis Joseph Fitzgerald
Cst. George Frances Kinney
Cst. Richard O'Hara Taylor
Cst. Francis Walter Davies
Cpl. Maxwell George Bailey
Cst. Michael James Fitzgerald
Cst. Alexander Lamont
S/Sgt. George Henry Leopold Bossange
Cpl. Ernest Usher
Sgt. Arthur George Searle
Cpl. William Andrew Doak

Cst. Ian M. MacDonald
Cst. Leo Francis Cox
Cst. Frederick Rhodes
Sgt. Richard Henry Nicholson
Cst. Donald Ross MacDonell
Cst. Edgar Millen
Cpl. Leonard Victor Ralls
Cpl. John Lorne Halliday
Insp. Lorne James Sampson
Cpl. Michael Moriarity
Cst. John George Shaw
Cst. George Campbell Harrison
Sgt. Thomas Sellar Wallace
Cst. Daniel Miller
Cst. George Edward Horan
Cst. William George Boorman
Cst. Willis Edward Rhodeniser
Cst. Norman Alfred Gleadow
Sgt. Arthur Julian Barker
Cst. Frederick Gordon Frank Counsell
Cst. H.G. Rapeer
Eng. 3rd Class Daniel Everett Gillis
Cst. Charles James Johnstone
Sgt. Louis Romeo Dubuc
Cst. C.F. Patterson
1st Officer Patrick Reginal Fairburn Milthorp
Cst. Peter Seddon Oliver
Master John Willard Bonner
Cst. J.H.D. Bedlington
Surgeon Maurice Powers, B.A., M.D., C.M.
Cst. Terence Graham Newcomen Watts
Cst. Edison Alexander Cameron
Cst. David Charles Gardner Moon
Cst. Gordon Evan Bondurant
Cst. Kenneth Laurence D'Albenas
S/Cst. John Terrence Hoey
Cst. John Francis Nelson
Cst. Donald Gilbert Stackhouse
Cst. Wilfred James Cobble
Cst. Carl Frizzle Wilson
Cst. Alexander Gamman
Cst. Joseph Kasimir Sander
Cst. Ronald Charles Bloomfield
Cst. William Lawrence Melsom
Insp. David James McCombe
Cst. John Roland Cobley

BEHIND THE BADGE

Cpl. Herbert Milton Smart
2/Cst. Maurice Melnychuk
2/Cst. Glen Frederick Farough
2/Cst. David Melvyn Perry
2/Cst. George Herbert Edward Ransom
S/Sgt. Stanley Samuel Rothwell
Cst. Richard William Green
S/Cst. Joseph Edouard Raymond Cormier
Cst. Colin Eric Lelliott
Cst. Ronald Arthur Ekstrom
S/Cst. Henry Clare Jarvis
S/Cst. Joseph Henry Kent
Cst. Albert Joseph Chartrand
Cpl. Laurence Percival Ryder
2/Cst. James Boyd Henderson
Cst. Herschel Taylor Wood
Cst. Stephen Kasper
Cst. Douglas Earl Ferguson
Cst. Roy Eldon Laird
Cst. Charles William Reay
2/Cst. Henry Charles Allington Chandler
Cst. Carl Lennart Sundell
Cst. Wayne Sinclair
Cst. Joseph Thor Thompson
Cst. Elwood Joseph Keck
Cst. Donald George Weisgerber
Cst. Gordon Eric Pedersen
Cst. Archille Octave Maxime Lepine
Cst. James Walter Foreman
Sgt. Kenneth Morley Laughland
Cpl. Robert William Asbil
Cst. Proctor Laurence Anthony Malcolm
Cst. William John David Annand
Cst. Joseph Pierre Francois Dubois
Cpl. Ervin Jack Giesbrecht
Cst. Robert Watson Amey
3/Cst. Reginald Wayne Williams
Cst. David Brian Robinson
Cst. Neil McArthur Bruce
Cst. Thomas Percy Carroll
3/Cst. Philip John Francis Tidman
Cst. Gordon Donald Pearson
3/Cst. Terry Eugene Tomfohr
Cpl. Donald Archibald Harvey
Cst. Alfred Perry
3/Cst. Robert William Varney
2/Cst. James Alexander Kerr
Cpl. Terry Gerrard Williams
Cst. William Joseph Green
Sgt. Robert James Schrader
Cst. Douglas Bernard Anson
Sgt. James Aldridge O'Malley
Cst. Derek Thomas Ivany
Cst. Harold Stanley Seige
Cst. Michael Robert Mason
Cst. Roger Emile Pierlet
Cst. Joseph Michel Benoit Letourneau
Cst. Joseph Henri Clément Tremblay
Cst. John Terrance Draginda

Cst. John Brian Baldwinson
Cst. Dennis Modest Nicklos Shwaykowski
Cpl. Barry Warren Lidstone
Cst. Joseph Perry Brophy
Dennis Anthony Onofrey
Cst. Thomas Brian King
S/Cst. George David Foster
Cst. Lindberg Bruce Davis
Cst. Mark Percy McLachlan
Cst. William I. Seward
Cst. Joseph Leon Michel Doucet
Cst. Gordon Alfred Brooks
S/Cst. Ningeoseak Etidloi
Cst. Roy John William Karwaski
Cst. Richard John Sedgwick
Cst. Thomas James Agar
Cpl. Ole Roust Larsen
Cst. James Franklin Thomas
Cst. Barry Flynn McKinnon
Cst. Douglas Ambrose Mark Butler
S/Cst. Wayne Graham Myers
Cpl. Frances Eugene Jones
Cst. Daniel Lincoln Keough
Cst. Robert Charles Anderson
Cst. Richard Allan Bourgoin
Cst. Allen Garry Giesbrecht
Cst. Michael Joseph Buday
S/Cst. W.P. Boskill
S/Cst. J.F. Wilson
S/Cst. Robert W.C. Thomas
Cpl. Budd Maurice Johanson
A/Cst. Frederick A. Abel
Cst. J.E.Mario Tessier
Cst. Scott G. Berry
S/Cst. Gordon Zigmund Kowalczyk
Cpl. Derek John Flanagan
Cst. D.S. Beyak

Cst. Christopher Colin Riglar
Cst. Gerald Vernon Maurice Breese
Sgt. Derek Cameron Burkholder
Cst. Joseph Ernest André Claude Gagné
Cst. Brian John Hutchinson
Gend. Joseph Luc François (Frank) Carrière
Cst. Dennis Douglas Strongquill
Cst. Christine Elizabeth Diotte
Cst. Wael Toufic Audi
S/Cst. Norman Massan
Cst. Jimmy Ng
Cst. Joseph Leo Ghislain Maurice
Cpl. James Wilbert Gregson Galloway
A/Cst. Joseph Ernest "Sam" Balmer
A/Cst. Glen Gregory Evely
Cst. Anthony Fitzgerald Orion Gordon
Cst. Lionide (Leo) Nicholas Johnston
Cst. Brock Warren Myrol
Cst. Peter Christopher Schiemann
Cst. J.M.J. (Jean) Minguy
Cst. Jose Manuel Agostinho

FOOTNOTES

Chapter One

Beginning

(1) RCMP Archives – Centennial Museum – Regina, Saskatchewan

(2) The Early Years of Depot Division, S.W. Horrall, *RCMP Quarterly*, Fall 1985, pages 8-9

Recruiting

(3) *The Pictorial History of the Royal Canadian Mounted Police*, S.W. Horrall, McGraw Hill Ryerson Ltd., Toronto, Canada, 1973, page 33

(4) Ibid, page 22

(5) The Early Years of Depot Division, S.W. Horrall, *RCMP Quarterly*, Fall 1985, page 15

(6) The Training Depot, Inspector C.E. Rivett-Carnac, *RCMP Quarterly*, July 1933, page 23

(7) www.rcmp-grc.ca/recruiting

Depot Division – Not a Favourite Place

(8) The Early Years of Depot Division, S.W. Horrall, *RCMP Quarterly*, Fall 1985, page 12

(9) *Edmonton Journal*, Sunday, October 3, 2004, Christopher Spencer

Hollywood

(10) The Premiere of the Northwest Mounted Police, Cpl. H.H. Radcliffe, *The Quarterly*, January 1941, page 277

(11) www.rcmp.ca/history/mountie_hollywood_e.htm

Socials

(12) Bands of the Force, *RCMP Quarterly*, October 1940, page 160

(13) Division Notes, *RCMP Quarterly*, April 1938, pages 278-279

(14) Division Notes, *RCMP Quarterly*, April 1934, page 179

(15) Division Notes, *RCMP Quarterly*, April 1938, page 278

(16) Divisional Dispatches, *RCMP Quarterly*, October 1970, page 55

(17) Division Notes, *RCMP Quarterly*, April 1959, page 331

Christmas

(18) Division Notes, *RCMP Quarterly*, April 1934, page 178

(19) Division Notes, *RCMP Quarterly*, April 1951, page 373

Chapter Two

"A" Block

(1) The Early Years of Depot Division, S.W. Horrall, *RCMP Quarterly*, Fall 1985, page 10

(2) Ibid

(3) Ibid

(4) *Federal Heritage Buildings Review Office Building Report – 11 Early Buildings at the RCMP Depot – Regina, Saskatchewan – FHBRO – No. 86-22*, page 4

Artisan

(5) *Federal Heritage Buildings Review Office Building Report- 11 Early Buildings at the RCMP Depot – Regina, Saskatchewan – FHBRO – No. 86-22*, page 31

(6) *Depot Today*, Cpl. W.K. Smith, *RCMP Quarterly*, Winter 1976, page 5

"B" Block

(7) The Early Years of Depot Division, S.W. Horrall, *RCMP Quarterly*, Fall 1985, page 10

(8) Ibid

(9) *RNWMP Annual Report 1907*, Superintendent G.E. Sanders, page 55

Barber

(10) *RCMP Academy at Depot Division – Basic Recruit Training Course*, 1987, pages 1-6

(11) The Recruit – Half a Century Ago, ex-Cst. G.V. Wellman, Reg. #9946, *RCMP Quarterly*, October 1973, page 47

(12) Looking Back, ex-Constable T. Jamieson Quirk, Reg. #11951, *RCMP Quarterly*, Winter 1989, page 28

(13) *Prelude to Duty*, 1947

Barracks

(14) Looking Back, ex-Constable T. Jamieson Quirk, Reg. #11951, *RCMP Quarterly*, Winter 1989, page 29

(15) *A Guide to Success* – compiled by the Training Branch, Ottawa 1960, page 11

(16) *Prelude to Duty*, 1950

(17) *NWMP Annual Report 1885*, Commander A.G. Irvine, page 9

(18) The Early Years of Depot Division, S.W. Horrall, *RCMP Quarterly*, Fall 1985, page 13

(19) *NWMP Annual Report 1886*, Commissioner L.W. Herchmer, page 12

(20) *NWMP Annual Report 1885*, Commander A.G. Irvine, page 8

(21) Ibid

(22) *NWMP Annual Report 1887*, Commissioner, L.W. Herchmer, page 12

(23) Looking Back, ex-Constable T. Jamieson Quirk, Reg. #11951, *RCMP Quarterly*, Winter 1989, page 32

(24) The Early Years of Depot Division, S.W. Horrall, *RCMP Quarterly*, Fall 1985, page 13

(25) *Behind the Scenes*, Supt. J. Religa (rtd.), Reg. #0.947, Oceanside Press, Pouch Cove, Newfoundland, 1997, page 9

Tent Living

(26) Depot 1935, S/Sgt. E.C.Parker (rtd.), Reg. #12640, *RCMP Quarterly*, Winter 1990, page 18

(27) Ibid, page 20

"C" Block

(28) *Federal Heritage Buildings Review Office Building Report – 11 Early Buildings at the RCMP Depot – Regina, Saskatchewan – FHBRO – No. 86-22*, page 9

(29) *Behind the Scenes*, Supt. J. Religa, (rtd.), Reg. #0.947, Oceanside Press, Pouch Cove, Newfoundland, 1997, pages 17-18

(29) *Depot Digest*, Depot Division, February/March, 2003, page 9

Centralized Training

(30) *Carpe Diem*, Depot Division, Communication Empowers, September 1998, Volume 2 No. 6, page 1

Chapel

(31) *Federal Heritage Buildings Review Office Building Report – 11 Early Buildings at the RCMP Depot, Regina, Saskatchewan – RCMP Depot – FHBRO – No. 86-22*, page 19

(32) Memo to the Commanding Officer of Depot Division from Supt. Bentham, Liaison Officer, 1976

(33) *Federal Heritage Buildings Review Office Building Report – 11 Early Buildings at the RCMP Depot, Regina, Saskatchewan – RCMP Depot – FHBRO – No. 86-22*, page 18

(34) Ibid

Crime Lab

(35) The Crime Detection Laboratory – Regina, Sask., Cst. C.C. Head, *RCMP Quarterly*, July 1953, page 29

(36) *The Pictorial History of the Royal Canadian Mounted Police*, S.W. Horrall, McGraw Hill Ryerson Ltd., Toronto, Canada, 1973, page 204

"D" Block

(37) *Federal Heritage Buildings Review Office Building Report – 11 Early Buildings at the RCMP Depot, Regina Saskatchewan – RCMP Depot – FHBRO – No. 86-22*, page 31

Drill Hall

(38) *Federal Heritage Buildings Review Office Building Report – 11 Early Buildings at the RCMP Depot, Regina, Saskatchewan – RCMP Depot – FHBRO – No. 86-22*, page 26

Guardroom

(39) *RNWMP Annual Report 1908,* Superintendent G.E. Sanders, page 48

Prisoners

(40) *RNWMP Annual Report 1908,* Superintendent G.E. Sanders, page 56

(41) *RNWMP Annual Report 1914,* Inspector R.S. Knight, page 174

(42) Ibid

(43) *NWMP Annual Report 1885,* Superintendent R.B. Deane

(44) *NWMP Annual Report 1885,* Superintendent R.B. Deane, page 64

(45) *NWMP Annual Report 1885,* Superintendent A.G. Irvine, page 19

Gym

(46) *Federal Heritage Buildings Review Office Building Report – 11 Early Buildings at the RCMP Depot, Regina Saskatchewan* – RCMP Depot – FHBRO – No. 86-22, page 34

(47) Ibid, page 36

(48) Divisional Dispatches, *RCMP Quarterly,* July 1973, page 58

Heating Plant

(49) *Federal Heritage Buildings Review Office Building Report – 11 Early Buildings at the RCMP Depot, Regina Saskatchewan* – RCMP Depot – FHBRO – No. 86-22, page 30

Lecture Hall

(50) *Federal Heritage Buildings Review Office Building Report – 11 Early Buildings at the RCMP Depot, Regina Saskatchewan* – RCMP Depot – FHBRO – No. 86-22, page 37

MTC

(51) The Early Years of Depot Division, S.W. Horrall, *RCMP Quarterly,* Fall 1985, page 10

(52) *Federal Heritage Buildings Review Office Building Report – 11 Early Buildings at the RCMP Depot, Regina Saskatchewan* – RCMP Depot – FHBRO – No. 86-22, page 38

Division Mess

(53) Division Notes, *RCMP Quarterly,* April 1942, page 454

(54) Looking Back, ex-Cst. T. Jamieson Quirk, Reg. #11951, *RCMP Quarterly,* Winter 1989, pages 35-36

(55) The Early Years of Depot Division, S.W. Horrall, *RCMP Quarterly,* Fall 1985, page 13

(56) *Behind the Scenes,* Supt J. Religa, Reg. #0.947, Oceanside Press, Pouch Cove, Newfoundland, 1997, page 12

(57) Mess Catering, Constable A.L. Alsvold, *RCMP Quarterly,* April 1936, page 270

(58) New Officers Mess – Regina, S/Sgt. C.J.W. Chester, *RCMP Quarterly,* July 1959, page 35

(59) The Old Order Changeth, Supt. H.A. Maxted, *RCMP Quarterly,* July 1958, pages 25 and 26

(60) Regina Sergeants' Mess, S/Sgt C.J. W. Chester, *RCMP Quarterly,* April 1963, page 265

(61) RCMP Corporals' Mess – Regina Sask, *RCMP Quarterly,* July 1960, page 39

(62) The Early Years of Depot Division, S.W. Horrall, *RCMP Quarterly,* Fall 1985, page 14

(63) Ibid,

RCMP Heritage Centre

(64) www.rcmpheritagecenter.com

Officers Residences

(65) *Depot Digest* Depot Division Regina, Saskatchewan, June 2002, page 6

Post Garage

(66) *Federal Heritage Buildings Review Office Building Report – 11 Early Buildings at the RCMP Depot, Regina Saskatchewan* – RCMP Depot – FHBRO – No. 86-22, page 28

(67) Ibid, page 12

(68) Ibid, page 28

Regina Town Station

(69) *The Early Years of Depot Division*, S.W. Horrall *The Quarterly*, Fall 1985, pages 12-13

(70) *Trooper and Redskin*, J. G. Donkin Sampson Low, Marston, Searle and Rivington, London, England, 1889, page 19

Resource Center

(71) *RCMP Libraries: An Historical Note*, Glen Gordon, March 1986, page 8

(72) Ibid, page 10

(73) *Carpe Diem*, Depot Division, December 1997, page 1

Riding School

(74) *The Early Years of Depot Division*, S.W. Horrall, *RCMP Quarterly*, Fall 1985, page 10

(75) Ibid, page 9

(76) Canada Parliament – House of Commons *Annual Report of the RCMP 1929*, Kings Printer, page 6

(77) *Federal Heritage Buildings Review Office Building Report – 11 Early Buildings at the RCMP Depot, Regina Saskatchewan* – RCMP Depot – FHBRO – No. 86-22, page 11

(78) Ibid, page 26

(79) Ibid, page 11

(80) Division Bulletin, *The Quarterly* January 1953, page 266

(81) *Depot Division Past and Present*

Stables

(82) Looking Back, ex-Cst. T. Jamieson Quirk, Reg. #11951, *RCMP Quarterly*, Winter 1989, page 29

(83) Ibid, pages 38-39

(84) Depot 1935, S/Sgt. E. C. Parker (rtd.), Reg. #12640, *The Quarterly*, Winter 1990, pages 18-19

Swimming Pool

(85) *Federal Heritage Review Office Building Report – 11 Early Buildings at the RCMP Depot Regina, Saskatchewan* – RCMP Depot – FHBRO – No. 86-22, pages 12-13

(86) Ibid, page 36

(87) Swimming Pool at Barracks Draws 16,000 People a Year – Regina *Leader-Post* – January 24, 1957

(88) Swimming at Depot, S/Cst. R.R. Canning, *The Quarterly*, October 1951, page 131

(89) *Federal Heritage Review Office Building Report – 11 Early Buildings at the RCMP Depot Regina, Saskatchewan* – RCMP Depot – FHBRO – No. 86-22, pages 12-13

Water Tower

(90) *The Early Years of Depot Division*, S.W. Horrall, *RCMP Quarterly*, Fall 1985, page 10

(91) Ibid, page 11

Chapter Three

Officers

(1) *Depot Digest*, Depot Division, September-October 2002

(2) *The Early Years of Depot Division*, S.W. Horrall, *RCMP Quarterly*, Fall 1985, page 16

Sergeant Major

(3) *The Early Years of Depot Division*, S.W. Horrall, *RCMP Quarterly*, Fall 1985, page 8

Church Parade

(4) *The Early Years of Depot Division*, S.W. Horrall, *RCMP Quarterly*, Fall 1985, page 12

(5) *Behind the Scenes*, Supt. J. Religa (rtd.), Reg. #0.947, Oceanside Press, Pouch Cove, Newfoundland, 1997, page 19

Sunset Ceremonies

(6) *Depot Digest*, Depot Division, January 2001

Musical Ride

(7) www.rcmp-grc.gc.ca/musicalride

(8) Ibid

(9) www.mountedpolicefnd.org/horse auction/pages/E-about1A.html

Chapter Four

Carden Estates

(1) Memo to the Commanding Officer – Depot Division from Supt. J. Bentham, Liaison Officer, dated June 10, 1976

Cemetery

(2) Memories – of the Way We Were, Sgt. Bill Poole (rtd.), *RCMP Quarterly*, Fall 2002, page 37

Entrance to Depot

(3) Division Notes, *RCMP Quarterly*, October 1940, page 228

St Roch

(4) *The Scarlet Horsemen*

Sleigh Square

(5) *In the Line of Duty – The Honour Roll of the RCMP Since 1873* – Robert Knuckle, General Store Publishing House, Burnstown, Ontario, 1994, page 42-44

(6) Ibid, page 44

(7) *CO's Communique* – Commanding Officer Depot Division, 2005-05-18

Street Names

(8) Street Names Commemorate Honour Roll, *RCMP Quarterly*, April 1960, page 315

(9) What's in a Name, S/M T.O. Lewis (rtd.), *RCMP Quarterly*, Summer, 1992 pages 39-42

Gardening

(10) Division Notes, *RCMP Quarterly*, April 1942, pages 454 and 455

(11) Division Bulletin, *RCMP Quarterly*, October 1952, page 166

Weather

(12) *NWMP Annual Report 1883*, Superintendent R.B. Deane, page 23

(13) *NWMP Annual Report 1900*, Commissioner A.B. Perry

(14) Divisional Dispatches, *RCMP Quarterly*, October 1971, page 56

(15) Looking Back, ex-Cst. T. Louiseize Quirk, Reg. #11951, *RCMP Quarterly*, Winter 1989, page 35

(16) Environment Canada www.climate.weatheroffice.gc.ca/climate_normals/results_e.html

Chapter Five

Curriculum

(1) The Early Years at Depot Division, S.W. Horrall, *RCMP Quarterly*, Fall 1985 pages 15-16

(2) *The Pictorial History of the Royal Canadian Mounted Police*, S.W. Horrall, McGraw Hill Ryerson Ltd., London, Canada, 1973, page 204

(3) *RCMP Brief – Recruit Training*, September 1962

Cadet Training Program

(4) *Cadet Training Program – Brief Overview – Program Training Standard* – June 11, 2004, page 1

(5) Ibid

(6) Cadet Training Handbook, *RCMP Quarterly*, Summer 1995

Dress/Deportment

(7) Memories – of the Way We Were, Sgt. Bill Poole (rtd.), *RCMP Quarterly*, Fall 2002, page 36

(8) *RCMP Academy at Depot Division Basic Recruit Training Course – Orientation and Reference Manual*, 1988, 5-1

Drill

(9) *The Drill Manual – Functions of Drill – RCMP*

(10) *NWMP Annual Report 1887*, Commissioner L.W. Herchmer

(11) *Depot Digest*, Depot Division, Regina, Saskatchewan, November 2001

(12) *Overview of the Cadet Training Program*, 2005, page 9

(13) *The Drill Manual – Calvary Drill* (dismounted), Ottawa, 1956

Facilitators

(14) *Rules and Regulations for the Government and Guidance of the Royal Canadian Mounted Police Force,* 1936

(15) *Career Management Manual,* Appendix 5-8, 2000-11-10

Firearms

(16) Division Notes, *RCMP Quarterly,* April 1938, page 278

(17) *Overview of the Cadet Training Program,* June 11, 2004, page 8

(18) *Martins Annual Criminal Code 2001,* Police Edition, Canada Law Book Inc., Aurora, Ontario, 2001, page 73

Regimental Numbers

(19) *Depot Digest,* Depot Division, March 2003

RCMP Families

(20) The Clare Brothers, S.W. Horrall, *RCMP Quarterly,* Winter 1986, page 41

Life at "Depot"

(21) *Behind the Scenes,* Supt. J. Religa, (rtd.), Reg. #0.947, Oceanside Press, Pouch Cove, Newfoundland, 1997, page 10

(22) Ibid, page 24

Leave Pass

(23) Looking Back, ex-Cst. T. Jamieson Quirk, Reg. #11951, *RCMP Quarterly,* Winter 1989, page 33

(24) *Behind the Scenes,* Supt. J. Religa (rtd.), Reg. #0.947, Oceanside Press, Pouch Cove, Newfoundland, 1997, page 10

(25) *Life at the RCMP Academy at Depot Division,* April 1977, Appendix C

Marriage

(26) Looking Back, ex-Cst. T. Jamieson Quirk, Reg. #11951, *RCMP Quarterly,* Winter 1989, page 33

(27) *A Career in Scarlet,* Ottawa, 1969, page 12

To the Wives

(28) *Life at the RCMP Academy at Depot Division,* April 1977

Native Special Constable Training

(29) RCMP Native Special Constable Program, Sgt. J.T. Hill, *RCMP Quarterly,* Winter 1978, page 16

(30) *Life at the RCMP Academy at Depot Division,* April 1977 – Appendix A

Pay

(31) *The National Parks and National Historic Sites of Canada*

(32) *RCMP Administration Manual,* Appendix II, 4-3 2005

(33) *Regulations and Orders for the Government and Guidance of the North West Mounted Police* 1889

(34) *The Recruit – Half a Century Ago,* ex-Cst. Glenn Victor Wellman, Reg. #9948, *RCMP Quarterly,* October 1973, page 47

(35) *Life at the RCMP Academy at Depot Division,* April 1977 – Appendix A

Pay Parade

(36) *Behind the Scenes,* Supt. J. Religa (rtd.), Reg. #0.947 Oceanside Press, Pouch Cove, Newfoundland, 1997, page 19

PT

(37) *Overview of the Cadet Training Program* June 11, 2004, pages 7 and 8

(38) Physical Training in the Force, Cpl. E.C. Curtain, *RCMP Quarterly,* April 1956, page 266

(39) *Behind the Scenes,* Supt. J. Religa (rtd.), Reg. #0.947, Oceanside Press, Pouch Cove, Newfoundland, 1997, page 22

(40) Ibid, pages 19-20

PDT

(41) *Overview of the Cadet Training Program,* June 11, 2004, page 7

(42) Self-Defence Training, Cpl. W.D. Pitcher, *RCMP Quarterly,* July 1973, page 36

Police Driving Unit

(43) *Overview of the Cadet Training Program* June 11, 2005, page 8

(44) New Driver Training Range at Depot, Sgt. James E. Scott, *RCMP Quarterly*, Summer 1983, page 26

(45) *Depot Digest,* Depot Division, Regina, Saskatchewan, Fall 2004

Recruit Training 1932

(46) Office of the Commissioner, Ottawa, Ontario, 1932

Reserves

(47) The Royal Canadian Mounted Police Reserve, Supt. V.A.M. Kemp, *RCMP Quarterly*, October 1937

Reveille

(48) *Behind the Scenes,* Supt. J. Religa (rtd.), Reg. #0.947, Oceanside Press Pouch Cove, Newfoundland, 1997, page 11

Saturday Inspection

(49) *Behind the Scenes,* Supt. J. Religa (rtd.), Reg. #0.947, Oceanside Press, Pouch Cove, Newfoundland, 1997, pages 18 and 19

Sports

(50) The Early Years of Depot Division, S.W. Horrall, *RCMP Quarterly*, Fall 1985, page 14

(51) Ibid,

(52) *The NWMP and the Development of Rugby Football in Western Canada, 1873-1908,* Patrick H. Lamb, University of Alberta, Edmonton, Alberta

(53) Division Notes, *RCMP Quarterly*, April 1938, page 278

(54) Division Notes, *RCMP Quarterly*, April 1939, page 291

(55) Ibid

(56) *RNWMP Annual Report 1915*

(57) Division Notes, *RCMP Quarterly*, April 1934, page 178

(58) *RCMP Quarterly,* July 1935

(59) *Ottawa Citizen,* July 1st, 2004

(60) Division Notes, *RCMP Quarterly*, October 1941, page 215

Swimming Pool

(61) Swimming at Depot, Spl. Cst. R.R. Canning, *The Quarterly,* October 1951, page 131

(62) Divisional Dispatches, *RCMP Quarterly*, Summer 1979, page 47

Training

(63) *Behind the Scenes,* Supt. J. Religa (rtd.), Reg. #0.947, Oceanside Press, Pouch Cove, Newfoundland, 1997, page 22

(64) *Life at the RCMP Academy at Depot Division,* April 1977, page 4

(65) *RCMP Academy At Depot Division – Basic Recruit Training Course,* 1987

(66) RCMP website address – www.rcmp-grc.ca/depot 2005

Chapter Six

Badge

(1) www.rcmp.ca/about/badges_insignia_e.htm

Guidon

(2) Calvary Guidons and Standards, R. Maurice Hill, *RCMP Quarterly*, October 1936, page 106

(3) www.rcmp.ca/national_memorial/guidon_e.htm

Divisions

(4) How the Divisions Came to Have Their Letters, Brenda Zanin, *RCMP Quarterly*, Summer 1999, pages 17 and 18

RCMP Ensign

(5) The RCMP Corps Ensign, *RCMP Quarterly*, Summer 1991, page 10

Mountie

(6) www.rcmp.ca/history/mountie_hollywood_e.htm

(7) *The Canadian Magazine – Leader-Post*, Regina, Saskatchewan, January 27, 1973, page 15

Chapter Seven

Horses

(1) The Recruit – Half a Century Ago, ex-Cst. G.V. Wellman, Reg. #9948, *RCMP Quarterly*, October 1973, page 48

(2) Looking Back, ex-Cst. T. Jamieson Quirk, Reg. #11951, *RCMP Quarterly*, Winter 1989, page 38

(3) www.rcmp.ca/musicalride

(4) Division Notes, *RCMP Quarterly*, October 1973, page 60

(5) *Friendly Notes,* Friends of the Mounted Police Museum, Fall 1999

Fun at Depot Division

(6) Fun At Depot Division, ex-Cst. Dave Mason, *RCMP Quarterly*, Spring 1980

Horse Troughing

(7) Looking Back, ex-Cst. T. Jamieson Quirk, Reg. #11951, *RCMP Quarterly*, Winter 1989, pages 37 and 38

(8) *Behind the Scenes,* Supt. J. Regila (rtd.), Reg. #0.947, Oceanside Press, Pouch Cove, Newfoundland, 1997, pages 16-17

Horse Auction

(9) *The Horses of the Royal Canadian Mounted Police*, William and Nora Kelly, Doubleday Canada Ltd., Toronto, Ontario, 1984, page 122

Cars

(10) *Depot Digest*, Depot Division, December 2001

(11) Ibid

Band

(12) Bands of the Force, *RCMP Quarterly*, October 1940, page 160

(13) Ibid, page 161

(14) *RCMP Quarterly,* April 1939, page 276

(15) Their Majesties in Saskatchewan, A/Comm C.D.LaNauze, *RCMP Quarterly*, July 1939, page 38

The Nine-Pound Field Guns

(16) *Friendly Notes*, Friends of the Mounted Police Museum, Summer 2000

The Seven-Pound Bronze Mark II

(17) *Friendly Notes*, Friends of the Mounted Police Museum Summer 2002

Chapter Eight

Uniforms

(1) *Red Coats on the Prairies – The North-West Mounted Police 1886-1900*, William Beahen and Stan Horrall, PrintWest Publishing, Regina, Saskatchewan, 1998

The Stetson

(2) *NWMP Annual Report 1885,* Superintendent R.B. Deane, page 9

The Buffalo Coat

(3) *NWMP Annual Report 1885,* Superintendent R.B. Deane, page 13

(4) *NWMP Annual Report 1887* Commissioner L.W. Herchmer

Kit – Stores

(5) *Depot Digest,* Depot Division, February/March 2003, page 9

(6) *A Guide to Success* – compiled by the Training Branch, Ottawa 1960, page 10

(7) Shine On, *RCMP Quarterly*, Spring 1993, page 14

(8) *The Canadian Magazine – Leader-Post*, Regina, Saskatchewan, January 27, 1973, page 16

BIBLIOGRAPHY

Articles

Alsvold, Cst. A.L., Mess Catering, *RCMP Quarterly,* April 1936

Canning, S/Cst. R.R., Swimming at Depot, *RCMP Quarterly,* October 1951

Chester, S/Sgt. C.J.W., New Officers Mess – Regina, *RCMP Quarterly,* July 1959

Chester, S/Sgt. C.J.W., Regina Sergeant's Mess, *RCMP Quarterly,* April 1963

Curtain, Cpl. E.C., Physical Training in the Force, *RCMP Quarterly,* April 1956

Head, Cst. C.C., The Crime Detection Laboratory – Regina, Saskatchewan, *RCMP Quarterly,* July 1953

Hill, Sgt. J.T. *RCMP,* Native Special Constable Program, *RCMP Quarterly,* Winter 1978

Hill, R. Maurice, Calvary Guidons and Standards, *RCMP Quarterly,* October 1936

Horrall, S.W., Lady Dewdney's Own – The Beginnings of the RCMP Musical Ride, *RCMP Quarterly,* Summer 1994

Horrall, S.W., The Clare Brothers, *RCMP Quarterly,* Winter 1986

Horrall, S.W., The Early Years of Depot Division, *RCMP Quarterly,* Fall 1985

Kemp, Supt. V.A.M., The Royal Canadian Mounted Police Reserve, *RCMP Quarterly,* 1937

LaNauze, A/Commr. C.D., Their Majesties in Saskatchewan, *RCMP Quarterly,* July 1939

Lewis, S/M T.O., What's in a Name?, *RCMP Quarterly,* Summer 1992

McCann, Edward, Sergeant G.W. Brinkworth: Historian with a Camera, *RCMP Quarterly,* 1982

Mason, ex-Cst. Dave, Fun at Depot Division, *RCMP Quarterly,* Spring 1980

Maxted, Supt. H.A., The Old Order Changeth, *RCMP Quarterly,* July 1958

Parker, S/Sgt. E.C., Depot 1935, *RCMP Quarterly,* Winter 1990

Pitcher, Cpl. W.D., Self-Defence Training, *RCMP Quarterly,* July 1973

Poole, Sgt. Bill, Memories of the Way we Were, *RCMP Quarterly,* Fall 2002

Quirk, ex-Constable T. Jamieson, Looking Back, *RCMP Quarterly,* Winter 1989

Radcliffe, Cpl. H.H., The Premiere of the Northwest Mounted Police, *RCMP Quarterly,* January 1941

Rivett-Carnac, Inspector C.E., The Training Depot, *RCMP Quarterly,* July 1933

Scott, Sgt. James E., New Driver Training Range at Depot, *RCMP Quarterly,* Summer 1983

Smith, Cpl. W.K., Depot Today, *RCMP Quarterly,* Winter 1976

Wake, Malcolm, Down to Earth, *RCMP Quarterly,* January 1972

Wellman, Cst. G.V., The Recruit – Half a Century Again, *RCMP Quarterly,* October 1973

Zanin, Brenda, How the Divisions Came to Have Their Letters, *RCMP Quarterly,* Summer 1999

Bands of the Force, *RCMP Quarterly,* October 1940

Cadet Training Handbook, *RCMP Quarterly,* Summer 1995

Looking Back, *RCMP Quarterly,* April 1975

RCMP Corporals' Mess – Regina, Saskatchewan, *RCMP Quarterly,* July 1960

Shine On, *RCMP Quarterly,* Spring 1993

Street Names Commemorate Honour Role, *RCMP Quarterly,* April 1960

The RCMP Corps Ensign, *RCMP Quarterly,* Summer 1991

The RCMP Police Band, *RCMP Quarterly,* April 1939

Training & Duties in the Force, *RCMP Quarterly,* April 1947

Books

Beahen, William and Horrall, S.W., *Red Coats on the Prairies – The North-West Mounted Police 1886-1900*, (1998) PrintWest Publishing, Regina, Saskatchewan

Boulton, James, *Uniforms of the Canadian Mounted Police*, (1990) Turner-Warwick Publications, North Battleford, Saskatchewan

Chisolm, Bill, Cunningham, Garth & Sheehan, Dale, *Depot 1998 – 125th Anniversary of the RCMP* (1998)

Donkin, J.G., *Trooper and Redskin* (1889) Sampson Low, Marston, Searle & Rivington, London, England

Horrall, S.W., *The Pictorial History of the Royal Canadian Mounted Police*, (1973) McGraw Hill Ryerson Ltd., Toronto, Ontario

Kelly, William *Policing the Fringe: A Young Mountie's Story*, (1998) PrintWest Publishing Regina, Saskatchewan

Kelly, William and Nora, *The Horses of the Royal Canadian Mounted Police*, (1984) Doubleday Canada Ltd., Toronto, Ontario

Knuckle, Robert, *In the Line of Duty – The Honour Roll of the RCMP since 1973*, (1994) General Store Publishing House, Burnstown, Ontario

Martins Annual Criminal Code 2001 Police Edition, (2001) Canada Law Book Inc. Aurora, Ontario

Religa, Supt. J., *Behind the Scenes*, (1997) Oceanside Press, Pouch Cove, Newfoundland

Booklets

Canada Parliament – *House of Commons Annual Report of the RCMP 1929* – Kings Printer

Chapel on the Square 100th Anniversary 1895-1995

Federal Heritage Buildings Review Office Building Report – 11 Early Buildings at the RCMP Depot – Regina, Saskatchewan – FHBRO – No. 86-22

Gordon, Glen, *RCMP Libraries: A Historical Note*, March 1986

Lamb, Patrick H. *The NWMP and the Development of Rugby Football in Western Canada 1873-1908*, University of Alberta, Edmonton, Alberta

Tyler, Grant *Northwest Mounted Police* (2004) Copyright Her Majesty the Queen in the Right Of Canada

Newspapers

Edmonton Journal, Spencer, Christopher, Sunday October 3, 2004

Regina *Leader Post*, Swimming Pool at Barracks draws 16,000 People a Year, January 24, 1957

Ottawa Citizen July 1st, 2004

Regina *Leader-Post*, Churchill Welcomed Here, August 22, 1929

Regina *Leader-Post, The Canadian Magazine*, January 27th, 1973

RCMP Publications

RCMP Annual Reports

NWMP Annual Report 1883
– Superintendent R.B. Deane

NWMP Annual Report 1885,
– Commissioner A.G. Irvine

NWMP Annual Report 1885,
– Superintendent R.B. Deane

NWMP Annual Report 1885,
– Superintendent A.G. Irvine

NWMP Annual Report 1886
– Commissioner L.W. Herchmer

NWMP Annual Report 1887
– Commissioner L.W. Herchmer

NWMP Annual Report 1887
– Superintendent R.B. Deane

NWMP Annual Report 1891

NWMP Annual Report 1900
– Commissioner A.B. Perry

RNWMP Annual Report 1907
– Superintendent G.E. Sanders

RNWMP Annual Report 1908
 – Superintendent G.E. Sanders

RNWMP Annual Report 1909

RNWMP Annual Report 1911

RNWMP Annual Report 1913

RNWMP Annual Report 1914
 – Inspector R.S. Knight

RNWMP Annual Report 1915

RCMP Annual Report 1929

RCMP Annual Report 1937

RCMP Booklets

A Career in Scarlet

A Guide to Success – Training Branch Ottawa 1960

Depot Division – Past and Present

Prelude to Duty 1947

Prelude to Duty 1950

The National Parks and National Historic Sites of Canada

The Scarlet Horsemen

Carpe Diem

December 1997

September 1998 Volume II

Commanding Officer's Communique

Depot Division May 18th, 2005

Depot Digest – Depot Division

January 2001

November 2001

December 2001

June 2002

September/October 2002

February/March 2003

Fall 2004

Correspondence

Memo to the Commanding Officer of Depot Division from Supt. Bentham, Liaison Officer, 1976

Office of the Commissioner Ottawa, Ontario, 1932

Office of the Commissioner – Training – Circular Memorandum No. 44E, September 1932

RCMP Brief – Recruit Training, September 1962

RCMP Quarterly,

Division Notes, July 1933

Division Notes, April 1934

Division Notes, July 1935

Division Notes, April 1936

Division Notes, January 1937

Division Notes, April 1938

Division Notes, April 1939

Division Notes, July 1940

Division Notes, October 1940

Division Notes, January 1941

Division Notes, October 1941

Division Notes, April 1942

Division Notes, July 1942

Division Notes, July 1950

Division Notes, April 1951

Division Notes, April 1959

Division Notes, October 1973

Division Bulletin, April 1951

Division Bulletin, October 1952

Division Bulletin, January 1953

Division Bulletin, October 1959

Divisional Dispatches, October 1970

Divisional Dispatches, October 1971

Divisional Dispatches, July 1973

Divisional Dispatches, Summer 1979

Cadet Training Program – Overview – Program Training Standard – June 11, 2004

Career Management Manual, Appendix 5-8, 2000-11-10

Familiarization Booklet for Recruits – "Depot" Division 1967

Life at the RCMP Academy at Depot Division, April 1977, Appendix A and C

Overview of the Cadet Training Program, June 11, 2004

Overview of the Cadet Training Program, 2005

RCMP Administration Manual, Appendix II – 4-3 2005

RCMP Academy at Depot Division – Basic Recruit Training Course, 1987

RCMP Academy at Depot Division – Basic Recruit Training Course – Orientation and Reference Manual, 1988

RCMP Basic Recruit Training – Driver Training – Classroom Syllabus – Ten Hours – Individual Lesson Plan

Recruit Training Manual, 1932

Recruit Training Manual, 1962

Regulations and Orders for the Government and Guidance of the North West Mounted Police, 1889

Rules and Regulations for the Government and Guidance of the Royal Canadian Mounted Police Force, 1928

Rules and Regulations for the Government and Guidance of the Royal Canadian Mounted Police Force, 1935

Rules and Regulations for the Government and Guidance of the Royal Canadian Mounted Police Force, 1936

The Drill Manual – Calvary Drill (dismounted) Ottawa, 1956

The Drill Manual – Functions of Drill

RCMP Veterans Association

Friendly Notes – Friends of the Mounted Police Museum, Fall 1995

Friendly Notes – Friends of the Mounted Police Museum, Fall 1999

Friendly Notes – Friends of the Mounted Police Museum, Summer and Winter 2000

Friendly Notes – Friends of the Mounted Police Museum, Summer and Fall 2002

Friendly Notes – Friends of the Mounted Police Museum, Spring 2003

Web Sites

Environment Canada – www.climate.weatheroffice.gc.ca/climate_normals/results_e.html

RCMP Badges www.rcmp.ca/about/badges_insignia-e.htm

RCMP Depot www.rcmp-grc.ca/depot

RCMP Guidon www.rcmp.ca/national_memorial/guidon-e.htm

RCMP Heritage Center www.rcmpheritagecenter.com

RCMP Hollywood www.rcmp.ca/history/mountie_hollywood_e.htm

RCMP Horse Auction www.rcmp-grc.ca/mounted policefnd.org/horseauction/pages/E- about1A.html

RCMP Musical Ride www.rcmp-grc.ca/musicalride

RCMP National Memorial www.rcmp.ca/national_memorial/guidon_e.htm

RCMP Recruiting www.rcmp-grc.ca/recruiting

The authors of *Behind the Badge* have made every effort to provide the most current and accurate information, however, errors and omissions are inevitable in a book of this scope and magnitude. For any future printings, the authors would appreciate receiving information that would enhance or correct the content of this book. You can contact Redd Oosten at redd.oosten@rcmp-grc.gc.ca with any pertinent information.

ACKNOWLEDGMENTS

As noted in the Preface, researching and writing *Behind the Badge: History of the Royal Canadian Mounted Police – "Depot" Division* has been a challenging project. For over two and a half years, thousands of hours have been spent interviewing RCMP members and former members, pouring over documents and sifting through photographs in the RCMP Museum and Archives, "Depot" Learning Resource Centre and other libraries. As these Acknowledgements gratefully attest, many people have generously provided invaluable assistance in all aspects of creating this book.

Photo Credits
Learning Technology and Creative Services

Martin Castle
Chrystal Kruszelnicki
Jerry Paul
Tom Wieclawski

Karleen Bardal-Oconnor
Christopher Caverly
Rob Close
Liz Collum
C.J. Gibson
S/Sgt. R.B. Graham
Luc. S. Martel
Joshua Sawka

Assistance
Julie Belisle
Martin Castle
George Charlebois
Isabelle Chartrand
Elizabeth Chidlow
Derek Colson
Heather Crooks
Shannon Cunningham
Harvey Elson
Margaret Evans
Leslie Frei
Vicky Gosselin
Doug Graham
Carmen Harry
Preston Haynee
Kenneth Iles
Wendy Kraushaar
James McGinnis
Rick McIlvenna
Nancy McLaughlan
Arlene Sernich
Carol Spence
Vera Visnevskis
Tom Wieclawski
Susan Yanosik

A/Commr. D. Lafosse #0.1739
Supt. Edwin Langner (rtd.)
Supt. W.R. (Bill) MacRae (rtd.), #0.645
Supt. J. Religa (rtd.), # 0.947
C/S/M H.M. (Mel) Gilbey (rtd.), #15427
S/M Harry Armstrong (rtd.)
S/M A.R. (Sandy) Mahon (rtd.), #27966
Insp. Jeff Dowling
Insp. Craig Gibson
S/Sgt. Kenn Barker (rtd.), #14375
S/Sgt Brian Cook
S/Sgt. Gord Hadley (rtd.), #27689
S/Sgt. C.N. MacKinnon (rtd.), #26295
Sgt. Joanne Crampton
Sgt. Don Dupasquier
Sgt. R. Gill #43063
Sgt. Lyne Malette
Sgt. Janet Marquis
Sgt. Denis Murphy (rtd.), #19129
Sgt. Tammy Patterson
Sgt. Carol Peabody
Sgt. Steve Smedley
Sgt. Jamie Taplin
Cpl. Karen Adams (rtd)
Cpl. Jennifer Carroll
Cpl. Earl LeBlanc
Cpl. Dan Marquis
Cpl. Deborah Porter
Cpl. Terry Tycholis
Cpl. Grace Warkentine
Cst. M. Coulibaly #50610
Cst Rene Cyr #18907
Cst. Mark Hustins #44062
Cst. Yvonne Javorovic
Cst. L.M. Tuchscherer #44212
Cst. Tammy Um
Chaplain Fred Salerno
ex-Cst. Angela Schurr

RCMP Veterans Association
RCMP Quarterly – Bill Gidley and Nathalie Egan
Friends of the Museum – Regina, Saskatchewan,
RCMP Heritage Branch – Ottawa, Ontario

Photograph Scans
Wayne Standon – PrintWest Communications Ltd.

Garda Depot, Phoenix Park, Ireland

Garda Depot, Phoenix Park, Ireland – the training facilities of the Royal Irish Constabulary – this is the building that inspired Commissioner A.G. Irvine to recommend the establishment of "Depot" at Regina. "Depot" Division was created on November 1, 1885 as a training centre for the North-West Mounted Police

Other RCMP-Related Books

Published by Centax Books/Publishing Solutions
PrintWest Communications Ltd.

Sam Steele: Lion of the Frontier
Robert Stewart

The Kelly Trilogy

Policing the Fringe: A Young Mountie's Story
William Kelly with Nora Hickson Kelly

Policing in Wartime: One Mountie's Story
William Kelly with Nora Hickson Kelly

My Mountie and Me: A True Story
Nora Hickson Kelly

Red Coats on the Prairies : The North-West Mounted Police 1886-1900
William Beahen and Stan Horrall
(currently unavailable)

Les Tuniques Rouge dan la Prairie : Le Maintien de l'Ordre dans l'Ouest Pionnier 1886-1900
William Beahen and Stan Horrall
(currently unavailable)

visit www.centaxbooks.com to view the complete catalogue of Centax books